S0-ECQ-189

T H E
A L M A N A C
O F
EUROPEAN
POLITICS
1995

M A T T H E W
C O S S O L O T T O

Congressional Quarterly Inc.

Washington, D.C.

Congressional Quarterly Inc.
1414 22nd Street, N.W., Washington, D.C. 20037

Book and cover design: Anne Masters Design, Inc.
Typesetter: Jessica Forman

Printed in the United States of America

Library of Congress Cataloging-in-Publication Data

Cossolotto, Matthew.

  The almanac of European politics 1995 / Matthew Cossolotto.
     p.   cm.
  Includes index.
  ISBN 0-87187-914-X (hard) -- ISBN 0-87187-913-3 (paper)
  1. Europe--Politics and government--1989-   --Handbooks, man-
uals, etc.   I. Title.
JN44.A12C67   1994
909'.09821'0829--dc20   94-32762

This book is dedicated to
my mother, Virginia Butler,
my wife, Lora,
and our daughter, Katherine Hope

CONTENTS

ACKNOWLEDGMENTS

This book could not have been written without the active and enthusiastic support of numerous individuals.

I want to thank my wife, Lora, for putting up with me during this process. That she is still my wife today attests either to her undying love or to the fact that she is just as crazy as I am.

Mark W. Newman, an intelligent and talented student from Utah, made a major contribution to this book. Mark compiled material and helped to draft the nucleus of many chapters while working as an intern in the New York public relations firm of Hunter MacKenzie. Many thanks, as well, to Karen MacKenzie for assigning Mark to this project and to David Gilman, my friend and sometime golf partner, who displayed a real spark of genius by putting me in touch with Karen in the first place. Without this somewhat convoluted chain of contacts, this almanac might never have been published.

Many others contributed to the book at different times. Robert Richie, national director of the Center for Voting and Democracy in Washington, D.C., and his wife, Cynthia Terrell, helped in the early stages to compile information from various embassies, especially with regard to voting systems and the percentage of women in parliament. Jack Benetto made some very useful suggestions regarding tables and voting systems. Thanks also go to Rena Caughlin for her useful research and to Erin Rainaldi, who spent many hours going through stacks of newspapers clipping hundreds of articles.

I want to acknowledge a debt of gratitude to Michael Barone, author of the well-respected *Almanac of American Politics*. The Barone almanac, first started in 1972, served as the inspiration, if not the model, for this book. Barone himself has always encouraged me to pursue the project. I do not hold it against him that the way he encouraged me sounded like something of a threat. When I first told him about my idea of an international version of his almanac, he said he wished he could "beat me to it." That reaction has sustained, and occasionally prodded, me through this sometimes trying process. I want to thank the Washington-based embassies of all the countries covered in this book. They provided valuable information that contributed enormously to the accuracy and timeliness of each country chapter. In this regard, Lars Romert of the Swedish embassy deserves special praise. His help and encouragement a few years ago made the first edition of the almanac possible. I recall warmly the book party he hosted in Washington. I want to state for the record, however, that I did not seek, nor would these embassies want to provide, official approval of the book's content.

My editor, Kerry Kern, deserves high praise for her painstaking efforts to turn a sometimes chaotic manuscript into a much more orderly book. She was ably assisted by Talia Greenberg, who helped fill in many missing pieces, and Will Gardner and Chris Gleason, who did extensive fact-checking and research.

Finally, I reluctantly yet stoicly accept full responsibility for any factual errors contained in this book.

FLAGS

A nation's flag is its most recognizable symbol. It serves as a visible reminder of the sovereignty and autonomy of its people.

Most countries have a single flag design that is used in all national representations; a few maintain several designs that may be used for diplomatic or military purposes. We present here the officially recognized national flags, as designated by the countries to fly outside the United Nations building. A full-color version of the flag of each nation covered in *The Almanac of European Politics* appears on the front and back covers. In addition, a black-and-white rendition appears on the opening page of each individual country chapter for easy recognition.

The following pages highlight the flags from the nineteen democracies in this volume. The flag of the European Union (EU), the organization devoted to promoting economic and political cooperation between member countries, is also shown. This flag currently has twelve gold stars on a royal blue background. The stars represent the twelve members of the organization through 1994.

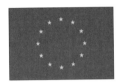

The European Union

France

Austria

Germany

Belgium

Greece

Denmark

Iceland

Finland

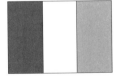

Ireland

Italy

Spain

Luxembourg

Sweden

Netherlands

Switzerland

Norway

Turkey

Portugal

United Kingdom

USER'S GUIDE

This *Almanac* focuses on the current political developments, governmental institutions, political parties, and leaders in the nineteen established democracies of Western Europe. Country-by-country analyses, arranged in alphabetical order, provide the reader with a broader and deeper understanding of each country and its contemporary political scene. The *Almanac* also acquaints the reader with the European Union (EU, formerly called the European Community), the organization devised to facilitate economic and political cooperation between the member states.

Europe, as defined for the purposes of this *Almanac*, includes all "West European" countries (as opposed to East European or Eurasian) with at least 1 million population or full membership in either the EU or the North Atlantic Treaty Organization (NATO). Thus, such small countries and ministates as Andorra (population: 50,000), Cyprus (population: 700,000), Liechtenstein (population: 28,000), Malta (population: 400,000), Monaco (population: 28,000), San Marino (population: 23,000), and Vatican City (population: 1,000) are excluded.

The countries of Western Europe that were selected for this volume are all full-fledged democracies, a prerequisite for inclusion in this *Almanac*. Even relatively new members of the club, like Turkey, Greece, and Spain, seem to have successfully made the transition from authoritarian states to stable, multiparty democracies.

Information on the United States is presented in the text and tables for comparative purposes.

COUNTRY CHAPTER OVERVIEW

Each country overview begins with a section called "The Country in Brief," which lists such information as the official country name, capital, currency, national day, language, religion, memberships, border countries, and the address and telephone number of the country's embassy in Washington, D.C.

This is followed by the "Political Profile," which provides information on the type of government, head of state, head of government, and legislature. The next section, entitled "Comparative Data," presents statistics on population, gross domestic product (GDP), GDP per capita, voting system, per capita representation rate (the number of people represented by each member of the national parliament), big government index (current government revenue as a percentage of GDP), percentage of women in parliament (elected to the lower house of parliament), and voter turnout (the percentage of people eligible to vote who actually do).

Following this factual introduction is the "Political Parties" overview. The history and philosophical orientation of each major group is discussed, as well as its popularity with the voters and its prominence in parliament. The parties are presented in the order they finished in the most recent election, from the highest percentage of the vote to the lowest. In many countries, an alphabetical listing of the most prominent minor parties is also included.

An in-depth discussion of the most recent national elections follows, presenting details on campaign issues, key political parties and candidates, and election results—the most vital elements in a country's political profile. Similar highlights from the previous national elections are also provided to give the reader a longer-term perspective of two election cycles.

The election coverage within countries is not a strictly chronological listing. Instead, it is arranged first by type of election: for president, parliament, European Parliament (EP), and miscellaneous. Within each type, the last two elections are detailed, with the most recent first. Of course, not all countries have each type of election (some countries are not members of the EU, for instance), but this order is used to standardize the information presented for all the countries. Information is provided for elections through the end of 1994. Previews of upcoming elections are provided for certain races that occur in early 1995.

Tables are included to summarize the votes and parliamentary seats won by each party in the given years. Additional tables supply the results of European Parliament elections in the twelve countries that belonged to the EU at the end of 1994. These tables provide information on the total number of seats held by each country, as well as party-by-party vote tallies.

Following the election highlights section is an "Election Lexicon"—a compilation of selected expressions, slogans, phrases, and terms that are common in the political vocabulary of each country. While it would be impossible to cover every such expression, these lexicons offer the reader quick and easy verbal entrée into a country's politics. A "Historical Synopsis" follows to brief the reader on key events in the country's modern political history.

The chapter on the EU follows a similar format. It begins with a rundown of the organization's membership and moves into an overview of the EU's history, evolution, components, and functions. The results of the latest election for seats in the European Parliament are discussed and a lexicon of terms is presented.

FREQUENTLY USED ACRONYMS

Following is a list of acronyms used throughout the *Almanac*. Many political parties are also referred to by initials, but these are defined within each individual country chapter.

BGI	Big government index
EC	European Community (renamed the EU in 1993)
ECU	European Currency Unit
ECSS	European Coal and Steel Community
EEA	European Economic Area
EEC	European Economic Community
EFTA	European Free Trade Association
EMU	Economic and monetary union
EP	European Parliament
EU	European Union (formerly the EC)
GDP	Gross domestic product
MMP	Mixed member proportional (voting system)
NATO	North Atlantic Treaty Organization
PCRR	Per capita representation rate
PLP	Party list proportional (voting system)
STV	Single transferable vote (voting system)
WTA	Winner take all (voting system)

A NOTE ON SOURCES

The Almanac of European Politics 1995 is a refined, refocused, and improved version of a volume entitled *The Almanac of Transatlantic Politics, 1991-1992* (Brassey's). This *Almanac* is a compilation of data from numerous sources, a fact that makes citing specific sources somewhat difficult. Among the most useful were *Western Europe 1993* (Stryker-Post Publications); *World Atlas of Elections* (The Economist); *Political Parties of the World* (Eastern Press Limited); *The Statesman's Year-Book* (St. Martin's Press); *The World Almanac and Book of Facts 1994* (Funk & Wagnalls); *The 1994 Information Please Almanac* (Houghton Mifflin); and *Political Handbook of the World*, 1991, 1993, and 1994 editions (CSA Publications).

Unless otherwise indicated, the economic data used in this *Almanac* are for 1991 and are intended to give the reader a basis for comparing the various countries vis-à-vis each other. For the West European democracies, the data are from a publication of the Organization for Economic Cooperation and Development (OECD) entitled "OECD in Figures: Statistics on the Member Countries," 1992 edition. Figures on the percentage of women elected to parliament were provided by Christine Pintat at the Inter-Parliamentary Union in Geneva and by Cynthia Terrell at the Center for Voting and Democracy in Washington, D.C. In addition, the center was helpful in supplying information on the voting systems used in Europe.

A small publication, *Twelve Democracies: Electoral Systems in the European Community*, by Enid Lakeman of the Electoral Reform Society in London, England, was an extremely useful reference. In addition, numerous periodicals have been invaluable sources of information. Of particular merit are *The Economist, Financial Times, Europe, Magazine of the European Community*, and the *Journal of Democracy*, published by the National Endowment for Democracy. Each country's embassy in Washington, D.C., provided information about its government officials and the political system.

INTRODUCTION

THE IMPORTANCE OF VOTING SYSTEMS

Students of European politics—or any country's politics, for that matter—would be well advised to pay close attention to the political impact of voting systems. The voting system used in a given country has a profound and far-reaching effect on the politics of that country, but too often it is taken for granted or overlooked. This is especially true in the United States, where serious political discussions about voting systems are about as common as sightings of the Sasquatch.

That prevalent American attitude stands in stark contrast to most of the rest of the democratic world. In many democracies in recent years (notably in Italy, New Zealand, Russia, Poland, South Africa, the United Kingdom, and Japan), the voting system has been one of the hottest topics of political debate. In fact, both Italy and New Zealand approved national referendums in 1993 that signal dramatic changes in their voting systems.

To the uninitiated, learning about voting systems can be a bewildering experience. This *Almanac* is designed to provide a general overview to acquaint the reader with the political structure of each country. No attempt has been made to cover the subject in excruciating detail. While the nuances of the various voting systems are important, it is more crucial for the uninitiated to grasp the general principles. Once those are understood, further reading can provide eager students or political practitioners with enough fascinating minutiae and subtle permutations to keep them occupied for a lifetime.

For the purposes of this *Almanac*, Europe is defined as European countries with at least one million in population or full membership in either the European Union (EU, formerly the European Community, EC) or the North Atlantic Treaty Organization (NATO). The data presented in the table on page 2 provide a standard statistical overview, for comparative purposes, of the nineteen countries covered in this *Almanac*. The population figures, combined with gross domestic product (GDP)—defined as the total value of all goods and services produced within each

Europe in Figures

Country	Population (Millions)	GDP (Billions)	Per Capita Income
United States	252.0	$5,600	$21,500
Germany	80.0	1,600	23,600
Italy	57.7	1,100	18,900
United Kingdom	57.4	1,000	17,000
Turkey	56.5	112	1,900
France	56.4	1,200	21,100
Spain	39.0	526	12,600
Netherlands	15.0	285	18,700
Greece	10.2	69	6,500
Belgium	10.0	197	19,300
Portugal	9.9	69	6,100
Sweden	8.6	235	26,700
Austria	7.9	162	20,400
Switzerland	6.8	230	33,100
Denmark	5.2	132	25,500
Finland	5.0	127	27,600
Norway	4.2	108	25,000
Ireland	3.5	43	12100
Luxembourg	0.4	9	22,900
Iceland	0.3	6	22,900

Note: GDP = gross domestic product. 1991 data in current dollars. U.S. data for comparison.

country—offer a fast and accurate way for the reader to evaluate each country's relative size and economic strength. The GDP per capita figure, arrived at by simply dividing GDP by total population, provides a statistical snapshot of the country's relative wealth. GDP and population figures are for 1991, the most recent figures available at the time the tables were developed.

The United States is included in tables and text throughout the *Almanac* for comparison purposes. Since the majority of this book's readers will be Americans, this addition is to provide a familiar reference point.

WHAT IS A VOTING SYSTEM?

Stripped down to the most basic level, a voting system determines how the votes of the electorate get translated into representation and political power. In fact, what we call *voting systems* really should be thought of as *vote-counting* systems, because different voting systems have everything to do with how votes are counted and very little to do with how people actually vote. The act of voting is roughly the same regardless of which voting system is used. It is how those votes are counted and then translated into representation that distinguishes one voting system from another.

There are two major categories of voting systems widely used in the world for electing national legislative assemblies: proportional representation and winner-take-all (WTA). By far the most widely used in Europe is some version of proportional representation. For the purposes of this *Almanac*, proportional systems are broken down into three categories: party list proportional (PLP), mixed member proportional (MMP), and single transferable vote (STV). The voting systems used in the countries in this book are shown in the table on page 4.

Proportional Systems

Party List Proportional. The PLP system is the most commonly used voting system in Europe. PLP systems vary a good deal, and these variations can profoundly affect the extent to which voters' ballot preferences actually result in the election of their candidates of choice.

Important variations include such things as which mathematical formula is used for allocating assembly seats to the competing political parties; the number of representatives elected from each electoral district (referred to as *district magnitude* by political scientists); and, perhaps most relevant for this *Almanac*, the *vote percentage threshold.* Most PLP countries require political parties to receive a certain percentage of the vote in order to win seats in parliament. Most countries employ a low threshold of 2 or 3 percent, while others employ a hefty 5 or 10 percent threshold (as in Germany and Turkey, respectively).

Voting Systems of Europe

Winner-Take-All (Plurality/Majoritarian)	Proportional		
	Party List	*Mixed Member*	*STV*
France	Austria	Italy	Ireland
United Kingdom	Belgium	Germany	
United States	Denmark		
	Finland		
	Greece		
	Iceland		
	Luxembourg		
	Netherlands		
	Norway		
	Portugal		
	Spain		
	Sweden		
	Switzerland		
	Turkey		

Note: STV = single transferable vote. U.S. entry for comparison.

Obviously, the lower the threshold, the easier it will be for parties to win seats in parliament. The higher the threshold, the more difficult it is for a party to win seats and the higher the percentage of "wasted" or "ineffective" votes for parties that do not reach the threshold. (The reader should note that district magnitude also imposes an inherent threshold. A five-member district requires a higher vote percentage—roughly 20 percent—for election than a ten- or twenty-member district.)

Despite these differences among the various PLP countries, they all share a common element: the political parties receive seats based on the percentage of votes they garner in the election. In other words, seats are distributed to parties *in proportion* to the votes they receive. For example, if a party wins 20 percent of the votes, it would be entitled to roughly 20 percent of the seats. The party then fills those seats with candidates from its party "list" or slate. Clearly, candidates at the top of the list stand the best chance of filling the seats allocated to each party.

Under the PLP system, voters tend to cast their votes in favor of a political party philosophy—and a party slate of candidates—as opposed to any one particular candidate. Thus, party list elections are seldom seen as popularity contests between competing candidates. A number of PLP countries use a "flexible" or "open" party list to allow voters to express candidate preferences, but in practice this tends to have little effect. By placing favored candidates near the top of the party list, the political parties themselves largely determine which candidates ultimately win seats.

Mixed Member Proportional. The MMP system was designed to overcome some of the shortcomings of WTA voting by combining the attributes of the PLP and the WTA systems. Under MMP, a portion (usually about 50 percent) of the legislative seats are elected by WTA—that is, by simple plurality—from districts with only one representative. The remaining seats are distributed to parties based on the PLP formula used. Each voter, therefore, casts two ballots: one for a district representative and one for a party. The first vote can be for a candidate from a different party than that of the second "party" vote.

There are two main variations of the MMP system. One version (used in Germany) is called *compensatory* because it ensures overall party list proportionality. In other words, the party list vote determines the percentage of total parliamentary seats the party receives. As an example, imagine an election to fill a 100-seat parliament, with 50 of those seats voted on under WTA rules as district seats. If Party A wins 40 percent of the party list votes, it is entitled to a total of roughly 40 seats (40 percent of the total seats). If Party A also wins 30 district seats, 30 of its 40 seats would be filled by the district results, and 10 party list seats would be added to make 40 seats total. If a party happens to win more district seats (first vote) than party list seats (second vote), the size of the assembly is sometimes increased to accommodate these additional district seats.

In the *noncompensatory* version (a variation of which was used in Italy in 1994), if Party A wins 30 of the 50 district seats, plus 40 percent of the 50 remaining party list seats (20 seats), it gets a total of 50 seats. With only 40 percent of the party list votes, it has won

50 percent of the seats. Thus, the noncompensatory variety fails to ensure overall party proportionality.

In 1993 the MMP system emerged as one of the world's most widely used voting systems. Italy, New Zealand, Russia, Mexico, and Japan all adopted or have moved close to adopting the MMP system, thus joining existing MMP users Germany, Hungary, and Bulgaria. If all these countries ultimately adopt MMP as expected, more than half a billion people will soon be electing their national representatives via this method.

Single Transferable Vote. This system (sometimes called the Hare System after its originator, Thomas Hare) is not widely used for electing national assemblies. This is an extremely fair voting system that, like the PLP system, minimizes the number of wasted votes. STV voting enables voters to rank individual candidates in order of preference (1, 2, 3, 4, etc.). The first preference votes for all candidates are counted first. If the voter's first-choice candidate cannot be helped by the vote (i.e., if the candidate has already been elected or eliminated), then the voter's second-ranked candidate receives that vote.

All seats are filled through a process of candidate elimination and vote transfers. This system ensures that a large percentage of voters will actually contribute to the election of a candidate.

Of the countries covered in this *Almanac*, only Ireland uses STV voting (see Ireland, page 162, for more details).

Winner-Take-All Systems

WTA systems are not widely used in Europe for electing legislative bodies. In Europe, only the United Kingdom and France use the WTA system. The United Kingdom (along with the United States) uses the *plurality* version (also called First Past the Post), in which the candidate with the most votes wins. France has opted for the second-ballot (majoritarian) version of WTA, in which a candidate must win an absolute majority of votes cast to win election in the first round. Failing that, the top two vote-getters face each other in a subsequent two-candidate run-off election, thus guaranteeing a majority winner. Because only one representative is elected per geographic district, all

WTA systems by definition often fail to represent the full range of voter preferences within a given district. In a two-person race, up to 49 percent of the electorate can be denied representation. Under the plurality system, in a three-person contest up to 66 percent of voters can see their candidates of choice defeated. WTA voting frequently results in a very high percentage of votes being wasted within each district. As a result, WTA usually fails to ensure representation of the full range of voter viewpoints or candidate preferences.

The U.S. System

Why include a discussion of the United States in this *Almanac of European Politics?* Since a large portion of the audience for this book will be from the United States, a brief overview of the major distinguishing features of the U.S. political system is provided for comparison with those of most European countries.

The most important difference between politics in the United States and most European countries derives from the unique governmental structure in the United States. The U.S. Constitution provides for a "separation of powers" between the executive and legislative branches that does not exist in most European countries.

In the United States, unlike any of the European countries covered in this *Almanac*, the president functions as both head of state and head of government. Combining those two functions in one office makes for an extremely powerful presidency. The more powerful the head of state, the closer the country comes to having a U.S. style presidency. The U.S. president is elected separately and apart from the national legislature. While the Constitution gives the U.S. Congress significant powers to keep the executive branch in check, the majority party or majority coalition in Congress does not directly determine who wields executive authority. Only twice in U.S. history, when no candidate for president gained the required majority in the electoral college, has the U.S. House of Representatives actually elected the president (Thomas Jefferson in 1801 and John Quincy Adams in 1825).

Most parliamentary systems differ markedly from the U.S. presidential system. Electing the head of government (usually a prime minister) is a primary role of parliaments in most European democracies. Within the parliamentary form of government, the executive branch depends for its very existence on the support of the legislative branch. Virtually all the European democracies covered in this *Almanac* have adopted some version of this form of government. Even in France, with its relatively strong presidency, a majority in the national assembly elects the prime minister, who actually forms the government and has extensive executive powers.

ROLE OF THE HEAD OF STATE

The nineteen European democracies in this *Almanac* are classified in the table on page 9 in terms of the role of the head of state. The more mature the democracy, the more likely it is to have a hereditary monarch or ceremonial president as head of state.

Eight of the countries are parliamentary democracies headed by a hereditary monarch. In every case, the political role of the sovereign is strictly limited. The head of state also has a very limited role in Germany, Greece, Italy, and Switzerland. These four countries are parliamentary democracies with a president who serves as a largely ceremonial head of state. Like the monarchs, the actual political power of these ceremonial presidents is severely restricted. In a sense, these monarchs and ceremonial presidents are heads of state oddly unattached to the *body politic* of the country.

The presidents in Austria, Iceland, Ireland, and Portugal are directly elected, but they yield only minor executive powers.

Only three established European democracies—Finland, France, and Turkey—have presidents who wield any significant executive powers. No European president has the same degree of authority to act independently as the U.S. president. For example, while President François Mitterand of France played an important role in foreign and defense policy, he was forced to share a considerable amount of power with the prime minister. President Bill Clinton, by contrast, has no competing "head of government" with whom he must share power.

Role of the Head of State

Exclusively Ceremonial [a]	Largely Ceremonial [b]	Powerful [c]
Belgium (monarch)	Austria	Finland
Denmark (monarch)	Iceland	France
Germany (president)	Ireland	Turkey
Greece (president)	Portugal	**United States**
Italy (president)		
Luxembourg (monarch)		
Netherlands (monarch)		
Norway (monarch)		
Spain (monarch)		
Sweden (monarch)		
Switzerland (president)		
United Kingdom (monarch)		

Note: U.S. entry for comparison.

[a] Monarch or indirectly elected president.

[b] Directly elected president with minor powers.

[c] Directly elected president with fairly extensive powers.

TWO-PARTY VERSUS MULTIPARTY SYSTEMS

Nothing in the Constitution says the United States can have only two viable political parties. Nor is there any law that requires other countries to have more than two active and influential parties. The United States seems to have more or less accepted the idea of a "two-party system" as something of an article of faith. Of the 535 senators and representatives in the 104th Congress, 534 are members of either the Democratic or Republican parties. Only Bernard Sanders, the lone representative from Vermont, was elected to the House as an independent.

Hence, on the left-right continuum from strong two-party system to strong multiparty system, the United States would be positioned far to the left as the quintessential two-party country. This is true even though Ross Perot, running as an independent candidate, managed to win 20 million votes (19 percent) in the 1992 presidential election. It is true even though nearly one-third of all U.S. voters call themselves "independents." Despite these clear signs of voter discontent with the two major parties, the Democratic and Republican parties effectively control the American political system.

By contrast, the two-party idea has not won many adherents in most of the democracies of Europe, where multiple parties compete for and regularly win large numbers of parliamentary seats. The one European country in which two parties still dominate is the United Kingdom, where the Labour and Conservative parties win virtually all parliamentary seats—even though the Liberal Democrats have received approximately 20 percent of the votes in recent elections.

Not surprisingly, the United States and the United Kingdom both use the WTA (plurality) system. In effect, and almost unbeknownst to many voters, the WTA voting system seems to work against the expressed wishes of voters in both countries for a greater range of parties to represent them.

In contrast, most European countries tend to have two to four major parties and quite a few smaller parties that compete for political power or build coalitions in order to form a government. All these multiparty parliamentary systems use a form of proportional voting, typically the PLP system described above, while the United States and the United Kingdom use the plurality variation of the WTA voting system to elect their national legislature. France uses the majoritarian variation. It is clear that proportional voting favors the creation of multiple political parties, while WTA voting tends to discourage the creation, growth, and survival of more than two political parties.

POLITICAL PARTIES AND IDEOLOGIES

Not surprisingly, the existence of multiple parties within a political system also tends to promote a sharpening of ideological distinctions. In the United States, while there clearly are differences in political philosophy between the two major parties, most politicians prefer to avoid ideological labels and run for office from a platform that is middle-of-the-road or vaguely left or right of center. Unlike European democracies, a large percentage of politicians in the United States run for office, and win election, as individuals who happen to be Republicans or Democrats.

The size and nature of a politician's political base are factors that affect political structure. A member of the U.S. House of Representatives, for instance, knows that he or she is the sole representative of a specific congressional district with approximately 600,000 residents. The need to attract a majority of votes cast (in a two-candidate race) from a large single-member constituency tends to drive candidates toward the center and away from the fringes.

The same applies to the Senate, where each senator must seek election from a statewide constituency that often amounts to many millions of voters. As a result, the ideological edges in American politics are rounded out by such large single-member constituencies and the need to attract at least a plurality—and in practice a majority—of votes cast. Some applaud this fact, while others decry it as producing politicians who fail to stand for anything more than bland platitudes and their own personal survival in office.

The same electoral facts of life do not face most European politicians. In Europe, most politicians get elected on the basis of proportional representation from multimember constituencies. This has a profound effect on the political dialogue and the range of viewpoints represented in parliament.

If one's political base is not a single-member district, but a political party whose total national or constituency-level percentage of the vote is used to "allocate" parliamentary seats, then one tends to toe the party line ideologically. Most significantly, parties that attract a relatively small percentage of votes can still win seats in parliament.

If the United States changed to a system of proportional representation, many smaller parties with emphatic views on key issues (for instance, environmentalists, ethnic or racial minorities, women's rights advocates, libertarians, etc.) would undoubtedly gain momentum across the country and win a number of seats in state legislatures and Congress. The ability to choose from among a wider range of parties might also increase voter turnout and possibly enhance the range of political issues debated and policy options considered. Proportional representation seems to yield markedly higher voter turnout rates than are typical in countries with the plurality system in effect.

Freeing parties from the need to attract large numbers of voters in order to win representation in parliament is one of the hallmarks of the proportional representation system. When parties do not need a plurality, let alone a majority, of votes cast to establish and maintain a stable political base, they can afford to define their ideological platform in terms that appeal to minority-issue or single-issue voters. The environmentalist Green parties, for example, have won election to a number of European parliaments in recent years by appealing to a select portion of the electorate. Under proportional representation, there is a proliferation of political parties that tend to stake out narrower, almost specialized, positions that appeal to their respective political bases.

In this regard, proportional representation allows political parties to play the role that interest groups do in the United States, where various interests band together to form groups to "lobby" largely nonideological parties and officeholders. Under proportional voting, smaller political parties seem to function as "elected" interest groups. By contrast, the mass parties in the United States have to envelop as many issues and interest groups as possible to win elections. Of course, governing is sometimes more difficult with a greater number of parties, especially if they espouse relatively extreme views and are unwilling to compromise. It is not necessarily a step forward to go from the occasional gridlock of two parties to the gridlock that sometimes occurs with many parties.

HOW THE COUNTRIES STACK UP

One of the main reasons for compiling an almanac of this kind is to gain insights into each country's political methods, not as isolated or discrete phenomena, but in comparison with other countries. For the purposes of developing useful comparative insights, the field has been narrowed down to four criteria: per capita representation rate (PCRR), big government index

(BGI), percentage of women in parliament, and voter turnout rates. These four subjects are highlighted in the following tables, not because they are the only important comparative criteria, but because taken together they can yield significant insights.

The individual statistics for these criteria are taken from the Comparative Data section in each chapter.

Per Capita Representation Rate

The PCRR is a simple calculation arrived at by dividing the country's total population by the number of members in the lower house of parliament. This yields the number of constituents per member. The data on how the European countries in the *Almanac* stack up in terms of per capita representation are presented in the table on page 14.

The PCRR figure offers some interesting insights into the nature and style of politics. In Iceland, for example, each member of parliament represents only 4,100 people. The political culture has a small-town feel: personal, direct, and open. By comparison, in the United States each member of the House of Representatives represents more than half a million people. The political culture is more distant, indirect, and impersonal, and go-betweens like lobbyists, interest groups, staff people, and the media play a significant role.

Between these two extremes, the countries of Europe can be arrayed along a continuum that has many of the smaller PCRR countries of Scandinavia closer to Iceland in terms of political style and culture, while larger PCRR countries like Germany and Turkey are closer to the middle of the spectrum. No European country came close to the PCRR rate of the United States, however.

Big Government Index

The BGI figure is based on one criterion: current government revenue, at all levels, as a percentage of GDP. This provides a fair indicator of the role of government in the country's overall economy. The lower the BGI, the less impact the central government has on the economy. A high BGI (greater than 50 percent) indi-

Per Capita Representation Rate

Country	PCRR
Iceland	4,100
Luxembourg	6,400
Ireland	21,000
Finland	25,000
Sweden	25,000
Norway	26,000
Denmark	29,000
Greece	33,000
Switzerland	34,000
Austria	43,000
Portugal	43,000
Belgium	47,000
United Kingdom	90,000
Italy	92,000
France	98,000
Netherlands	100,000
Spain	112,000
Germany	123,000
Turkey	125,000
United States	580,000

Note: U.S. entry for comparison.

cates a relatively intrusive role for the government in the economic affairs of the country.

The countries at the top of the BGI list are all highly developed "welfare state" countries—that is, countries that provide a full range of extensive health care, unemployment, and other social and education benefits for their citizens. In contrast, Turkey provides very little in the way of welfare state programs.

Compared with virtually every European country listed in the table on page 15, the United States has a relatively low BGI profile, indicating a comparatively low level of government intrusion in the economy. One reason for the low BGI figure in the United States is that the U.S. government is not responsible for the full

Big Government Index

Country	Government Revenue as Percentage of GDP
Sweden	64.0
Denmark	56.1
Norway	55.0
Luxembourg	53.0
Netherlands	50.0
France	46.5
Austria	46.4
Belgium	45.0
Germany	44.9
Italy	42.1
Finland	41.2
Ireland	40.1
United Kingdom	39.8
Portugal	38.7
Spain	36.0
Iceland	34.9
Switzerland	34.2
Greece	31.9
United States	31.8
Turkey	24.1

Note: GDP = gross domestic product. 1991 data in current dollars. U.S. entry for comparison.

range of health, employment, and welfare programs typically provided by the central governments in Europe. Nor does the United States, in contrast to many European countries, have state-run or state-owned enterprises in key industries such as telecommunications or transportation.

Percentage of Women in Parliament

Does the percentage of women elected to parliament correlate with other social or political variables? There certainly seems to be a relationship between the percentage of women elected to parliament and the voting system used by the country.

The table on page 17 ranks all European democracies on the basis of the percentage of women elected to the lower house of the country's national parliament and lists the appropriate voting system in place in each country. It is no accident that the countries with the highest percentage of women in parliament use some form of proportional representation. Three countries in the list (United Kingdom, France, and, for comparison purposes, the United States) use the WTA voting system and all have relatively low percentages of women elected to parliament.

Clearly, factors such as culture, religion, and the degree of maturity of a country's democratic institutions also play a role in determining how many women seek and win political office. This *Almanac* could not possibly discuss all the factors related to the voting system itself, such as district magnitude and vote percentage thresholds, that affect the degree to which women candidates seek and win office. However, these factors help at least partially to explain why some PLP countries have relatively low percentages of women in parliament.

Even taking these other factors into account, the fact remains that only those European countries using some variation of the proportional voting systems achieve female representation in the double-digits, up to nearly 40 percent. In marked contrast, the two WTA countries (United Kingdom and France) struggle to attain female representation above 10 percent.

Germany is a good example. Because of Germany's mixed member system, it is possible to compare the percentage of women elected from single-member districts with those elected using the PLP system. Doing so effectively controls for all the nonvoting system factors such as culture and socioeconomic conditions. Using WTA voting from single-member districts, only 12 percent of those elected to parliament in 1990 were women. Using PLP balloting, women comprised 28 percent of those elected. This discrepancy between two systems of voting within the same country offers convincing evidence that voting systems do matter.

The reader is invited to compare this table with others in this chapter to explore other possible relationships. For instance, those countries with the highest per capita incomes tend to have

Percentage of Women in Parliament

Country	Voting System	Percentage of Women Elected to Parliament
Sweden	PLP	41
Finland	PLP	39
Norway	PLP	36
Denmark	PLP	33
Netherlands	PLP	29
Iceland	PLP	24
Germany	MMP	21
Austria	PLP	21
Switzerland	PLP	18
Spain	PLP	16
Italy	PLP	13
Luxembourg	PLP	13
Ireland	STV	12
United States	WTA	11
Belgium	PLP	9
Portugal	PLP	9
United Kingdom	WTA	9
France	WTA	6
Greece	PLP	5
Turkey	PLP	2

Note: Figures are the percentage of women elected to the lower (or single) house of the country's national parliament. Percentages have been rounded to the nearest whole number. PLP = party list proportional, MMP = mixed member proportional, STV = single transferable vote, WTA = winner-take-all/plurality or majoritarian. U.S. entry for comparison.

Source: Inter-Parliamentary Union.

the highest percentage of women in parliament and the highest BGI rates. They also tend to have the lowest per capita representation rates and high voter turnout rates. While it is not the purpose of this *Almanac* to draw hard and fast correlations between such statistics, clearly the value in compiling comparative data of this kind is in being able to make comparisons that may lead to interesting and perhaps unexpected conclusions.

Voter Turnout Rates

Voter turnout rates refer to the percentage of eligible voters who actually vote in a given election. While experts are divided on the issue of what voter turnout says about a country's politics, most observers agree that high turnout is better than low turnout. Turning out to vote indicates, at a minimum, that the voter has decided that voting has some meaning or importance.

High voter turnout rates could be said to correlate with a number of factors, such as the voting system used, per capita income levels, the per capita representation rate, or interest in a particular election. It seems clear from the available data that countries using proportional voting systems enjoy much higher voter turnout rates than do France, the United Kingdom, and the United States—the three countries that use WTA voting (see table on page 19).

The one anomaly in this table is Switzerland. The low turnout rate among Swiss voters (47 percent) is atypical for a PLP country (compare this to Belgium with 93 percent). One possible explanation is the Swiss tradition of holding frequent referenda on most important questions. Voters participate directly in deciding major issues and paradoxically probably feel somewhat "burned out" by voting and at the same time sufficiently empowered that they do not need to vote for members of parliament.

Election Timetable

In most European countries, the parliament can be dissolved before its full term expires. This is just one reason why it is difficult to keep an accurate calendar of future European elections. Only in Norway and Switzerland are early elections strictly forbidden. Other countries tend to discourage early elections. In Sweden, for instance, the newly elected parliament merely serves out the remainder of the dissolved parliament's term.

The timetable presented on page 20 provides the best available schedules for the parliamentary and presidential elections that will be held in Europe from 1995 to 1999. For parliaments, the schedule is based on the year of the most recent election and

Voter Turnout Rates

Country	Voter Participation (in Percentages)
Belgium	93
Turkey	92
Italy	89
Luxembourg	87
Austria	86
Iceland	86
Sweden	86
Denmark	83
Norway	83
Netherlands	80
Germany	78
Greece	77
United Kingdom	76
Finland	72
Spain	70
Ireland	69
Portugal	68
France	65
United States	55[a]
Switzerland	47

Note: Figures are the percentage of eligible voters who actually voted in recent parliamentary elections. Percentages have been rounded to nearest whole number. U.S. entry for comparison.

[a] 1992 presidential election. Turnout for the 1994 congressional elections was 36 percent.

the maximum term of office for the existing parliament. Presidential terms are generally less variable, ranging from four to seven years.

Each country's upcoming parliamentary election is listed. Those countries that directly elect the president have an additional entry. For more information on specific elections, please see that particular country chapter.

Election Timetable, 1995-1999

Country	1995	1996	1997	1998	1999
Austria				● ■	
Belgium	●				●
Denmark				●	
Finland	●				
France	■			●	
Germany				●	
Greece			●		
Iceland	●	■			
Ireland			● ■		
Italy				●	
Luxembourg				●	
Netherlands				●	
Norway			●		
Portugal	●	■			
Spain				●	
Sweden			●		
Switzerland	●				
Turkey		●			
United Kingdom			●		
United States		● ■			

Note: European Parliament elections, held every five years, will take place in May 1999. ● = parliamentary elections; ■ = presidential elections.

WHAT'S LEFT AND WHAT'S RIGHT?

This *Almanac* includes information on election results and the key political parties and players in nineteen European countries located in what is generally referred to as "Western" Europe. Even though these are all reasonably well-established democracies, it is not always easy to keep track of who is in power in what country and where the government falls on the classic "left-right" ideological continuum.

Ideological differences tend to blur toward the middle of the spectrum. A center-left party may be difficult to distinguish from a center-right party. That being said, there are a few overarching ideological positions that tend to characterize the right and the left. Some of these positions are matters of degree rather than major differences in kind between parties.

Generally speaking, the parties on the right have tended to support the following positions: a strong belief in free market solutions and an equally strong suspicion of big government. This general view implies a dislike of welfare and other programs run by the central government, support for tax cuts or at least opposition to tax increases, and advocacy of deregulation and privatization of government-owned or government-run enterprises. Parties on the right also tend to support a comparatively strong commitment to higher levels of defense spending.

The parties on the left tend to support the following positions: reductions or slower growth in defense budgets; a greater role for government in the economy and in providing for the education and welfare of citizens; if not tax increases, then at least no or limited tax cuts so as to avoid reductions in social services; and continued government ownership, or at least regulation, of some parts of the economy. In Western Europe, parties on the left have begun to highlight environmental concerns, often opting for less economic growth if that is what it takes to protect the environment.

Given the number of countries involved, and the general state of political flux, the old adage that you need a scorecard to keep track of everyone is especially relevant. So, one is provided.

The European Political Scorecard 1994 on page 22 lists the government leaders for all the countries covered in this *Almanac*. These governments are arranged alphabetically by country in one of three columns.

The first column lists all European governments that can generally be classified as left or center-left in political outlook. The middle column, under the heading "cohabitation," lists all countries that are ideologically split, with a president of one philosophy sharing power with a prime minister of a different political persuasion. The term *cohabitation* was made famous by the French, who used it in 1986 to describe the power-sharing arrangement be-

European Political Scorecard, 1994

Left/Center-Left	*Cohabitation*	*Right/Center-Right*
DENMARK PM Rasmussen	**AUSTRIA** Pres. Klestil Chan. Vranitsky	**BELGIUM** PM Dehaene
GREECE PM Papandreou	**FINLAND** Pres. Ahtisaari PM Aho	**GERMANY** Chan. Kohl
NETHERLANDS PM Kok	**FRANCE** Pres. Mitterrand PM Balladur	**ICELAND** PM Oddsson
NORWAY PM Brundtland	**IRELAND** Pres. Robinson PM Bruton	**ITALY** PM Dini
SPAIN PM Gonzalez		**LUXEMBOURG** PM Juncker
SWEDEN PM Carlsson	**PORTUGAL** Pres. Soares PM Cavoco Silva	**TURKEY** Pres. Demirel PM Ciller
	SWITZERLAND Coalition with rotating presidency	**UNITED KINGDOM** PM Major
	UNITED STATES Pres. Clinton (Dem.) Congress (Rep.)	

Note: PM = Prime Minister, Chan. = Chancellor, Pres. = President, Dem. = Democratic, Rep. = Republican. U.S. entry for comparison.

tween Socialist President François Mitterrand and the rightist government of Jacques Chirac, leader of the coalition that won the national assembly elections that year (see France, page 104, for details). Clearly, such a split can only happen in countries that have a relatively strong president who is elected separately from the legislature. The third column displays those countries whose governing philosophy can be described as right or center-right.

The reader should bear in mind that few, if any, governments are ideologically "pure." Governing inevitably involves striking compromises and bargains. This is especially true when a government consists of a coalition of parties with differing views on important policy areas. Nonetheless, the student of European politics is well served by having at least a general idea of where the various governments of Europe fall on the left-right continuum.

It is clear from the Political Scorecard that the parties on the right and center-right are the dominant governmental force in the biggest and most influential countries of Europe today. During the preparation of this *Almanac,* seven of the nineteen countries had right or center-right governments in power, including the large countries of Germany, Italy, and the United Kingdom. Six smaller countries had governments that could be called left or center-left in orientation.

If the list of six cohabitation countries is examined further, four (Finland, France, Ireland, and Portugal) could be classified as leaning right as opposed to left since the prime minister and not the president is in charge of most functions of the government. In those cases, the president is the leftist element. In Austria, the prime minister is the leftist element, sharing power with a rightist president. Switzerland can fairly be classified as neither left nor right since the multiparty coalition rules in a collegial manner.

If you factor in the cohabitation countries in the left/right tallies, then eleven of the nineteen countries covered can be said to have right/center-right governments, with six falling into the left/center-left category. Switzerland stays firmly in the middle of the road.

Only two of these democracies use the WTA voting system. Both of these countries, France and the United Kingdom, also happen to have center-right governments, but this seems to be a mere coincidence. Countries using the PLP voting system are as likely to have a center-right as a center-left government.

It is noteworthy, perhaps, that three of the four largest European countries have had center-right governments throughout most of the 1980s and early 1990s. France is the exception, having twice experienced left-right cohabitation during the presidency of Socialist François Mitterrand.

The
European
Union

The European Union in Brief

Official Name: European Union (EU, as of November 1, 1993; formerly the European Community, EC)

Capitals: Brussels, Strasbourg, Luxembourg

Currency: European Currency Unit (ECU)

Languages: Danish, Dutch, English, Finnish, French, German, Greek, Italian, Portuguese, Spanish, Swedish

Constitution: Treaty of Rome (1957), amended by Single European Act (1987) and Maastricht Treaty (1993)

1995 Membership: Austria, Belgium, Denmark, Finland, France, Germany, Greece, Ireland, Italy, Luxembourg, the Netherlands, Portugal, Spain, Sweden, United Kingdom

Membership Pending: The following countries have applied to join the EU (the year of their application is in parentheses): Turkey (1987), Norway (1992), and Switzerland (1992).

U.S. Address: European Union Delegation of the European Commission, 2300 M St. N.W., Washington, D.C. 20037. Telephone: (202) 862-9542.

Executive (Joint):

European Commission

President: Jacques Santer (Luxembourg; Christian Democrat)

Assumed Office: 1995

Term of Office: Five years

Full Commission Membership: Martin Bangemann (Germany), Emma Bonino (Italy), Ritt Bjerregaard (Denmark), Sir Leon Brittan (United Kingdom), Edith Cresson (France), João de Deus Pinheiro (Portugal), Yves-Thibault de Silguy (France), Franz Fischler (Austria), Padraig Flynn (Ireland), Anita Gradin (Sweden), Neil Kinnock (United Kingdom), Erkki Liikanen (Finland), Manuel Marín (Spain), Mario Monti (Italy), Marcelino Oreja (Spain), Christos Papoutsis (Greece), Jacques Santer (Luxembourg), Hans van den Broek (Netherlands), Karel van Miert (Belgium), Monika Wulf-Mathies (Germany)

Council of Ministers

Presidency: Presidency rotates among member states in alphabetical order

Term of Office: Six months

Legislature: Unicameral European Parliament (EP), 567 members (pre-1995), elected according to the voting system in member states

Term of Office: Five years

Last Election: 1994

Next Election: 1999

Electorate: Universal, age 18

Voter Turnout: 56.4 percent (1994 EU average)

EUROPEAN UNION: HISTORY AND EVOLUTION

The European Union (EU), which has at various times been referred to as the EC, the European Communities, the European Economic Community (EEC), and the Common Market, is a complex, supranational institutional framework designed to facilitate economic and political coordination among its member states.

Membership swelled from twelve countries to fifteen on January 1, 1995, when Austria, Finland, and Sweden were formally admitted. The EU officially came into being on November 1, 1993, following the ratification of the Maastricht Treaty on European Union.

The EU grew out of the European Community (EC), which was the result of the 1967 merger of three then-existing organizations: the European Coal and Steel Community (ECSC), the European Atomic Energy Community (commonly referred to as Euratom), and the EEC.

The impetus for some form of regional cooperation in Europe sprang from the ravages of the two cataclysmic world wars in this century. In the aftermath of World War II, many Europeans became convinced that the best—and perhaps only—hope for the their region was to replace age-old national rivalries with a new spirit of European cooperation. Winston Churchill, in his famous speech in Zurich in 1946, urged the creation of a United States of Europe.

Two other men—both French—stand out as pioneers in turning the idea of a European community into reality. French foreign minister Robert Schuman and the noted pan-Europeanist Jean Monnet unveiled a plan in 1950 to combine the coal and steel production of France and Germany. The 1951 European Coal and Steel Community Treaty, signed in Paris by France, Germany, Belgium, Italy, Luxembourg, and the Netherlands, transferred powers of production and distribution of steel and coal to the ECSC High Authority. By binding the signatories—especially France and Germany—together into a limited but significant economic union, political stability in Europe was enhanced.

The success of the ECSC established a solid foundation for further economic cooperation and encouraged the same six nations to create two additional integrating institutions on March 25, 1957—the European Atomic Energy Community and the EEC. The earlier Treaty of Paris and the two Treaties of Rome form the three pillars upon which an elaborate structure for European economic cooperation has been constructed.

The initial excitement about European integration began to wane in the mid-1960s, and the process toward unification was mired in bureaucratic inertia and economic distractions until the mid-1980s. Real momentum toward fuller economic and political integration has only emerged in recent years. Beginning in the mid-1980s, a discernable sense of common purpose began to take hold within the EC countries.

The Rocky Road from Community to Union

Without much enthusiasm, with much turmoil, the Maastricht Treaty on European Union finally limped into effect November 1, 1993. Danish voters had nearly scuttled the whole thing by narrowly rejecting the treaty in the EC's first national referendum on the subject, held June 2, 1992. Given a second chance, and some convenient exemptions from the treaty, the Danes later reversed themselves and approved Maastricht in a 1993 referendum.

In another near fatal shock to the system, the French, who had seemed for so long the most intensely pro-European country in Europe, barely passed Maastricht with 51 percent of the vote in their 1992 national referendum.

What happened to the great expectations about European Union? Europe's long recession dampened enthusiasm considerably. Adding to Europe's woes were declining and, in 1993, even negative gross domestic product (GDP) growth rates, coupled with an alarmingly high unemployment rate of roughly 11 percent.

According to Eurobarometer, the prominent European opinion research organization, at the end of 1990 about 73 percent of the public thought EC membership was "a good thing." By 1993, only 60 percent held that opinion. Meanwhile, the percentage of people who thought their country had benefited from EC membership had dropped from about 60 percent in 1990 to 47 percent in 1993. That same 1993 poll showed that the Maastricht Treaty itself enjoyed the support of a clear majority of the public in only three countries: Ireland, the Netherlands, and Denmark. Maastricht was favored by less than 40 percent of British citizens and between 40 and 45 percent in Portugal, Spain, Germany, and Italy. On average, 42 percent of citizens in then-EC countries were in favor of the treaty, 22 percent were against, and 36 percent were undecided.

With less than overwhelming public backing, the great surprise is that Maastricht managed to win ratification at all.

What Is the Maastricht Treaty?

The Maastricht Treaty was signed in a small Dutch town by that name in December 1991. In creating the European Union, Maastricht essentially added two new elements to the existing institutions of the European Community: a common foreign and security policy and cooperation in matters related to police and justice. Both additions will take some time to put into place. The first element, in particular, will prove a vexing goal. One need only consider Europe's divergent views on what to do about the ongoing slaughter in the former Yugoslavia to recognize the difficulty of creating a common foreign and security policy for all EU members.

The other goals advanced by Maastricht—having to do with Economic and Monetary Union (EMU), reducing the "Democratic Deficit" by strengthening the European Parliament (EP), and granting new powers to EU institutions in Brussels with regard to industrial policy, consumer affairs, health, and education—will all be pursued within the institutional apparatus that already existed within the EC. The path toward EMU— complete with a common currency throughout the EU—will no doubt prove as difficult for the EU as creating a common foreign policy.

In many ways, the Maastricht Treaty was born of a certain amount of panic. With turmoil and uncertainty sweeping the Eastern part of Europe, leaders of the EC wanted to "deepen" the drive toward unity without delay. They jumped on the Maastricht bandwagon but almost forgot about the need to bring their respective publics along for the ride.

Debate has been raging among the EU member states about whether to expand (broaden) membership now or to integrate more fully (deepen) the economies of the existing members. The rationale for deepening centers on the difficulties inherent in implementing existing goals, such as the Single Market program that went into effect on January 1, 1993. Essentially, the Single Market created a European free-trade zone that would effectively eliminate all barriers to the free exchange of goods, services, and labor among EU member states. To broaden membership before that program was completed would have complicated, and possibly short-circuited, the process of achieving a single market.

Supporters of broadening have argued that delaying admission will make it more difficult for new members to fully integrate their economies into the EU. Proponents pointed to revolutionary events in Eastern Europe and suggested that the then-EC should expand its membership in order to serve as a magnet, drawing these countries closer to the world of economic and political pluralism.

With the Single Market in place and with Maastricht ratified, the EU must begin the difficult task of making a more complicated organization work. It must do so while also dealing with the enormous issue of broadening the membership in the next few years. Three countries acceded to the European Union in 1995 (Austria, Finland, and Sweden). Norway had applied, but voters rejected (52.8 percent versus 47.2 percent) Norway's membership in the November 28, 1994, national referendum.

Turkey and Switzerland also formally applied for membership, but for different reasons are unlikely to join the EU anytime soon. Although Turkey is eager to join the EU, the chances are almost nil that this officially secular, yet largely Muslim country will be admitted for many years to come. Reasons for this range from the backward state of Turkey's economy to alleged human rights violations to the often unstated but very real religious issue. While Switzerland applied for EU membership in 1992, Swiss voters set back the idea in December 1992 by narrowly defeating a referendum calling for Swiss membership in the proposed European Economic Area, which would link European Free Trade Association (EFTA) countries with the EU.

The EU must also deal with the question of opening its doors to the new democracies in Central and Eastern Europe. Countries like Hungary, the Czech Republic, and Poland already have expressed their desire to join.

In order to expand from an organization of fifteen members to possibly twenty, the EU will first have to revamp its outmoded decision-making structure. In particular, the current voting formula for the powerful Council of Ministers (see discussion below) will have to be changed so as not to give even more disproportionate power to smaller countries.

INSTITUTIONAL OVERVIEW

Four key institutions are largely responsible for legislative and judicial decision-making and for running the European Union: the Council of Ministers, the European Commission, the European Parliament, and the European Court of Justice. Each will be discussed below.

Council of Ministers

The Brussels-based Council of Ministers, made up of representatives of the governments of the fifteen member states, is the decision-maker of the EU. Representatives to the council change according to the subject matter under discussion, but the senior representatives are the foreign ministers, who meet once a month to discuss the main issues before the council. The ministers of agriculture and finance also hold monthly meetings, while the "specialist councils" of ministers of the environment, transportation, and other departments meet less often (usually every three to six months).

A meeting of the heads of government is referred to as the European Council or an EU Summit. Such meetings usually occur every June and December, at the end of each presidency of the Council of Ministers. The European Council is now officially recognized by the Single European Act (SEA), which mandates that the European Council meet at least twice a year.

The Council of Ministers is charged with adopting EU legislation, which takes the form of decisions, directives, and regulations. The council provides member governments with their greatest leverage on EU decision-making, but the council can act only on proposals submitted to it by the commission.

With the reforms contained in the SEA, the Council's decision-making ability has been enhanced. Prior to the SEA, any member state held veto power over any decision of the council. The council can now make certain decisions based on a "qualified" majority of 54 votes of the 76 possible. France, Germany, Italy, and the United Kingdom possess 10 votes each; Spain has 8; Belgium, Greece, the Netherlands, and Portugal have 5 each; Denmark and Ireland have 3 each; and Luxembourg has 2.*

The five biggest countries in the EU, which have roughly 84 percent of the EU's population, only have 48 votes (or 63 percent of the voting strength) in the Council of Ministers—6 short of the qualified majority. Thus, the five biggest countries cannot impose their will on the smaller countries. This, in effect, gives the smaller countries a disproportionate share of power within the EU. The qualified majority rule was designed so that any decision of the council must have the support of at least two of the smaller EU countries. The rule also means that a voting "bloc" of 23 or more votes can prevent the council from adopting a particular decision.

While the qualified majority rule applies to most internal market proposals, decisions relating to taxation, the free movement of persons, and the rights and interests of employees were exempted from the SEA and still require a unanimous vote of the council.

The presidency of the council rotates alphabetically (according to the spelling of the member state in its own language) among the countries. The six-month duration means each country will hold the council presidency once every seven and one-half years.

The European Commission

The European Commission—which, like the Council of Ministers, is seated in Brussels—is the only EU body with the power to initiate policies by submitting proposals to the Council of Ministers. It thus functions as something of a U.S.-style executive branch of government. The commission proposes and the Council of Ministers, with some help from the European Parliament, disposes. Nineteen of the twenty commissioners are appointed by agreement among the EU countries. Each country is represented, but the "big four" countries—the United Kingdom, Germany, France, and Italy—supply two commissioners each. The twentieth commissioner serves as president of the commission and can be from any member country. The commission includes twenty directorate generals, which are essentially large bureaus or divisions

---

* This discussion does not include voting changes made after January 1, 1995, with the addition of Austria (4 votes), Finland (3 votes), and Sweden (4 votes).

with authority over various policy areas and a staff of 17,000, making the commission the largest of the EU institutions.

The commission's major responsibility is to oversee the implementation of the EU treaties. Unlike the Council of Ministers, the members of the commission do not represent their national governments. In fact, commissioners are to remain scrupulously independent of their governments, and this independence accounts for much of the EU's supranational influence.

Before sending proposals to the Council of Ministers, the commission gets feedback on draft proposals from the Committee of Permanent Representatives (COREPER). The draft proposals must also be sent to the European Parliament for comment, which gives the parliament an opportunity to exercise one of its primary powers: the power to kill a proposal by refusing comment. Comments on proposals are also required from the Social and Economic Committee, but this committee does not have the power to derail the process by refusing to comment.

Once a proposal has made it through this preliminary process, it gets sent to the Council of Ministers where it is either approved, referred back to the commission, or rejected.

Other responsibilities of the commission include collecting and dispersing revenue, overseeing EU administration, and negotiating with nonmembers about terms for joining the EU. Maastricht also gave the commission greater authority in the area of foreign and military policy.

The European Parliament

The European Parliament is the legislative arm of the EU, comprised in 1994 of 567 members (this number rose to 626 on January 1, 1995, when 21 members for Austria, 16 for Finland, and 22 for Sweden were added after official membership was granted). It holds sessions and committee meetings and maintains offices in Brussels, Strasbourg, and Luxembourg.

The June 1994 elections for the European Parliament marked the fourth direct elections to this legislative body. The first direct elections took place in 1979. Despite the fact that these are direct elections by popular suffrage throughout the EU countries, elections in each country are held according to national voting rules.

The European Parliament has tried to promote a uniform electoral system throughout the EU for electing its members, as is required by the Treaty of Rome, but to no avail. The parliament prefers a system of proportional representation with regional constituencies within the larger countries and national constituencies for the smaller countries.

The Council of Ministers, however, has never managed to agree on how to change the voting system. As in other areas, such as the social charter, the United Kingdom has been the major obstacle to change. The European Parliament, on March 10, 1993, finally took matters into its own hands by adopting a proposal by Karel De Gucht, a member of the European Parliament (MEP) from Belgium. The proposal, which passed 207 to 79, requires member states to use some form of proportional voting to elect their MEPs. Use of the British winner-take-all (WTA) system is specifically ruled out. If the parliament's proposal ultimately is endorsed by the Council of Ministers, the 1994 European Parliament elections could turn out to be the last time Britain uses its WTA voting system for European elections.

At present, most of the EU's member countries use some form of party list proportional representation for European elections. The exceptions are Italy and Germany, which use the mixed member system; France and the United Kingdom, which use majoritarian/WTA systems; and Ireland, which uses the single transferable vote method (see Introduction, p. 1, for a discussion of voting systems).

For the 1994 elections, the European Parliament's 567 seats were apportioned by population among the then-twelve EU member countries in the following manner: Germany, 99; France, Italy, and the United Kingdom, 87 each; Spain, 64; the Netherlands, 31; Belgium, Greece, and Portugal, 25 each; Denmark, 16; Ireland, 15; and Luxembourg, 6. The number of seats had been 518 for the 1989 election. The seat count rose to 626 with the admission of Austria, Finland, and Sweden in 1995.

Main Functions. The EP's main functions are to approve the EC's budget, to debate and review the European Commission's proposals, and to pose questions to the commission and the Council of Ministers. It does not initiate legislation. However, because the commission must receive the advice of the EP on its proposals, the parliament is able to influence policy by delaying or threatening to delay giving its advice to the commission.

The SEA gave the EP the power to amend the commission's proposals in a number of areas, including facilitating the completion of the internal market, research and technology policy, regional policy, and social policy. This process is known as the "cooperation procedure." The Maastricht Treaty strengthened the role of the EP slightly, as the EP's support is needed for the seating of the European Commission.

It seems inevitable that the European Parliament will gain a greater share of power as the EU evolves toward economic and political unification. That was German Chancellor Helmut Kohl's message at a summit at Strasbourg when he, with strong Italian backing, came out in favor of creating a more powerful European Parliament. The idea has opposition, however. There are those who feel a more powerful European Parliament would siphon power away from national parliaments and lead to further erosion of national sovereignty.

The EP Elections of June 1994. Some 245 million people were entitled to cast ballots for candidates to fill the 567 seats in the European Parliament. The EP electorate is the second largest in the world, after India's. Only 56 percent of those entitled actually voted in the 1994 elections, a much lower turnout than usually occurs in most European national elections.

The 1994 EP elections were held June 9 in the United Kingdom, Ireland, Denmark, and the Netherlands and on June 12 in the eight remaining EU countries. The first EP election since ratification of the Maastricht Treaty on European Union did not produce many major changes in the relative strength of the various established party groupings, but there were a few surprises in individual countries.

Apathy was the big winner in the elections, with voter turnout sliding to its lowest level (56.4 percent in 1994 compared with 58.6 percent in 1989) in the history of Euro-elections. The declining turnout is odd juxtaposed against the fact that the size and powers of the EP had been enlarged somewhat by the Maastricht Treaty. Assuming voters ever had good reason for voting in European

European Parliament Election Results

Party	1994	1989
European Socialist Party (PES)	199	197
European People's Party (EPP, Christian Democrats)	148	162
Liberal and Democratic Reform Group (LDR)	43	44
European Democratic Alliance (EDA)	24	20
Greens	22	27
European Right (ER)	14	12
Left Unity (LU)	13	13
Rainbow Group	8	16
Independent and nonattached (NA)	96	27
Total	567	518

Note: Party totals tend to be provisional in nature, fluctuating over time due to shifts in the affiliation of some members from certain countries. These totals should, therefore, be used as only a close approximation of the composition of the EP.

Parliament elections, they had even more reason to vote in 1994.

In general, the established political parties—especially governing parties—lost substantial support, as indicated by the surge in support for the independent and nonattached (NA) group. The NA group gained 69 seats, jumping from 27 seats in 1989 to 96 seats in 1994.

Nonetheless, the European Socialist Party (PES) remained the EP's largest grouping with 199 seats, compared with 197 in the outgoing parliament. However, the combined strength (242 seats) of the various leftist parties (PES, Greens, Left Unity, Rainbow Group) dropped 11 seats from where it had been after the 1989 election (253). Likewise, the combined seat total for the rightist parties (EPP, LDR, EDA, ER) also slipped, from 238 seats in 1989 to 229 in 1994.

This loss of seats for the leftist and rightist party groupings, while significant in absolute terms, is magnified by the fact that the size of the parliament itself increased by 49 seats, from 518 seats in 1989 to 567 seats in 1994. It can be said, on balance, that the left suffered a bit more than the right, with the solid showing of the

Labour Party (44.2 percent of the vote) in the United Kingdom being the left's only significant victory. Socialist party results in Spain, Germany, Italy, and France were disappointing at best, if not outright humiliating.

From the vantage point of the governing party or parties, the Euro-elections of 1994 sent a loud and clear message of voter discontent. Compared with their showing in the most recent general election, governing parties in Belgium, Denmark, France, Luxembourg, the Netherlands, Spain, and the United Kingdom lost considerable voter support. In the cases of Spain and the United Kingdom, the swing against the government was dramatic. Only in Germany (Kohl) and Italy (Berlusconi) did the prime minister's party receive anything resembling a vote of confidence.

A brief rundown of the June EP election results follows.

Belgium (25 seats, +1 vs. 1989). Prime Minister Jean-Luc Dehaene's center-left coalition government (Socialists and Christian Democrats from both the French and Flemish language groups) captured 12 seats in the 1994 balloting, translating into a 3-seat loss. Meanwhile, the Liberals won 6 seats, a 2-seat increase reflecting substantial voter support versus their showing both in the 1991 general election and in the 1989 Euro-election. The Greens won 2 seats, while the Radicals captured 1. The ultra-nationalist group Vlaams Blok won 2 seats, with the remaining 2 seats going to minor parties.

Denmark (16 seats, same as 1989). The anti-Maastricht forces—People's Movement Against the EU and the June Movement—scored well, garnering 25.5 percent of the vote and 4 seats. The ruling Social Democrats, which had the largest share of the vote in 1989, lost support in 1994, winning only 15.8 percent and 3 seats (a 1-seat loss). They fell behind the Liberals, who won 18.9 percent and 4 seats (a 1-seat gain), and the Conservatives, with 17.7 percent and 3 seats (a 1-seat gain). The Socialist People's Party and the Radical Liberals each secured 1 seat.

France (87 seats, +6 vs. 1989). The center-right government comprised of the Rally for the Republic and the Union for French Democracy lost support (-3.4 percent), but ended up winning 29 seats—a 3-seat gain over 1989. The big story was the surprisingly strong showing by the anti-Maastricht party called the Other Europe, which won 12.3 percent of the vote and 13 seats. The National Front again captured 10 seats, and the French Communist Party won 6, one less than in 1989. Michel Rocard, the Socialist Party leader and one-time hopeful presidential candidate in 1995, presided over the worst showing for the Socialists in a Euro-election; they received just 14.5 percent of the vote and 16 seats—a 6-seat loss. Rocard later resigned from the party leadership. Minor parties won 13 seats.

Germany (99 seats, +18 vs. 1989). As if to underscore his own popularity, Chancellor Helmut Kohl led his CDU-CSU coalition to a resounding victory in the June elections, capturing 15 additional seats in 1994 than in 1989—the majority of the 18 extra seats Germany was awarded after German unification. Kohl's coalition partner, the Free Democrats, fared poorly in the election, losing all of the 4 seats they had held. Meanwhile, voter support for the Social Democrats declined sharply, from 37.4 percent to 32.2 percent, but they still managed to win 40 seats, 9 more than in 1989. The Greens did well, winning 12 seats, a 4-seat increase over 1989. The right-wing Republicans lost all 6 seats they had previously held. Minor parties captured approximately 10 percent of the vote but no seats.

Greece (25 seats, +1 vs. 1989). Prime Minister Andreas Papandreou's Socialist Party (PASOK) lost substantial voter support since the 1993 general election. Nonetheless, the Socialists remained the most popular party, winning 10 seats (a 1-seat increase over their 1989 EP seats) and 37.6 percent of the vote, followed by New Democracy with 9 seats and 32.7 percent. Gaining ground were the Communists and the Ex-Communist Left Alliance (winning 2 seats each and a combined 13.1 percent of the vote) and, most dramatically, Political Spring, the new right-wing nationalist party that garnered 8.7 percent of the vote and 2 seats.

Ireland (15 seats, same as in 1989). Prime Minister Albert Reynolds led his Fianna Fáil Party to a first-place showing, although support for it slid 4.1 percent from the general election in 1992. With 35 percent of the vote, Fianna Fáil captured 7 seats, one more than in 1989, while the opposition Fine Gael Party held steady with 4 seats. The big surprise was the Green Party, which captured 2 seats—its first in the European Parliament from Ireland. The Labour Party retained its 1 seat and independents won 1 seat.

Italy (87 seats, +6 vs. 1989). Newly elected Prime Minister Silvio Berlusconi's party, Forza Italia, came out on top with 30.6 percent of the vote (and 27 seats), a substantial increase over its tally in the general elections in March. The former Christian Democrats won only 10 percent of the vote, entitling them to 8 seats, a stunning 18-seat decline versus 1989. The Socialists continued their dramatic slide into near political oblivion, losing 10 of their 12 seats. Italy's second largest party continues to be the Ex-Communists, who won 19.1 percent of the vote and 16 seats, down 6 seats from 1989. Forza Italia's coalition partners, the National Alliance (NA) and the Northern League (NL), lost voter support compared with the March general election, but managed to gain seats. The NA won 11 seats, a 7-seat increase over 1989, while the NL secured 6 seats, a 4-seat increase. The remaining 17 seats went to various minor parties.

Luxembourg (6 seats, same as 1989). The Greens won their first EP seat by garnering 10.9 percent of the vote. This slight shift was at the expense of the ruling Christian Democrats, who relinquished the seat and fell to just 2 seats. The Socialists held onto their 2 seats, and the Liberals retained the remaining seat.

The Netherlands (31 seats, +6 vs. 1989). The Christian Democrats, after being humiliated in the May 3 general elections where they polled only 22.2 percent of the vote, gained voter support and won 30.8 percent of the Euro-vote. This was enough for the Christian Democrats to capture 10 seats, versus 8 for the second-place Socialists. The Liberals won 6 seats and the D66 (Social Democrats) won 4, a 3-seat increase for each party, leaving 3 seats for the Political Reformed Party and the Greens.

Portugal (25 seats, +1 vs. 1989). The opposition Socialists picked up 10 seats—a 2-seat increase—and 34.7 percent of the vote to inch ahead of the ruling Social Democrats, who won 9 seats and 34.3 percent. That showing for the Social Democrats was down sharply from the 1991 general election when they won 50.4 percent of the vote. The Social Democratic Center Party, which ran an anti-EU campaign, won 12.4 percent of the vote and 3 seats. A new Communist-Green alliance garnered the support of 11.2 percent of the vote and won 3 seats.

Spain (64 seats, +4 vs. 1989). The opposition Popular Party collected an impressive 40.2 percent of the vote and 28 seats—a gain of 13—in dealing the ruling Socialists a stunning defeat. In capturing 30.6 percent of the vote, the Socialists lost 5 of their previous 27 seats. The Communists and allied left parties scored well with 13.4 percent of the vote and 9 seats, a 5-seat increase. Minor parties accounted for 5 seats.

United Kingdom (87 seats, +6 vs. 1989). Prime Minister John Major's Conservative Party suffered a staggering defeat, winning only 27.8 percent of the vote and just 18 seats—14 seats less than its 1989 tally. The Conservatives had won 41.9 percent of the vote in the 1992 general election. Meanwhile, the Labour Party enjoyed its best showing in many years, collecting 44.2 percent of the vote—nearly 10 percent above its 1992 general election results—and 62 seats, a gain of 17 over 1989. The Liberal Democrats, with 16.7 percent of the vote and 2 seats, finally managed to win Euro-representation. Various minor parties garnered the remaining 5 seats.

Aftermath. Following the June balloting, the new European Parliament took two notable actions in July. First, on July 19, 1994, the EP elected German Social Democrat Klaus Haensch to the post of president. Haensch received an overwhelming 365 votes from the 534 MEPs (of 567 total) who participated, well above the 227 votes that would have given him the required majority.

The second significant action taken by the EP was the "consultative" vote taken July 21 in favor of Jacques Santer's nomination to succeed Jacques Delors as European Commission president. Santer's margin of victory was extremely small: 260 for, 238 against, with 23 abstentions. While the vote was technically no more than a consultative exercise, had the EP voted against Santer's nomination, most observers agree that his nomination could not have survived. Under the Maastricht Treaty, the EP is granted the power to approve or reject the entire commission that the president nominates. On January 18, 1995, the EP voted 416 to 103 in favor of the twenty-member commission proposed by Jacques Santer.

The EP Elections of June 1989. Average turnout in the 1989 election was 58 percent. While that was low by European standards, it far exceeded the dismal 36.2 percent turnout registered in the United Kingdom. Bad as that was, British turnout had been nearly 4 percentage points lower in the 1979 and 1984 European Parliament elections.

After holding presidential and parliamentary elections in 1988, voter fatigue may have been a factor in France's poor 48.9 percent showing at the polls. The 1979 tally had been 60.7 percent, which fell to 56.7 percent in 1984.

Overall, the previous center-right majority was replaced by a majority of the center-left. The Socialists, Greens, and the Left Unity Group (Communists) enjoyed an absolute majority. The Socialists became the largest single group in the parliament, increasing their seats from 166 to 197. Meanwhile, the Greens and allied Rainbow Group more than doubled their seats, growing from 20 to 43.

The center-right parties did not do well. In Germany, the Christian Democrats lost support to the extreme right wing, which won 6 seats. In France, the center-right lost 9 seats, lowering their total to 32 seats. In the United Kingdom, Margaret Thatcher's Conservative Party surrendered 13 seats to Labour, bringing its total down to 32, while Labour raised its total to 45 seats.

European Court of Justice

The European Court of Justice is the EU's supreme court. It sits in Luxembourg and in 1994 consisted of thirteen justices—a president and a judge from each of the member states who serve by agreement of the member states. Justices serve renewable six-year terms.

The court determines whether EU laws, as embodied in the treaties, are interpreted and implemented properly. Complaints about treaty violations by member states can be addressed to the court by other members states or by the European Commission. Member governments, EU institutions, and private individuals also have redress to the court to contest commission and council actions.

The court resolves conflicts between community and national laws, and its decisions are binding on all parties and may not be appealed. The court's decisions have generally strengthened EU institutions and promoted the process of EU integration. It has played a major role in the removal of barriers to the free movement of goods and people among the member states.

Because the court has become overloaded with cases in recent years, the SEA created a new Court of First Instance. This lower-level court has jurisdiction over such things as antitrust matters and suits brought by employees of the EU.

LEXICON

Accession: The process whereby new member states become full members of the EU.

"Battle of the seat": Derisive name given to the jurisdictional dispute raging between Belgium, Luxembourg, and France about which country ultimately will be home to a consolidated European Parliament.

Broadening versus deepening: Debate raging in the EU about whether to expand (broaden) membership now or integrate more fully (deepen) the economies of the EU members.

The Bureau: Executive Committee of the European Parliament, composed of the president and vice presidents. It establishes agenda and organizes work of the parliament.

CAP: Common Agricultural Policy. A controversial and expensive system of agricultural subsidies by the EU that currently consumes 65 percent of the EU's total budget.

The commission: Common term for the European Commission, the initiator of EC policies.

COREPER: Committee of Permanent Representatives. These are ambassadors from member states to the EU in Brussels.

The council: Common term for the Council of Ministers.

Decisions: The commission and council can issue binding "decisions" directed at specific governments, enterprises, or individuals. Decisions have the force of law but are not generalized in their application.

The Delors Plan: Named after European Commission president Jacques Delors, the plan establishes stages for implementation of a European Economic and Monetary Union (EMU).

Directives: The commission and council can issue "directives" that are binding on member states. Such directives establish only the results to be achieved and leave the specific methods for achieving those results to the member states.

ECU: European Currency Unit. Accounting unit used by the EU, with limited business and private use as well, that may become the single currency for a fully integrated EU.

EDC: European Defense Community. Aborted attempt in the 1950s to create an integrated European military force.

EEA: European Economic Area. Created in 1992 to link the free-trade zones of the EU and the European Free Trade Association (EFTA). Free-trade benefits were extended to non-EU members, but such members were not included in EU decision-making. Swiss voters decided in December 1992 against participation in the EEA.

EFTA: European Free Trade Association. Established in 1960 by the Stockholm Convention and headquartered in Geneva, this association currently has four members: Iceland, Liechtenstein, Norway, and Switzerland. Six former members (Austria, Denmark, Finland, Portugal, Sweden, and the United Kingdom) have left the EFTA and joined the EU.

EMS: European Monetary System. Established in 1979, this system of fixed exchange rates is an important building block toward eventual economic and monetary union. A key element of EMS is the Exchange Rate Mechanism (ERM).

EMU: Economic and Monetary Union. Scheduled for full implementation in 1999, EMU is a plan to integrate the economies of the EU countries, with economic and monetary policy directed from Brussels, utilizing a European Central Bank and a single currency, probably the ECU.

EPC: European Political Cooperation. Forum in which EU ministers of foreign affairs discuss coordination of foreign policy among member countries.

ERM: Exchange Rate Mechanism. The central feature of the European Monetary System (EMS), this control measure allows member currencies to fluctuate within two specified bands. The British pound left the ERM in September 1992, followed by the Italian lira, and the entire EMS process has been in considerable disarray since that time.

ESCB: European System of Central Banks. Part of the Delors Plan for European Economic and Monetary Union (*see* EMU).

Europe 1992: The then EC's program for economic integration, launched in a 1985 White Paper. Also referred to as EC-'92, "1992," Europe Without Frontiers, and the Single Market.

European Council: A "summit" meeting of the EU heads of government that takes place twice a year.

European Union (EU): The organization established in 1993 by the Maastricht Treaty. The EU adds a common foreign and security policy and cooperation on justice and police matters to the existing EC structure.

Europhoria: The new mood of optimism in Europe spurred on by excitement about the Single Market of 1992.

Eurosclerosis: A mood of impotence and malaise that gripped Europe during the late 1970s, the early 1980s, and reappeared in the 1990s. Economic and political stagnation was thought to portend an end to Europe's central role in world events.

Fortress Europe: Term used in the United States and elsewhere by those concerned that the Single Market would create open borders within the EU and closed borders to the outside world. EU officials have steadfastly denied any protectionist intent.

Harmonization: Process of bringing member-state laws or policies into line with a norm or directive of the EU.

Maastricht Treaty: Far-reaching and controversial treaty that went into force on November 1, 1993. Maastricht created the European Union (EU) and established a timeframe for moving toward a common European currency and a common foreign and security policy.

MEP: Member of the European Parliament.

Monnet, Jean: French economist and advocate of a "United States of Europe." He helped found the European Coal and Steel Community (ECSC), serving as its president from 1952 to 1955.

"Mountains of butter, lakes of wine": Derisive reference to the surpluses that resulted from the Common Agricultural Policy (CAP).

Party group: Members of the European Parliament are organized by sometimes fluid groupings of ideologically like-minded members from various countries instead of by national delegations.

Schuman, Robert: French foreign minister in 1950 who, together with Jean Monnet, proposed creation of the ECSC and served as president of the European Assembly in 1958.

Single European Act (SEA): Ratified in 1987, this act amended the Treaty of Rome to provide a legal framework and streamlined decision-making for implementation of the EC's integrated market of 1992.

Single Market. See Europe 1992.

Social dimension: The social and economic disruptions that were expected to result from increased competition, mergers, and acquisitions throughout Europe. The Council of Ministers adopted a social charter that offered protection against "social dumping" and guaranteed certain health, safety, and labor rights throughout the EU.

Social dumping: Attempts in EU countries to devalue wages and labor laws to attract investment. A social charter was designed to prevent abuse of worker rights.

Subsidiarity: Principle of decentralization in the EU that encourages that decisions be made by the lowest level of government—the "subsidiary" rather than headquarters level. British prime minister Thatcher stressed this principle in opposing too much power being amassed by "Brussels."

"Traveling circus": Nickname for the European Parliament, which holds sessions and committee meetings and maintains offices in Brussels, Strasbourg, and Luxembourg.

Treaties of Rome: Treaties signed in 1957 establishing the European Economic Community (EEC) and European Atomic Energy Community (Euratom).

Treaty of Paris: Treaty signed in 1952 establishing the ECSC.

VAT: Value-added tax, the most common form of indirect taxation in most European countries.

Weighted or qualified majority: Under the Single European Act, the Council of Ministers can adopt most legislation by "weighted" or "qualified" majority. Before this amendment to the Treaty of Rome, all decisions had to be approved by unanimous vote, giving any member state an effective veto.

Austria

The Country in Brief

Official Name: Republic of Austria (*Republik Osterreich*)
Capital: Vienna
Currency: Schilling
National Day: October 26 (anniversary of declaration of neutrality)
Language: German
Religion: Roman Catholic
Memberships: Non-NATO; officially joined EU January 1, 1995
Border Countries: Czech Republic, Germany, Hungary, Italy, Liechtenstein, Slovakia, Slovenia, Switzerland
Embassy in Washington, D.C.: 3524 International Court, N.W., 20008. Telephone: (202) 895-6700.

Political Profile

Government Type: Federal republic/parliamentary democracy
Head of State: Federal President Thomas Klestil
Political Party: People's Party (OVP)
Assumed Office: 1992
Election Method: Directly elected, second ballot
Term of Office: Six years
Next Election: 1998
Head of Government: Federal Chancellor Franz Vranitzky

Political Party: Social Democratic Party (SPO)
Assumed Office: 1986
Reelected: 1994
Next Election: 1998
Legislature: Bicameral, Federal Assembly
(*Bundesversammlung*)
Upper Chamber: Bundesrat, 63 members, indirectly elected by
the nine state legislatures (*Länder*)
Term of Office: Four to six years, depending on state
Lower Chamber: Nationalrat, 183 members, elected by propor-
tional representation, has most legislative powers. The government
is formed by the party that controls a majority of Nationalrat
members.
Term of Office: Four years
Last Election: 1994
Next Election: 1998

Comparative Data

Population: 7.9 million
GDP: $162 billion
GDP Per Capita: $20,400
Voting System (Lower Chamber): Party list proportional
Per Capita Representation Rate: 43,000
Big Government Index: 46.4%
Women in Parliament: 21%
Voter Turnout Rate: 86%

MAJOR POLITICAL PARTIES

Social Democratic Party of Austria
(*Socialdemokratshe Partei Osterreichs*, SPO)

Founded in 1889 as the Social Democratic Party, the SPO was
subsequently renamed the Austrian Socialist Party before returning to its original name in 1991. It retains a center-left orientation.
Its base of support is from workers and the lower middle class.

Austrian People's Party (*Osterreichische Volkspartei*, OVP)

Founded in 1945, the People's Party evolved from the Christian Social Party. It has a center-right orientation, with its base of support coming from farmers and business people.

Austrian Freedom Party (*Freiheitliche Partei Osterreichs*, FPO)

The Freedom Party evolved in 1956 from the National Socialist Party. It retains a right-wing orientation, but has tried to moderate its policies and has become something of a traditional "liberal" party while stressing strong anti-immigration positions.

Green Alternative (*Grüne Alternative*, GA)

The Green Alternative was founded in 1987 as a coalition of three environmental groups. It focuses on environmental issues and has a left orientation.

MINOR POLITICAL PARTIES

Austrian Alternative List (*Alternative Liste Osterreich*, ALO)
Liberal Forum (*Liberales Forum*, LF)
United Greens of Austria (*Vereinigte Grüne Osterreichs*, VGO)

ELECTION REVIEW

1992 Presidential Elections: Acceptance Regained

For six years, beginning in 1986, Austria endured the agony of having a federal president who was something of as an international pariah. Those were the Kurt Waldheim years. Accused of participating in war crimes during World War II, Waldheim was informed by such countries as Belgium, Canada, Japan, Switzerland, and the United States that he would not be welcome on state

1992 Presidential Election Results		
Candidate	First Round (% Votes)	Runoff (% Votes)
Rudolf Streicher (SPO)	41	43
Thomas Klestil (OVP)	37	57
Heide Schmidt (FPO)	16	
Robert Jungk (Greens)	6	

Note: Percentages may not add up to 100 due to rounding. SPO = Social Democratic Party, OVP = People's Party, FPO = Freedom Party.

visits. In April 1987, the U.S. Justice Department placed Waldheim's name on its "watch list" because of evidence that he had "assisted or otherwise participated in the persecution of persons because of race, religion, national origin or political opinion." Feeling the brunt of this international cold shoulder was particularly difficult for Austrians, since their country, officially neutral, was home to so many United Nations facilities and the site of numerous international conferences and negotiations.

For many Austrians, the 1992 presidential elections could not have come too soon. After all, Austria had officially applied to join the EC (now EU). It certainly did their cause no good to have an alleged Nazi war criminal in the presidential palace. The priority in 1992 was to elect a president who had a clean record and would be accepted in international circles. Enter Thomas Klestil, a conservative, who was heralded as having international contacts and a spotless reputation.

Austrians knew very little about Klestil, but what they did know reassured them. An economist, he was the top career diplomat at the foreign office and had served as an ambassador in Washington, D.C.

Klestil easily defeated Social Democrat Rudolf Streicher (57 percent to 43 percent) in a runoff election on May 24, 1992. The Freedom Party's candidate received 16 percent of the vote in the first round of elections and dropped out of the running. Jörg Haider, the Freedom Party leader, indirectly endorsed Klestil, thus giving him the support needed to secure the victory. Klestil took office July 8, 1992.

1986 Presidential Elections: The World Is Watching

Intense worldwide attention focused in 1986 on the Austrian presidential and parliamentary elections. This was unusual for a country whose national elections frequently come and go without the world community taking much notice. However, former United Nations General Secretary Kurt Waldheim's bid to become Austria's president changed all that, shining an unwanted spotlight on a dark episode in Austrian history. Revelations about his World War II service in the German army opened old wounds and dominated his presidential campaign.

Some Austrians resented what was seen as foreign intrusion into Austria's domestic political process, and Waldheim probably benefited from this nationalistic reaction. Waldheim bested his Socialist opponent, Kurt Steyrer, in the first round of voting on May 4, but his 49.65 percent tally was just short of the required majority. He won the June 8 runoff convincingly, garnering 54 percent of the vote against 46 percent for Steyrer.

The next day, Socialist Chancellor Fred Sinowatz resigned and the SPO leadership elected Franz Vranitzky to replace him. Waldheim was sworn in as president on July 8, 1986, the first non-Socialist since 1945 elected to the presidency.

1986 Presidential Election Results

Candidate	First Round (% Votes)	Runoff (% Votes)
Kurt Waldheim (I)	49.7	53.9
Kurt Steyrer (SPO)	43.7	46.1
Freda Meissner-Blau (Greens)	5.4	
Otto Scrinzi (ND)	1.2	

Note: Percentages may not add up to 100 due to rounding. I = Independent, SPO = Socialist Party, ND = National Democratic Party.

1994 Parliamentary Election Results

Party	% Votes	Seats
Social Democratic Party (SPO)	35	65
People's Party (OVP)	28	52
Freedom Party (FPO)	23	42
Greens	7	13
Liberal Forum (LF)	6	11
Total Seats		**183**

Note: Percentages may not add up to 100 due to rounding.

1994 Parliamentary Elections: The Right Surges

The ruling coalition was stunned on October 9 with the worst election results either party had received since 1945. For the first time in the postwar period, these two parties combined to win less than 80 percent of the vote.

Despite this dismal outcome, the two ruling parties, the Social Democrats (renamed from the Socialists in 1991) of Chancellor Franz Vranitzky and the People's Party of Erhard Busek, remained Austria's two largest parties. The Social Democrats won 35.2 percent of the vote and 65 seats (down from 80 seats in 1990), while the People's Party garnered 27.9 percent of the vote and 52 seats (down from 60 seats). Combined, they still enjoy a comfortable majority in the 183-seat Nationalrat.

The big surprise of the election was the surge in support for Jörg Haider's far-right Freedom Party. Haider's party, which campaigned on a strong anti-immigration platform, picked up 9 additional seats, for a total of 42, on the strength of roughly 22.6 percent of the vote. The Greens won 7 percent of the vote and 13 seats and the Liberals secured 5.7 percent of the vote and 11 seats.

1990 Parliamentary Elections: How Grand a Coalition?

The Freedom Party directly affected the 1992 presidential elections by endorsing Klestil. The party's influence in the 1990 parliamentary elections was much less direct.

Past Parliamentary Election Results

Party	1990 % Votes	1990 Seats	1986 % Votes	1986 Seats	1982 % Votes	1982 Seats	1979 % Votes	1979 Seats
SPO	43	80	43	80	48	90	51	95
OVP	32	60	41	77	43	81	42	77
FPO	17	33	10	18	5	12	6	11
VGO/ALO[a]	5	10	5	8	—	—	—	—
Total Seats		183		183		183		183

Note: Percentages may not add up to 100 due to rounding. SPO = Socialist Party, OVP = People's Party, FPO = Freedom Party, VGO/ALO = United Greens of Austria/Austrian Alternative List.

[a] These parties formed the Green Alternative in 1987.

During the campaign, the People's Party (OVP) said it would not rule out the possibility of forming a coalition with the Freedom Party (FPO). The Socialist Party (SPO), on the other hand, made it clear that it would not enter a coalition that included the Freedom Party. Thus, many liberals and socialists decided to vote for the SPO rather than take the risk of a coalition government that included the right-wing FPO.

That was not the only selling point for the SPO. Franz Vranitzky, the incumbent federal chancellor and Socialist Party leader, was immensely popular. His name was placed on the top of the party list in all nine electoral districts. The SPO used his popularity to mask some of the scandal and internal conflicts brewing within the party. The SPO even encouraged voters to write in Vranitzky's name on the ballot if they wanted to avoid voting directly for the SPO. The Socialist Party ended up with 43 percent of the vote—the same percentage as in 1986—and 80 of the 183 available seats. Vranitzky was reappointed chancellor.

During the campaign, Vranitzky emphasized "safety first" and "no experiments," hoping to reassure an electorate that had become anxious in light of the unprecedented instability that was sweeping much of Eastern Europe.

For its part, the People's Party suffered from having a less than flamboyant leader in a campaign highlighted by personalities. Josef Riegler had a farm boy image, a stark contrast to the SPO's Vranitzky and the FPO's Haider. In the end, the OVP garnered only 32 percent of the vote and 60 seats.

Playing against the ambiguous immigration record of the People's Party, the Freedom Party stood firm against immigration. The FPO argued that tighter controls would help solve the country's increasing crime and unemployment problems and warned Austrians that "Vienna must not become Chicago."

The FPO, with almost 17 percent of the vote and 33 seats, received support from the working-class districts in Vienna, thereby taking votes away from the Socialists. Meanwhile, the environmentalist Green parties, which had formed a coalition in 1987 called the Green Alternative (GA), won nearly 5 percent of the votes and captured 10 seats.

ELECTION LEXICON

Active neutrality: Austria's brand of neutrality, which it interprets as militarily neutral but not politically neutral. This enables Austria to join international political organizations.

Anschluss: Literally, "joining." Refers to the union of Austria and Germany after Hitler absorbed Austria in 1938.

Antifreeze Crisis: The government of Franz Sinowatz was shaken in 1985 by revelations that toxic antifreeze was being added to sweeten Austrian wines.

Austrian State Treaty: Treaty signed May 15, 1955, by the four Allied foreign ministers: Molotov (U.S.S.R.), McMillan (United Kingdom), Dulles (United States), and Pinay (France), as well as by Austrian Foreign Minister Figl. The treaty granted Austria full sovereignty, provided it remained neutral.

Bundesrat: The 63-seat upper house of parliament.

Bundesversammlung: Term for the Federal Assembly, which is a special meeting of both chambers of parliament.

Grand coalition: Governing coalition between the Social Democratic and People's parties.

"Hitler's grandson": Unflattering reference to Jörg Haider, leader of the right-wing Freedom Party.

Kreisky era: The period from 1970 to 1983, when the Socialists controlled the government, under Chancellor Bruno Kreisky.

Land/Länder: A state or province. Nine states, or *Länder*, comprise the Federal Republic of Austria: Vienna, Salzburg, Vorarlberg, Carinthia, Upper Austria, Lower Austria, Burgenland, Styria, and Tirol.

"A man the world trusts": Kurt Waldheim's unintentionally ironic campaign slogan during the 1986 presidential campaign.

"Marriage of the elephants": Derisive term used by Freedom Party chairman Jörg Haider to describe the SPO-OVP grand coalition.

Nationalrat: The 183 member lower chamber of parliament.

"Prisoner of the Vienna Hofburg": Unkind reference to former president Kurt Waldheim. Unable to travel on state visits, Waldheim spent much of his presidency stuck at the Vienna Hofburg, the president's residence.

"Proper employment policies of the Third Reich": These words of Jörg Haider led to his removal from the governorship of Carinthia in 1991.

Proporzsystem: Austrian version of the spoils system in which jobs and other state-controlled benefits are distributed according to party affiliation and electoral strength. Until 1966, the SPO and OVP divided up cabinet and other government jobs according to this "proportional system."

"Safety first" and "No experiments": 1990 campaign appeals of Federal Chancellor Franz Vranitzky. They struck a responsive chord with voters increasingly concerned about growing instability in Eastern Europe.

Social partnership: The policy of cooperation rather than confrontation between labor and industry. This approach has provided jobs and minimized strikes, but has shown signs of weakening under the pressure of rising unemployment.

UN on the Danube: Reference to the many United Nations agencies located in the Vienna International Center.

HISTORICAL SYNOPSIS

Austria became a separate nation with the collapse of the Austro-Hungarian Empire in World War I. During the two decades between the wars, there was little sense of national identity, aggravating the political and economic turmoil that characterized the period.

1919 The Treaty of St. Germain with the victorious Allies establishes the German-speaking provinces of the former Austro-Hungarian Empire as an independent republic. Union with Germany is prohibited.

1938 German troops enter Austria. *Anschluss* incorporates Austria into Hitler's Third Reich.

1945 Allied forces from both East and West take control of Austria. The country is divided into occupation zones, with Vienna under joint administration.

1947 The People's Party and the Socialist Party set up a "grand coalition."

1955 Austrian State Treaty ending the occupation is concluded. The Austrian parliament declares the country neutral.

1970 Elections give a plurality to the Socialist Party, which forms a minority government with Bruno Kreisky as chancellor.

1983 The Socialist Party loses its majority in elections but forms a coalition government with the Freedom Party. Kreisky resigns as chancellor and is succeeded by Fred Sinowatz.

1986 Kurt Waldheim, running as an independent with the support of the People's Party, is elected president. Radical nationalist Jörg Haider takes command of the

Freedom Party. The Socialist Party refuses to continue the coalition. Franz Vranitzky becomes chancellor and calls for early elections. The Socialist Party is returned with a reduced plurality. The People's Party also loses seats, while the Freedom Party gains. The Greens enter parliament for the first time.

1987   A new "grand coalition" takes office with Vranitzky as chancellor and People's Party leader Alois Mock as vice chancellor and foreign minister.

1989   Austria submits an application for membership in the European Economic Community, which becomes the European Union (EU) in 1993.

1991   The Socialist Party decides to moderate its image by renaming itself the Social Democratic party.

1992   Thomas Klestil succeeds Kurt Waldheim as president.

1994   Austrians on June 12 overwhelmingly pass referendum to join the EU.

1995   On January 1, Austria (along with Finland and Sweden) officially joins the EU.

Belgium

The Country in Brief

Official Name: Kingdom of Belgium (*Royaume de Belgique* [French], *Koninkrijk België* [Flemish/Dutch], *Konigreich Belgien* [German])
Capital: Brussels
Currency: Belgian franc
National Day: July 21 (Independence Day)
Languages: Flemish/Dutch, French, German
Religion: Roman Catholic
Memberships: NATO and EU
Border Countries: Federal Republic of Germany, France, Luxembourg, the Netherlands
Embassy in Washington, D.C.: 3330 Garfield Street, N.W., 20008. Telephone: (202) 333-6900.

Political Profile

Government Type: Constitutional monarchy
Head of State: King Albert II
Succeeded to Throne: August 1993
Head of Government: Prime Minister Jean-Luc Dehaene
Political Party: Christian Social Party (CVP)
Assumed Office: 1992
Next Election: 1995
Legislature: Bicameral, Parliament

Upper Chamber: Senate, 181 members (106 directly elected by proportional representation; remainder indirectly elected, 50 by provincial councils, 25 by Senate).

Lower Chamber: Chamber of Representatives, 212 members, elected by proportional representation. Although the Senate and the Lower Chamber technically have roughly equal powers, the Lower Chamber forms the government and is regarded as the more influential body.

Term of Office: Five years

Last Election: 1991

Next Election: 1995

Comparative Data

Population: 10 million

GDP: $197 billion

GDP Per Capita: $19,300

Voting System (Lower Chamber): Party list proportional

Per Capita Representation Rate: 47,000

Big Government Index: 45%

Women in Parliament: 9%

Voter Turnout Rate: 93%

MAJOR POLITICAL PARTIES

Because linguistic and regional divisions are of particular importance in Belgium, the major political parties all have Flemish and French branches.

CHRISTIAN DEMOCRATIC PARTIES (*Christelijke Vokspartij*, CVP—Flemish; *Parti Social Chrétien*, PSC—Francophone)

While similar in orientation to other European Christian democratic parties, these parties have evolved from the original Catholic Party, but they are now nondenominational. Their support comes from both commercial and working-class interests.

SOCIAL DEMOCRATIC PARTIES (*Parti Socialiste*, PS— Francophone; *Socialistische Partij*, SP—Flemish)

Both branches of the Socialist Party are pragmatic, social democratic in outlook. Their focus tends to be on industrial democracy and social welfare issues.

LIBERAL PARTIES (*Freedom and Progress Party, Partij voor Vrijheid en Vooruitgang*, PVV—Flemish; *Liberal Reform Party, Réformateur Libéral*, PRL—Francophone)

These offshoots of the former Belgian Liberal Party present traditional "liberal" programs, such as commitment to free enterprise and restraints on government spending. The PVV was founded in 1970 and the PRL was founded in 1979.

Flemish Bloc (*Vlaams Blok*, VB)

Founded in 1979, the VB is an ultranationalist Flemish group that seeks an independent Flanders and the repatriation of non-Flemish immigrants.

MINOR POLITICAL PARTIES

Ecologists (*Ecologistes*, Ecolo)
Francophone Democratic Front
    (*Front Démocratique de Bruxellois Francophones*, FDF)
Live Differently (*Anders Gaan Leven*, Agalev)
People's Union (*De Volksunie*, VU)

ELECTION REVIEW

1991 Parliamentary Elections: Head to the Fringes

Because Belgium consists of three main regions (Flanders, Wallonia, and Brussels) and three language groups (Flemish/Dutch,

1991 Parliamentary Election Results		
Party	% Votes	Seats
Flemish Christian People's (CVP)	17	39
French Socialist (PS)	14	35
Flemish Socialist (SP)	12	28
Freedom and Progress (PVV)	12	26
Liberal Reform (PRL)	8	20
French Social Christian (PSC)	8	18
Vlaams Bloc (VB)	7	12
Peoples Union (VU)	6	10
Ecologists (ECOLO)	5	10
Others	11	14
Total Seats		212

Note: Percentages may not add up to 100 due to rounding.

French, and German), Belgian politics for years has revolved around constitutional reforms to protect these regions and language groups. The linguistic issues are often referred to as "community problems." While other policy issues are discussed, community problems tend to dominate the political landscape and create the most tensions within the government.

In general, due to a proportional voting system that allows smaller parties to win seats in parliament—and because voting is compulsory (a small fine is levied against nonvoters)—voter turnout is extremely high. High turnout and numerous parties make for a volatile and complicated political scene.

In 1991, Belgians were fed up with the traditional political parties. When they went to the polls on November 24, they registered a powerful protest vote against business as usual. As a result, Prime Minister Wilfried Martens, who had served continuously since December 17, 1981, was forced to turn over the reins of government.

Martens's Flemish Christian Democratic Party dropped to an all-time low of 16.7 percent of the vote and 39 seats—a 4-seat loss in the 212-member parliament. All the mainstream parties, including the Flemish and French-speaking Socialists, French-speaking Christian Democrats, Flemish Peoples Union, and the French-speaking Liberals lost voter support and a combined total of 19 seats.

Meanwhile, significant gains were made by parties previously considered to be on the fringes of the political spectrum. In Wallonia, the Green Party (Ecolo) went from 3 to 10 seats in parliament. In Flanders, the extreme nationalist Vlaams Blok jumped from 2 seats to 12. Vlaams Blok had campaigned for an independent Flanders and to return non-European immigrants to their countries. This party received significant support in cities with large immigrant populations, even earning a plurality of the vote (25 percent) in Antwerp.

Another party made its presence felt in 1991—the antipolitical party headed by former stock exchange guru Jean-Pierre Van Rossem. His party, whose slogan was "Vote Libertine," called for the abolition of the monarchy, privatization of the social security system, and higher taxes on the wealthy. Arrested the week before the election on charges of investment fraud, Rossem nonetheless entered parliament, along with two of his colleagues.

Following the election, it took many months of negotiating behind the scenes before Jean-Luc Dehaene, a Flemish Christian Democrat, was able to form a new government. Dehaene had been deputy prime minister from 1988 to 1992.

When Dehaene took over, he faced two major tasks: stabilizing the economy and continuing the constitutional reforms implemented by Martens. In dealing with the economy, he had to decide on issues of public finances and the budget deficit to put the country on course for the European Economic and Monetary Union (EMU) in 1996. His solutions were to tighten up on welfare fraud, close loopholes in the tax system, and introduce a 1 percent social security tax.

Obtaining the proposed constitutional reforms would prove tougher to achieve. Dehaene's four-party coalition—Socialists and Christian Democrats from both language groups—did not command enough votes to guarantee passage of the government's programs.

Adding to the political uncertainty in Belgium was the death of the country's long-serving and respected King Baudouin, who died of a heart attack July 31, 1993, while vacationing in Spain.

Although the Belgian king has only limited political authority, he plays an important symbolic role. King Baudouin was particularly beloved by his subjects. Because succession is based on direct male heirs, and since Baudouin and his wife were childless, his younger brother, Prince Albert, ascended to the throne on August 1, 1993.

The power and to some extent the legitimacy of the king came under attack in April 1990 on an issue related to abortion. Tradition holds that the king must sign all legislation passed by democratic methods. But King Baudouin, a devout Catholic, was morally opposed to a bill that allowed abortion within the first trimester of pregnancy and would not act against his conscience.

Invoking Article 79 of the Constitution on April 3, 1990, the government announced that the king was "temporarily incapable of ruling." The abortion law was then approved by ministerial signature. Less than thirty-six hours later, a joint session of parliament invoked Article 82, placing the king back in power.

This process has led to renewed debate about the proper role of the king in politics. While it is unlikely that a significant reduction in his power will occur, it is likely that the prerequisite of his signature on new legislation will be eliminated.

1987 Parliamentary Elections:
Of Languages, Constitutions, and Martens

The 1987 election occurred only two years into the parliament's four-year term—precisely because of a controversy about languages. The so-called Happart Affair involved the mayor of Voeren (*Fouron* in French), a historically French-speaking city that was transferred in 1963 into the jurisdiction of Flemish-speaking Limburg province. French-speaking Jose Happart was elected mayor in 1983. He refused to use the official language of the province (Flemish) and, in 1986, the Limburg administrative court ruled that Happart should be removed from office for failing to speak Flemish. The case lingered for some time, causing tension and strain throughout the political system.

It became clear in the midst of this crisis that the constitutional structure of the state needed further reform. The only apparent solution to the longstanding tensions in Voeren was to continue the federalization of the country, a process started in the 1970s.

Past Parliamentary Election Results

Party	1987 % Votes	1987 Seats	1985 % Votes	1985 Seats	1981 % Votes	1981 Seats	1978 % Votes	1978 Seats
CVP	19	43	21	49	19	43	26	57
PS	16	40	14	35	13	35	13	32
SP	15	32	15	32	12	26	12	26
PRL/PVV	21	48	21	46	22	52	16	37
PSC	8	19	8	20	7	18	10	25
VU	8	16	8	16	10	20	7	14
Others	13	14	13	14	18	18	15	11
Total Seats		**212**		**212**		**212**		**202**

Note: Percentages may not add up to 100 due to rounding. CVP = Flemish Christian People's Party, PS = French Socialist Party, SP = Flemish Socialist Party, PRL = Liberal Reform Party, PVV = Freedom and Progress Party, PSC = French Social Christian Party, VU = Peoples Union.

Unable to make progress on any of his economic policy initiatives, such as cutting the budget deficit and reducing unemployment, and facing a possible "no confidence" vote even among Flemish-speaking members of his own party, Prime Minister Martens submitted his resignation to the king. The resignation was accepted, and the king charged Martens with creating a new government to pursue further constitutional reforms needed to solve the Voeren problem—in other words, the "community problem." The two chambers of parliament were dissolved and new elections were held on December 13, 1987.

Results. A number of trends can be detected in the election results. Flemish-speaking Flanders moved to the right, while French-speaking Wallonia veered leftward. In addition, for the first time since 1936, the Socialist parties (PS and SP) emerged as the country's foremost political force, with the Christian parties (CVP and PSC) second and the Liberal parties (PVV and PRL) third. The Socialists received 30.6 percent of the 1987 vote, compared with 28.4 percent in 1985. The Christian parties garnered 27.5 percent in 1987, down from 29.3 percent in 1985. The Liberals stayed the same at 20.9 percent in both elections.

These three principal political families represented a growing portion of the electorate, having grown from 73.1 percent in 1981 to 78.6 percent in 1985 and 79 percent in 1987.

1994 European Parliament Elections

As usual, Belgians turned out to vote in large numbers in the European Parliament elections, held June 12, 1994. In general, Prime Minister Jean-Luc Dehaene's ruling left coalition (Socialists and Christian Democrats from both language groups) lost support compared with the 1989 Euro-election while the right gained.

The vote for the center-left parties declined 5 percent, resulting in a 3-seat loss. The Christian Democratic parties captured 6 seats, a 1-seat loss. The Socialists also won 6 seats, dropping 2 seats from the 1989 elections. Support for the Greens also tapered off, leaving them with 2 seats.

Gaining strength were the Liberals, who captured 6 seats for a 2-seat gain. The ultranationalist group Vlaams Blok won 2 seats.

European Parliament Election Results

Party	1994		1989		1984		1979	
	% Votes	Seats	% Votes	Seats	% Votes	Seats	% Votes	Seats
CVP/PSC	24	6	29	7	27	6	38	10
PS/SP	22	6	27	8	30	9	23	7
PRL/PVV	20	6	18	4	18	5	16	4
Others	34	7	26	5	25	4	22	3
Total Seats		25		24		24		24

Note: Percentages may not add up to 100 due to rounding. CVP = Flemish Christian People's Party, PSC = French Social Christian Party, PS = French Socialist Party, SP = Flemish Socialist Party, PRL = Liberal Reform Party, PVV = Freedom and Progress Party.

ELECTION LEXICON

Article 79: Constitutional provision that allows parliament to temporarily declare the king incapable of ruling. It was used in 1990 to enact a new abortion law.

Article 82: Constitutional provision that returns power to the king after Article 79 has been invoked.

Avenue of the law: *Rue de la Loi,* in French; *Wetstaat,* in Flemish. Common expression for the parliament.

BENELUX: The Belgium, Netherlands, and Luxembourg economic union, founded in 1948.

BLEU: The Belgium-Luxembourg Economic Union, established in 1922. Expanded in 1948 to include the Netherlands (*see* BENELUX).

"Bulldozer" or "Carthorse": Nicknames given to Jean-Luc Dehaene's government because of its ability to fix problems.

"Capital of Europe": Nickname for Brussels, the headquarters city for the European Union and NATO. About one in three residents of Brussels is non-Belgian.

"Community problems": Catchall term that covers the linguistic and cultural frictions resulting from Belgium's multilingual and multicultural society.

Devolution: Shifting of political power from the national government to the linguistic regions.

"Happart Affair": Jose Happart, the French-speaking mayor of Voeren elected in 1983, refused to use the official language of the region, Flemish. The administrative court ruled in 1986 that Happart should be removed from office because of this refusal. Prime Minister Wilfried Martens resigned over the issue, leading to the 1987 elections.

Hertoginnendal: Expression for the central government, referring to the castle where major government meetings take place.

Kiesplicht: Duty to Vote. Every Belgian eighteen or older has the legal obligation to vote in local, national, and European elections.

"Our people first": Anti-immigrant campaign slogan of Vlaams Blok in 1991.

"Out of self-defense": Another anti-immigrant Vlaams Blok campaign slogan during the 1991 election. Posters containing the slogan showed a pair of boxing gloves.

"Pacte Communautaire": Also known as the "Egmont Pact," this complex constitutional reform plan from the late 1970s provided for a Senate, with voting requirements to protect minority French speakers, to represent community interests.

"Plumber": Nickname for Prime Minister Jean-Luc Dehaene, earned because of his reputation as a "Mr. Fixit."

"Roman-blue" coalition: Popular name of the previous coalition, headed by Prime Minister Wilfried Martens. Roman refers to the Flemish Christian Democratic Party and blue refers to the trademark color of the liberal Freedom and Progress Party.

"Royal question": After World War II, the Belgian monarchy was rocked by accusations—never proved—that King Leopold III was a Nazi collaborator during World War II.

"TGV": Nickname for Prime Minister Jean-Luc Dehaene, referring to the French TGV express train.

Treaty of Rome: Treaty signed in 1957 by Belgium and the other five original members of the European Economic Community.

"Vote Libertine": Slogan for the antipolitical party headed by Jean-Pierre Van Rossem.

HISTORICAL SYNOPSIS

A successful revolution in 1830 against Wilhelm I of the Netherlands resulted in Belgium gaining its independence in 1831.

1922	The Belgium-Luxembourg Economic Union (BLEU) is formed.
1940	Germany invades Belgium.
1944	Belgium is liberated from German occupation.

1944–1950	The "Royal Question" dominates Belgian politics. Suspicion is raised against King Leopold III that he had prematurely surrendered to the Germans in 1940 and then collaborated with the Nazis.
1948	Women are granted suffrage. Britain, France, the Netherlands, Belgium, and Luxembourg sign the Brussels Treaty, creating a fifty-year alliance against armed attack. Belgium, the Netherlands, and Luxembourg form the BENELUX economic union.
1949	Belgium becomes a founding member of NATO.
1950	Referendum in favor of the king passes with 57.7 percent of the vote. The Flemings vote overwhelmingly in support of the king's return from exile during the Nazi era, with a narrow majority of Walloons (Francophone residents of Wallonia) opposed.
1951	On July 16, after massive demonstrations and violence in Wallonia, King Leopold III abdicates in favor of his eldest son, Baudouin (*Boudewijn* in Flemish).
1957	Belgium is among the original six countries signing the Treaty of Rome and establishing the European Economic Community, effective January 1, 1958.
1960	The Congo Republic obtains its independence on June 30. (In 1971, it changed its name to Zaire.)
1962	The linguistic border is officially established by a law requiring that all education in the Flemish-speaking areas be conducted in Flemish, except for the bilingual area of Brussels, which is officially declared a bilingual city.
1968	Language-related riots and tensions at the Catholic University of Louvain in Flanders cause the downfall of the national government headed by Paul Vanden Boeynants. His government is the first, but not the last, national government to fall due to "community problems."
1970	Constitution is amended to recognize the linguistic communities and regions.
1980	"Reform of the State," the so-called revision to the Constitution that began to institutionalize a federal structure, allowing Flanders and Wallonia to establish

elected regional legislatures with authority over local matters, such as public health, roads, and housing.

1987   Wilfried Martens resigns as prime minister in the fall-out over the Happart Affair. Elections are held on December 13, 1987, in order to develop new constitutional reforms.

1988   On August 8, the parliament passes the revision of the Constitution, which transferred major economic and transportation matters to jurisdiction of the communities and regions.

1990   In April, government passes abortion law by releasing King Baudouin from his office for thirty-six hours so he would not have to sign a law against his conscience.

1992   Three months after the November 24, 1991, elections, Jean-Luc Dehaene forms a center-left coalition and succeeds Wilfried Martens, who had been prime minister since 1979.

1993   On July 31, King Baudouin dies and is succeeded by his younger brother, Prince Albert.

1995   Prime Minister Dehaene announces a May 21 date for new parliamentary elections, seven months earlier than required.

Denmark

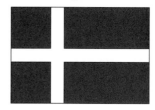

The Country in Brief

Official Name: Kingdom of Denmark (*Kongeriget Danmark*)
Capital: Copenhagen
Currency: Krone
National Day: April 16 (birthday of Queen Margrethe II)
Language: Danish
Religion: Lutheran
Memberships: NATO and EU
Border Countries: Germany, Sweden
Embassy in Washington, D.C.: 3200 Whitehaven Street, N.W., 20008. Telephone: (202) 234-4300.

Political Profile

Government Type: Constitutional monarchy/parliamentary democracy
Head of State: Queen Margrethe II
Succeeded to Throne: 1972
Head of Government: Prime Minister Poul Nyrup Rasmussen
Political Party: Social Democrat
Assumed Office: 1993
Legislature: Unicameral. Folketing, 179 members (plus 2 members each from Greenland and the Faroe Islands), elected by proportional representation.

Term of Office: Four years
Last Election: 1994
Next Election: 1998

Comparative Data

Population: 5.2 million
GDP: $132 billion
GDP Per Capita: $25,500
Voting System: Party list proportional (2% threshold)
Per Capita Representation Rate: 29,000
Big Government Index: 56.1%
Women in Parliament: 33%
Voter Turnout Rate: 84%

MAJOR POLITICAL PARTIES

Social Democratic Party (*Socialdemokratiet*, SD)

Founded in 1871, the Social Democrats have been Denmark's largest and most important political party since 1924. The party is nonideological and reform-minded. In 1961, the party excised all references to Karl Marx from its party programs. Because of splits within its ranks, the party had been slowly losing support until the 1990 elections.

Liberal Party (*Venstre*, L)

The Liberal Party, founded in 1870, advocates decentralizing government and direct participation of the electorate in local and community affairs. It favors worker participation in management councils, tax reform to aid consumers, and continued membership in NATO.

Conservative People's Party (*Konservative Folkeparti*, KF)

The Conservative party has grown toward the center of the political spectrum since its inception in 1916 as a reactionary party of the right. Its basic orientation is to seek "balance" between the public and private interests. It sets a priority on reducing taxes and taking away any disincentives for work.

Socialist People's Party (*Socialistisk Folkeparti*, SP)

The party was founded in 1958 by Aksel Larsen, former chairman of the Communist Party of Denmark. Larsen had been expelled from the Communist Party after calling for "independence" from Moscow and opposing the Soviet invasion of Hungary in 1956. The fastest growing party of the left, the SP opposes membership in NATO and the EU and draws most of its support from disaffected Social Democrats.

MINOR POLITICAL PARTIES

Center Democrats (*Centrum Demokraterme*, CD)
Christian People's Party (*Kristeligt Folkeparti*, KrF)
June Movement/Rainbow Group (*Juni Bevaegelsen*, JB)
People's Movement Against the EU
    (*Folksbevaegelsen mod EF-Union*, FB)
Progress Party (*Fremskridtspartiet*, PP)
Social (Radical) Liberal Party (*Radikale Venstre*, RV)
Union Common List (*Faglig Faellesliste*, UL)

ELECTION REVIEW

1994 Parliamentary Elections: Stay the Course, Lean Left

As predicted by pre-election opinion polls, Prime Minister Poul Nyrup Rasmussen's Social Democrats (SD) and their center-left governing coalition of the Radical Liberals (RV), Center Democrats (CD), and Christian People's Party (KrF) lost the 1-seat majority they had enjoyed before the September 21 election, but they managed to win just enough votes to remain in office. One coalition partner, the KrF, failed to reach the 2 percent threshold and so lost its 4 seats.

1994 Parliamentary Election Results

Party	% Votes	Seats
Social Democratic Party (SD)	35	62
Liberal Party (L)	23	42
Conservative People's Party (KF)	15	27
Socialist People's Party (SP)	7	13
Progress Party (PP)	6	11
Radical Liberal Party (RV)	5	8
Union Common List (UL)	3	6
Center Democrats (CD)	3	5
Others	3	5
Total Seats		179

Note: Percentages may not add up to 100 due to rounding.

Altogether, the new, more rickety, SD-led coalition garnered just under 42 percent of the vote and will have to rely on the tacit support of two left-of-center parties, the Socialist People's Party (SPP) and the Union Common List Party (UL), which together won 10.5 percent of the vote and a crucial 19 seats. The new SD-led governing coalition parties (SD, RV, CD, plus one of four members elected from Greenland/Faroe Islands) hold a mere 76 seats in the 179-seat Folketing (parliament), but by being able to rely on the two leftist parties for support on certain issues, the Rasmussen government commands at least the tacit support of 95 members—a slim majority of the Folketing.

The three main center-right opposition parties (Liberal, Conservative People's, and Progress), led by the Liberal Party's Uffe Ellemann-Jensen, won 44 percent of the vote and 80 seats. Although support for the Liberals rose to an all-time high of 23.3 percent of the vote and 42 seats, the Conservatives and the Progress Party lost a combined total of 4 seats—just enough to allow Rasmussen's center-left coalition to cling to power.

This delicate balancing act continues Denmark's longstanding tradition of installing cobbled-together coalition governments that have only minority support in the Folketing, forcing them to rely on tacit backing from nongovernment parties to stay in power.

It also continues the pivotal role played by the small Radical Liberal Party (RV), which, like the Free Democrats in Germany, has traditionally had enormous influence in Danish politics. Occupying the middle of the political spectrum, the RV often holds the balance of power because it can shift its support to the right or left depending on the issues of the moment. Those shifts have often meant the difference between a center-right or a center-left government coming to power. For example, the shift of RV support to the SD enabled Poul Rasmussen to come to power in 1993.

1990 Parliamentary Elections: Schlüter Slips, Then Falls

In 1990, Denmark continued its tradition of calling early elections, this time over an economic plan to lower the tax rate on higher incomes. During autumn, Conservative, Liberal, and Radical Liberal coalition members began negotiating with leading Social Democrats on a new economic package.

The two sides disagreed on many points, but they worked through most of their differences and were nearly in agreement on the plan in November. However, the Liberals called for the tax rate on higher incomes to be lowered from 68 percent to 64 percent. The Social Democrats did not want the rate lowered below 66 percent.

The negotiations broke down over this relatively minor point, and when the debate opened in parliament on the morning of November 22, Prime Minister Poul Schlüter announced that elections would take place in three weeks, on December 12.

Schlüter tried to make the tax-cut proposal the issue of the campaign, but the Danish voters did not see it that way. In fact, many felt the debate over how much to lower the tax rate was trivial. Two-thirds of the electorate would not benefit from the tax cut, but they might be affected by the accompanying reduction of welfare expenditure that would result from the measure.

It is not clear why Schlüter wanted an early election. There was no indication from poll data that his political situation would be improved by an election. Additionally, had he let the minor differences run their course, the parliamentary committees would probably have balanced out the proposals without the whole budget being rejected.

Past Parliamentary Election Results

Party	1990 %Votes	1990 Seats	1988 %Votes	1988 Seats	1987 %Votes	1987 Seats	1984 %Votes	1984 Seats
SD	37	69	30	55	29	54	31	56
L	16	29	12	22	11	19	12	22
KF	16	30	19	35	22	38	23	42
SP	8	15	13	24	15	27	11	21
PP	6	12	9	16	5	9	4	6
RV	4	7	6	10	6	11	5	10
CD	5	9	5	9	5	9	4	8
KrF	2	4	2	4	2	4	3	5
Others	5	4	4	4	5	8	8	9
Total Seats		**179**		**179**		**179**		**179**

Note: Percentages may not add up to 100 due to rounding. SD = Social Democratic Party, L = Liberal Party, KF = Conservative People's Party, SP = Socialist People's Party, PP = Progress Party, RV = Radical Liberal Party, CD = Center Democrats, KrF = Christian People's Party.

The Liberals and Social Democrats figured to score well in the early election. The Liberals had been receiving favorable public exposure, in large part due to party leader and Foreign Minister Uffe Ellemann-Jensen's highly visible role in the months leading up to the Gulf War and his promotion of European unity. The Social Democrats expected to benefit from the general weakness and disarray among other leftist parties.

In the end, Schlüter's Conservative People's Party (KF) captured 30 seats (a 5-seat loss), while its coalition partners, the Liberals, recorded a 7-seat gain to bring its total to 29 seats. The other coalition party, the Radical Liberals, tumbled from 10 to 7 seats. Schlüter's center-right coalition emerged with a total of 66 seats, a modest decline from the 67 seats it held after the 1990 elections.

The Socialist People's Party declined sharply, dropping from 24 to 15 seats. The right-wing Progress Party also lost support, slipping from 16 to 12 seats.

Meanwhile, the Social Democrats captured 69 seats, registering an impressive 14-seat gain and more than doubling the number of seats taken by any other party. Despite winning more seats than the ruling coalition, the Social Democrats and the other leftist parties were unable to unite to form a government, leaving things open for another center-right coalition.

Interestingly, while environmental issues had become a high priority in Denmark in light of the 1986 Chernobyl disaster and a Swedish power plant located near Copenhagen, the environmentalist Green Party failed once again to win any seats in the parliament.

After the elections, Schlüter managed to continue as prime minister, but he lost the Radical Liberals as part of the coalition. The new government was a Conservative-Liberal coalition, relying on tacit support from the various center-right parties, including the Radical Liberal and the Progress Party. With that, the government had a narrow majority of seven seats over the leftist bloc.

Aftermath. In January 1993, Poul Schlüter resigned as prime minister after a government inquiry determined that his government had lied to parliament about blocking visas for immigrants from Sri Lanka. The resignation ended Schlüter's surprisingly long tenure of more than ten years in office. With Radical Liberal support, the Social Democrats were able to create a ruling coalition, elevating Poul Nyrup Rasmussen to prime minister.

1994 European Parliament Elections

The ruling Social Democrats, which had the largest share of the vote in 1989, took a real drubbing in the 1994 Euro-elections, winning only 15.8 percent and 3 seats (a 1-seat loss). They fell behind the Liberals, who won 18.9 percent and 4 seats (a 1-seat gain), and the Conservatives, with 17.7 percent and 3 seats (a 1-seat gain).

The big story of 1994, however, was the 25.5 percent win by two anti-Maastricht parties, the environmentalist June Movement and the People's Movement Against the EU. These forces collectively captured 4 seats.

European Parliament Election Results

Party	1994 % Votes	1994 Seats	1989 % Votes	1989 Seats	1984 % Votes	1984 Seats	1979 % Votes	1979 Seats
L	19	4	17	3	13	2	15	3
KF	18	3	13	2	21	4	14	2
SD	16	3	23	4	20	3	22	3
JB	15	2	—	—	—	—	—	—
FB	10	2	19	4	21	4	21	4
SP	9	1	9	1	9	2	5	1
CD	1	0	8	2	7	1	6	1
Others	11	1	11	0	9	0	17	2
Total Seats		16		16		16		16

Note: Percentages may not add up to 100 due to rounding. L = Liberal Party, KF = Conservative People's Party, SD = Social Democratic Party, JB = June Movement, FB = People's Movement Against the EU, SP = Socialist People's Party, CD = Center Democrats.

The Socialist People's Party and the Radical Liberals each secured 1 seat.

Ratifying Maastricht: Second Time's a Charm

In June 1992, Danish voters narrowly rejected the Maastricht Treaty on European Union, voting 50.2 percent against the referendum. The unexpected rejection struck a blow to the European Community's drive for economic and political union because, according to EC rules, all members had to ratify the treaty for it to become effective.

Before the referendum, government officials said voting against Maastricht would cause a severe drop in Denmark's living standards. Rejection of the treaty might also force Denmark to withdraw from the EC entirely.

But the EC and the Danish government refused to take no for an answer. The EC moved ahead with ratification efforts in other countries and negotiated a number of exemptions, or "opt-outs," for Denmark. These were significant exemptions that excluded Denmark from the EC's planned economic and monetary union, and from common citizenship, environmental, and defense policies.

In May 1993, the Danish government presented an amended Maastricht Treaty to the voters. Despite winning 57 percent approval, the treaty battle clearly had divided Denmark on the question of European integration.

ELECTION LEXICON

"Alternative security majority": Phrase used to describe the cooperation exhibited by the Socialist People's Party, the Radical Liberal Party, and the Social Democratic Party in votes concerning security policy, thereby thwarting the proposals of the conservative coalition government in the period 1982 to 1988.

Borgen: Literally, "castle." Refers to Christiansborg, where the Folketing (parliament) is located.

Christiansborg Castle: Meeting site for the Folketing (parliament). "Christiansborg" is another colloquial reference to the Folketing.

"Earthquake election" of 1973: In this parliamentary election, five previously unrepresented political parties captured 36 percent of the total vote. This changed the political landscape by shattering the dominance of the four existing major parties (the Social Democrats, Radical Liberals, Liberals, and Conservative People's parties).

Folketing: The 179-member unicameral parliament.

"Footnote nation": A reference to Denmark's insistence that a"footnote" be added to NATO agreements and communiqués registering Denmark's dissenting opinion. This footnote strategy was necessary because the conservative coalition government faced a hostile "alternative security majority" in parliament. The term also applies to Denmark's request for exemptions from the Maastricht Treaty on European Union.

"Four leaf clover": The coalition government formed in 1982 by Poul Schlüter with the Conservative People's, Liberal, Center Democrats, and Christian People's parties. Schlüter was the first Conservative prime minister since 1894.

June Movement: An anti-Maastricht organization dedicated to defeating the treaty when it came up for a vote in June 1992.

"Majority for the occasion": Refers to the method of governing required in minority governments. No Danish government has had a majority in parliament this century, so the parties have become adept at governing with majorities that shift depending on the issue at hand.

Nordic Council: An organization created in 1952, consisting of the parliaments and cabinets of Denmark, Finland, Iceland, Norway, and Sweden. Its goal is to coordinate policy on economics, foreign affairs, social welfare, and cultural affairs. It has succeeded in facilitating substantial uniformity in the legislation of these countries.

Nuclear-free zone: A proposal, supported by Social Democrats and various Green parties, that Denmark should join with the other Scandinavian countries to establish a zone that would be devoid of nuclear weapons.

"Potato cure": Reference to the Conservative coalition government's economic program in 1986 aimed at restraining domestic consumption.

"Scandinavian Model": The common mixed-economy approach in Denmark, Sweden, and Norway which consists of a mixture of the traditional welfare state, a stable negotiated labor market, and the cooptation of the various unions in the public administration.

Slotsholmen: The area of Copenhagen where the parliament and most of the ministries are located.

Snapstinget: Term once used to describe the place in Christiansborg where the parliamentary decisions were made. Now it mainly refers to a restaurant by that name.

"Tamilgate": Scandal created when Prime Minister Schlüter's justice minister ordered civil servants to delay issuing entry visas

to the wives and children of Tamil refugees, breaking Danish law. The scandal helped bring down Schlüter's government in 1993.

Ten Ore coin: Danish coin, worth about one cent. When a member of parliament gives an exceptional speech, fellow members quietly hand the speaker a 10 Ore coin as a sign of appreciation.

HISTORICAL SYNOPSIS

Denmark's first liberal constitution establishing a democratically elected parliament was drafted in 1849. Sixty-six years later a revised constitution granted the franchise to women and servants.

1940   On April 9, Germany occupies Denmark.

1945   Denmark is liberated on May 4.

1949   Denmark becomes a member of NATO.

1953   In a constitutional amendment, the Landsting (upper house of parliament) is abolished; Margrethe, current queen of Denmark, achieves the right of succession, which previously had been the exclusive privilege of sons of the royal family.

1973   Denmark joins the EC, along with Great Britain and Ireland.

1992   Referendum on ratifying the Maastricht Treaty for Economic Union is narrowly defeated.

1993   In January, Conservative prime minister Poul Schlüter resigns and his government is replaced by that of Social Democrat Poul Nyrup Rasmussen. In a May referendum, 57 percent of Danish voters reverse the 1992 decision and vote in favor of an amended version of the Maastricht Treaty that includes significant exemptions for Denmark.

1994   Prime Minister Poul Rasmussen continues in office following parliamentary elections on September 21. Although his coalition loses its 1-seat majority, tacit support from two leftist parties allows the SD-led coalition to stay in power.

Finland

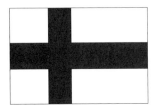

The Country in Brief

Official Name: Republic of Finland (*Suomen Tasavalta*)
Capital: Helsinki
Currency: Markka
National Day: December 6 (Independence Day)
Languages: Finnish, Swedish
Religion: Lutheran
Memberships: Non-NATO; officially joined the EU January 1, 1995
Border Countries: Norway, Russia, Sweden
Embassy in Washington, D.C.: 3216 New Mexico Avenue, N.W., 20016. Telephone: (202) 298-5800.

Political Profile

Government Type: Presidential/parliamentary democracy
Head of State: President Martti Ahtisaari
Political Party: Social Democrat
Assumed Office: 1994
Election Method: Popularly elected (since 1988). Majority required or election held in 301-member electoral college.
Term of Office: Six years
Next Election: 2000
Head of Government: Prime Minister Esko Aho
Political Party: Center Party

Assumed Office: 1991
Legislature: Unicameral. Eduskunta, 200 members, elected by proportional representation.
Term of Office: Four years
Last Election: 1991
Next Election: 1995

Comparative Data

Population: 5.0 million
GDP: $127 billion
GDP Per Capita: $27,600
Voting System (Parliament): Party list proportional (candidate preferences required)
Per Capita Representation Rate: 25,000
Big Government Index: 41.2%
Women in Parliament: 39%
Voter Turnout Rate: 72%

MAJOR POLITICAL PARTIES

Center Party (*Keskustapuolue*, KP)

Established in 1906 as the Agrarian Union to promote the interests of the rural sector, this party has been a major force in Finnish politics. Most of Finland's prime ministers and presidents have been members of this party. With industrialization, the party's base of support gradually began to dwindle. In response, the party changed its name in 1965 to Center Party to broaden its appeal. Until the recent growth of the National Coalition, the KP had been the leading nonsocialist party. It has a middle-of-the-road ideology and has cooperated in government with all of the major parties.

Finnish Social Democratic Party
(*Suomen Sosialidemokraattinen Puolue*, SDP)

This Scandinavian-style Social Democratic Party, founded in 1899, has dominated Finnish politics throughout the twentieth century. Drawing its main support from the working and middle classes and small farmers, the SDP advocates moderate, reformist policies.

National Coalition (*Kansallinen Kokoomus*, KoK)

This moderately conservative party, founded in 1918, is anti-Communist and pro-western. Prior to 1987, this ideological mix had made it unacceptable as a coalition partner to left and center parties.

Left-Wing Alliance (*Vasemmistoliito*, Vas)

This party was formed in 1990 as an alliance of former Communist and various other leftist parties, including the People's Democratic League (SKDL).

MINOR POLITICAL PARTIES

Finnish Christian League (*Suomen Kristillinen Lütto*, SKL)
Finnish People's Democratic League
   (*Suomen Kansan Demokraasttinen Lütto*, KDL)
Finnish Rural Party (*Suomen Maaseudun Puolue*, SMP)
Green Union (*Vihreä Lütto*, VL)
Liberal People's Party (*Liberaalinen Kansanpuolue*, LKP)
Swedish People's Party (*Svenska Folkpartiet*, SFP)

ELECTION REVIEW

1994 Presidential Elections: "Cohabitation" Continues

On January 16, 1994, Finnish voters went to the polls to begin the process of selecting a successor to president Mauno Koivisto, who was elected in 1982. This was the first election in which voters were able to directly elect the president, using a two-ballot, majoritarian method that is similar to the French system. As it turned out,

1994 Presidential Election Results

Candidate	First Round (% Votes)	Runoff (% Votes)
Martti Ahtisaari (SDP)	25.9	54.0
Elizabeth Rehn (SFP)	22.0	46.0
Paavo Väyrynen (KP)	19.5	
Raimo Ilaskivi (KoK)	15.2	
Others	17.5	

Note: Percentages may not add up to 100 due to rounding. SDP = Social Democratic Party, SFP = Swedish People's Party, KP = Center Party, KoK = National Coalition.

no candidate in 1994 came anywhere near winning a majority of votes cast in the first round, so a second-round, runoff election had to be held three weeks later on February 6.

In the first round, Social Democrat Martti Ahtisaari placed first with 25.9 percent of the vote. Defense Minister Elizabeth Rehn, candidate of the Swedish People's Party, came in second with 22 percent. Paavo Väyrynen, representing Prime Minister Esko Aho's Center Party, was third with 19.5 percent. The former mayor of Helsinki, Raimo Ilaskivi of the National Coalition, won 15.2 percent for a fourth-place finish. Seven minor party candidates also competed in the election, accounting for more than 17 percent of the vote.

The race narrowed to a two-way contest between Ahtisaari, a former senior Finnish diplomat, and Rehn, whose Swedish People's Party represented the small Swedish-speaking minority in Finland. Largely for that reason, her candidacy was not expected to amount to much. Her second-place showing in the first round was something of a shock.

Public opinion polls taken soon after the first round showed Rehn slightly ahead of Ahtisaari. Indeed, had the second round of voting occurred one week after the first round instead of three weeks later, there is a good chance that Rehn might have been elected president.

As it turned out, Ahtisaari gained momentum leading up to the February 6 balloting. He ended up winning the election with a solid 54 percent of the vote against Rehn's 46 percent. A major reason for his success was the fact that Rehn, the sitting minister of defense in the center-right government of Prime Minister Aho, was saddled with Aho's record on domestic policy. Even though the Finnish president is largely powerless to take any action in domestic affairs, with the economy in recession and with unemployment above 20 percent, voters seemed eager to support the opposition candidate.

Rehn also made a few remarks before the election that were viewed as being insensitive to the plight of the unemployed. At one point, she referred to jobless people as the "new helpless." She also spoke out against Finland's "welfare state," referring to it as the "nanny state."

In the field of foreign policy, which is within the president's area of responsibility, very little separated the two candidates. Both expressed strong support for Finland's application to join the European Union (EU)—the hottest foreign policy issue on the national agenda.

1988 Presidential Elections: Koivisto Reelected

The reelection of Social Democrat Mauno "Manu" Koivisto to another six-year term as president was in itself not surprising. Personally popular, Koivisto had been at the center of Finnish political power for more than a decade. After serving as prime minister in 1979, he succeeded long-time president Urho Kekkonen in that office in 1982. But Finnish politics had been shifting slowly rightward in the 1980s, culminating in the 1987 parliamentary elections that brought the conservative National Coalition Party (KoK) into a governing coalition for the first time in twenty-one years.

After the March 1987 parliamentary elections, the Center Party pressed for a nonsocialist government. As a result, the Center Party was dropped from the coalition government in favor of the KoK. President Koivisto, exercising one of the key powers of the presidency, chose KoK member Harri Holkeri as prime minister. This placed a future presidential challenger to Koivisto in the prime minister's office at the head of a "red-blue" (SDP/KoK) government. Curiously, this situation closely mirrored develop-

1988 Presidential Election Results

Candidate	Popular Ballot (% Votes)	Electoral College Votes (First Ballot)	Electoral College Votes (Second Ballot)
Mauno Koivisto (SDP)	47.9	144	189
Paavo Väyrynen (KP)	20.1	68	68
Harri Holkeri (KoK)	18.1	63	18
Kalevi Kivistö (KDL)	10.5	26	26
Total		301	301

Note: Percentages may not add up to 100 due to rounding. SDP = Social Democratic Party, KP = Center Party, KoK = National Coalition, KDL = People's Democratic League.

ments in France when President Mitterand was forced to "cohabit" with conservative prime minister Jacques Chirac from 1986 to 1988 (see France, p. 104, for more details).

Less than a year before his appointment as prime minister, Holkeri had been touting himself not only as the nonsocialist alternative to Koivisto, but also as the man who would stop the "Social Democrats' disproportionate exercise of power."

Holkeri did, in fact, challenge Koivisto in 1988 in the first Finnish presidential election that gave the voters a direct voice in deciding the outcome. Before 1988, a 301-member electoral college, popularly elected by proportional representation, actually selected the president. In the 1988 election, Finns voted both for the candidate of their choice and for electoral college members who had pledged to support specific candidates. Using this system, if a candidate won a majority of the popular vote, he or she was elected president; if no candidate won a popular majority—as happened in 1988—then the electoral college had to be convened to elect the new president. (The 1994 election election discussed above was the first one that did not use the electoral college.)

The Center Party nominated Paavo Väyrynen as its presidential candidate, although political insiders saw this as nothing more than a foundation for the 1994 election. There was a brief moment of hope for the 1988 Väyrynen candidacy when the nonsocialist parties considered making Väyrynen their joint candidate. However, this scenario never came to pass because the KoK felt that if it was to become a real contender in the 1994 race, it would have to make an independent showing in 1988. Hence, the Holkeri candidacy came about.

The People's Democratic League and the Communist Party, which had recently split with hard-line Communists, united behind the candidacy of Kalevi Kivistö. He was portrayed not as a party candidate but as the leader of a broad movement. Kivistö's candidacy was supported by left-wing intellectuals who were dissatisfied with Finnish consensus politics. He was also supported by Stalinists and environmentalists. The extreme left supported Jouko Kajanoja, the fringe Communist leader.

In the presidential balloting, Mauno Koivisto won 47.9 percent of the vote. Since no candidate won an absolute majority, the popularly elected electoral college was convened. On the second ballot, Koivisto received 189 votes, an absolute majority of the 301 electors. Väyrynen drew 68 votes, Kivistö 26, and Holkeri a mere 18. Koivisto's popularity had withstood Finland's ideological shift to the right.

1995 Parliamentary Election Preview

Elections scheduled for March 19 seemed likely to result in a major loss for Prime Minister Aho and his Center Party. The Social Democratic Party was expected to reemerge as Finland's largest party and name Paavo Lipponen as the next prime minister. The National Coalition was also likely to lose some support, mainly to the advantage of the Left-Wing Alliance.

1991 Parliamentary Elections: The Center Triumphs

The March 17, 1991, parliamentary election was not a big news story in Finland. In fact, the elections received very little attention in the media. The nation and the world were preoccupied with the Persian Gulf War and the unrest in the Baltics.

The election did result in one of the most significant upheavals in Finnish politics, however. At 72 percent, voter turnout continued its downward trend, compared with 76 percent in 1987. Ap-

1991 Parliamentary Election Results		
Party	*% Votes*	*Seats*
Center Party (KP)	24	55
Social Democratic Party (SDP)	22	48
National Coalition (KoK)	19	40
Left-Wing Alliance (Vas)	10	19
Green Union (VL)	7	10
Swedish People's Party (SFP)	5	12
Rural Party (SMP)	5	7
Others	7	9
Total Seats		**200**

Note: Percentages may not add to 100 due to rounding.

proximately two-thirds of the incumbents were rejected at the polls, reflecting the public's widespread disaffection toward politics as usual. In general, women candidates did exceptionally well, winning 77 of the 200 available seats, or slightly more than 38 percent.

This was the first election following the formation, in 1987, of the Social Democratic/National Coalition government under the leadership of Prime Minister Harri Holkeri. The coalition did not fare well in the election.

The Social Democratic Party captured 22 percent of the vote and 48 seats, an 8-seat loss, while the National Coalition Party (KoK) dropped to 19 percent of the vote and 40 seats, a loss of 13 seats. The Rural Party was also a loser, claiming only 7 seats, compared with 9 seats after the 1987 election.

The big winner was the Center Party, led by Esko Aho. It claimed nearly 25 percent of the vote and 55 seats, a 15-seat increase, thereby becoming the largest party in parliament. Dropped from the ruling coalition in 1987 because Aho had pressed for a nonsocialist government, the Center Party suddenly became the senior party in a ruling coalition, with Aho as prime minister.

The Green Party also did well, winning almost 7 percent of the vote and increasing from 4 to 10 seats.

Past Parliamentary Election Results

	1987		1983		1979		1975	
Party	% Votes	Seats	% Votes	Seats	% Votes	Seats	% Votes	Seats
KP	18	40	18	38	17	36	18	39
SDP	24	56	27	57	24	52	25	54
KoK	23	53	22	44	22	47	19	35
SFP	5	12	5	10	4	10	5	10
SMP	6	9	10	17	5	7	4	2
SKL	3	5	3	3	5	9	3	9
SKDL	9	16	13	26	18	35	19	40
Others	12	9	3	5	6	4	8	11
Total Seats	**200**		**200**		**200**		**200**	

Note: Percentages may not add up to 100 due to rounding. KP = Center Party; SDP = Finnish Social Democratic Party; KoK = National Coalition Party; SFP = Swedish Peoples Party; SMP = Finnish Rural Party; SKL = Finnish Christian League; SKDL = Finnish Peoples Democratic League.

1987 Parliamentary Elections: Shift Right, Sort Of

On paper, the parliamentary elections of March 1987 resulted in a sharp move toward the right. For the first time in twenty-one years the conservative National Coalition Party (KoK) became part of the governing coalition, having captured 11 additional parliamentary seats.

In effect, though, little changed. The major Finnish parties tend to be consensus-oriented and nonideological. The issues and the parties' positions have been essentially the same for many years. In fact, Finland's modern politics have been described as being a "supermarket" where one can find a little of all ideologies. However, despite the broad areas of agreement, each party has its own nuances and constituencies.

During the 1987 campaign, KoK officials accused the SDP government of withholding information about radioactive fallout over Finland after the Chernobyl accident. The loss of the SDP's overall majority in parliament following the election is attributed to his accusation. In the wake of the disaster, the cries for a continuation of the nuclear-free policy intensified.

Both the SDP and the KoK supported legislation to lower tax rates and reduce the number of tax brackets. With the Finnish population becoming increasingly urban and upwardly mobile, there was more political pressure to lighten the tax burden and free the economy from public controls and nationalized industries in favor of a free market.

The recent baby boom, especially in Helsinki, caused many to call for an improved system of child and health care. Finland found itself experiencing the same demographic dilemmas that face nearly every industrialized nation on the globe: women are working and demanding affordable child care and the population is living longer and demanding adequate health care and housing into retirement. These issues were championed by the Social Democrats in the 1987 election.

1994 European Union Referendum: Finns Opt for Europe

On October 16, Finnish voters opted to join the European Union. With a 57 percent positive vote, this endorsement was expected to influence the Swedish and Norwegian referendums scheduled for November 13 and November 28, respectively. In the end, Sweden voted to follow Finland into the EU, but Norway voted narrowly against joining.

Whether or not Finland should join the EU had become a major topic of political debate. Given the background of Finland's attempts to maintain a neutral foreign policy, the decision about EU membership was a difficult one for many Finns. Nevertheless, a 1991 opinion poll showed that Finns favored joining the EU by a two-to-one margin. Following suit, the Aho government announced in 1992 that Finland would apply for EU membership.

Prime Minister Aho, in an address to the Finnish parliament in 1992, said the decision to join the EU was one of "the most important and far-reaching decisions ever taken by Finland as an independent state." President Koivisto urged support of the proposal because "it is better that we have a voice where the decisions are made." The Finns officially joined the EU January 1, 1995.

Soviet Relations. The political upheaval in the former Soviet Union also caused concerns for Finland. There was considerable fear that hundreds of thousands of Russians would flee their homeland and cross into Finland. Helsinki debated whether it could, or should, seal its borders with Russia.

After the 1991 Soviet coup, Prime Minister Aho renegotiated the Soviet-Finnish Treaty, which had been signed in 1948. In 1990, Finland had abandoned a section of the treaty that limited the size of its military. One element of the treaty had also called for Finland to be neutral. Aho was afraid that this agreement could have been a hurdle to Finland's efforts to join the European Union.

The new treaty would be valid for ten years. It called for each party to respect existing borders, protect one another's citizens, and renounce the use of force against the other. With the signing of this treaty, Finland became the first Western country to ratify a treaty with independent Russia.

With regard to the Baltic States, Finland remained officially neutral during their quest for independence. Once independence was declared, Finland became one of the first countries to recognize the new nations.

ELECTION LEXICON

Active neutrality: Term used to describe the consensus vision of Finnish foreign policy, especially concerning the Soviet Union. Finland wanted to be seen by the Soviets as strictly neutral militarily, but with some political independence.

Coalition government: The Finnish electoral system is such that it is virtually impossible for any one party to win a majority of seats and thereby control a clear majority in the Eduskunta. The need to build coalitions has contributed to Finland's noncombative style of politics.

Collegiality: The spirit of cooperation and consensus-building that has prevailed in most Finnish governments, virtually all of which have been multiparty coalition governments.

Council of State: Term for the Finnish cabinet, which is appointed by the president and headed by a prime minister who has less power than most other European heads of government.

Eduskunta: The 200-seat unicameral parliament.

Electoral college: Prior to 1988, a popularly elected, 301-member electoral college chose Finland's president. In 1994, voters for the first time elected the president directly, using a French-style, two-round, majoritarian system.

"Extinguishing lights": Allusion to the behind-the-scenes process used by the electoral college before 1988. Prior to reform, electors did not have to announce their allegiance to a certain candidate.

FCMA: The Treaty of Friendship, Cooperation, and Mutual Assistance between Finland and the Soviet Union, signed in 1948, which remained a cornerstone of Finnish foreign policy until renegotiated in 1990.

"Finlandization": Metaphor for a country that has lost virtually all its independence and only goes through a kind of charade of sovereignty. It alludes to Finland's relationship to its one-time powerful and often domineering neighbor, the former Soviet Union.

"Forgotten countryside" and the "Small man": Terms used by the Rural Party in 1987 to attack the other parties' neglect of poor farmers and the lower classes.

"Invisible wall": Term used to describe Finnish soldiers wearing white clothing who fought Russians during the "Winter War." They would fight fiercely and then disappear into the landscape of drifting snow.

"Kekkonen line": Term used to describe longtime president Urho Kekkonen's belief that as East-West tensions grew worse, Finland would be compelled to side with the Soviet Union. This led to Finland taking an active role in trying to reduce world tensions.

"Moral conservatives" and "Pietists": Historically, members of the National Coalition used these terms to describe their political and social philosophy. Since the 1980s, the desire of Finnish voters

for upward mobility and economic progress has reduced the popularity of such harsh-sounding rhetoric. These phrases were not the basis for the KoK's electoral campaign in 1987.

Nordic Council: An organization created in 1952, consisting of the parliaments and cabinets of Denmark, Finland, Iceland, Norway, and Sweden. Its goal is to coordinate policy on economics, foreign affairs, social welfare, and cultural affairs. It has succeeded in facilitating substantial uniformity in the legislation of these countries.

Nuclear-free zone: Widely supported concept whereby all nuclear weapons would be banned from Scandinavia.

"The only 'real' monarchy in Scandinavia": During the twenty-five-year reign of former Center Party president Urho Kekkonen, Finland was frequently referred to ironically as the only "real" monarchy in Scandinavia. Denmark, Norway, and Sweden are all constitutional monarchies.

"Paasikivi line": Name given to a campaign by President J. K. Paasikivi (1946-1956) to eliminate anti-Russian views among the Finns.

"Quality of life": Slogan adopted by the Center Party to appeal to the upscale, young, urban voters and encourage them to vote for Center Party candidates.

Red-blue coalition: The coalition of the Social Democratic and National Coalition parties established in 1987 when Harri Holkeri became prime minister.

Red-green coalition: The coalition of the Social Democratic and Center parties during the middle 1980s.

"Supermarket": Term describing Finland's diversity of political parties, because a voter can find a little bit of everything.

"Winter War": 1989 marked the fiftieth anniversary of the so-called Winter War between Finland and the Soviet Union. The episode continues to have a profound impact on the collective memory of many Finns. For 105 days (November 30, 1939 to March 13, 1940), Finland's outnumbered forces valiantly fought the invading Red Army to a virtual standstill. An estimated 25,000

Finnish troops died and 45,000 were wounded; as many as 220,000 Russians perished and 800,000 were wounded.

HISTORICAL SYNOPSIS

A grand duchy of the Russian empire for nearly a century, Finland in 1906 adopted a constitution providing for proportional representation and universal suffrage. Following the Russian Revolution a decade later, Finland declared its independence from the Russian empire.

1939-1940	The Soviet Union defeats Finland in the Winter War.
1941-1944	The Soviet Union defeats Finland in the Continuation War.
1946	Finland establishes policy of neutrality in international politics.
1955	Finland joins the United Nations and the Nordic Council.
1960	Finland joins the European Free Trade Association (EFTA) as an associate member.
1973	Finland and other EFTA members enter into free-trade agreements with the European Community.
1981	President Urho Kekkonen resigns from office due to ill health after serving for twenty-five years.
1982	Social Democrat prime minister Mauno Koivisto is elected president.
1987	Finland experiments with French-style "cohabitation" when the conservative National Coalition (KoK) party leader, Harri Holkeri, becomes prime minister under Social Democrat Koivisto.
1988	Koivisto is elected to a second six-year term as president.
1991	The Center Party ends twenty-five years of government dominance by the Social Democrat Party. On March 17, Center Party leader Esko Aho, age thirty-six, becomes Finland's youngest prime minister.

1992	Finland announces it will seek membership in the then European Community.
1994	Finns elect Social Democrat Martti Ahtisaari president. In October, 57 percent vote in favor of joining the European Union.
1995	On January 1, Finland (along with Austria and Sweden) officially joins the EU.

France

The Country in Brief

Official Name: Republic of France (*République Française*)
Capital: Paris
Currency: Franc
National Day: July 14 (Bastille Day)
Language: French
Religion: Roman Catholic
Memberships: NATO and EU
Border Countries: Andorra, Belgium, Germany, Italy, Luxembourg, Monaco, Spain, Switzerland
Embassy in Washington, D.C.: 4101 Reservoir Road, N.W., 20007. Telephone: (202) 944-6000.

Political Profile

Government Type: Presidential/parliamentary democracy
Head of State: President François Mitterrand (until May 1995)
Political Party: Socialist
Assumed Office: 1981
Reelected: 1988
Election Method: Directly elected, with majority requirement. Second ballot runoff if necessary.
Term of Office: Seven years
Next Election: 1995

Head of Government: Prime Minister Edouard Balladur (until May 1995)
Political Party: Rally for the Republic (Neo-Gaullist)
Assumed Office: 1993
Legislature: Bicameral, Parliament (*Parlement*)
Upper Chamber: Senate, 321 members, indirectly elected to nine-year terms by municipal councils and the National Assembly.
Lower Chamber: National Assembly, 577 members, elected by majoritarian system from single-member districts.
Term of Office: Five years
Last Election: 1993
Next Election: 1998

Comparative Data

Population: 56.4 million
GDP: $1.2 trillion
GDP Per Capita: $21,100
Voting System (Lower Chamber): Majoritarian/Second ballot from single-member constituencies
Per Capita Representation Rate: 98,000
Big Government Index: 46.5%
Women in Parliament: 6%
Voter Turnout Rate: 65%

MAJOR POLITICAL PARTIES

The French are passionate about their politics and historically have strongly identified themselves with a particular party. Increasingly, however, party labels are losing their significance.

Rally for the Republic
   (*Rassemblement pour la République*, RPR)

This Neo-Gaullist party was founded by Jacques Chirac in 1976. It is a direct descendent of de Gaulle's *Rassemblement du Peuple Français* (RPF). This party has usually been allied with the Union for French Democracy, but is further to the right on the political spectrum and has been less enthusiastic about European unification.

Union for French Democracy
(Union pour la Démocratie Française, UDF)

A federation of several center-right parties inspired by Valéry Giscard d'Estaing in 1978. The UDF includes the *Parti Républicain* and the *Centre des Démocrates Sociaux* (CDS), in addition to other diverse centrist political groups such as the followers of Raymond Barre ("Barristes"). The UDF has a free-market and pan-European orientation.

Socialist Party (*Parti Socialiste*, PS)

While historically dating back to 1905, the present Socialist Party was reformed and revitalized under the leadership of François Mitterrand at a congress of various Socialist groups held in Epinay in 1971. Lionel Jospin took over as leader of the party upon Mitterrand's accession to the presidency in 1981. The party has traditionally been committed to transforming France into a socialist society using nationalization and other means to do so, but the party has moved away substantially from this stance under Mitterrand's leadership.

French Communist Party
(Parti Communiste Français, PCF)

This Marxist-Leninist party was founded in 1920 and until the demise of the Soviet Union remained faithful to Moscow. In the postwar era, it has gone from a position of great importance when it captured 28 percent of the vote in the November 1946 National Assembly elections to a marginal position today, capturing just 5 percent of the vote in the 1993 National Assembly elections.

National Front (*Front National*, FN)

This extreme right-wing nationalist party was founded by Jean-Marie Le Pen in 1972. Its electoral platform is built mainly on an anti-immigrant stance. The FN became a credible party in 1984 when it won 11 percent of the French vote in the elections to the

European Parliament. Its support comes from the traditional right, as well as from the Communist left in working-class areas. Its main base of support is in Marseilles.

MINOR POLITICAL PARTIES

Greens (*Les Verts*, V)
Left Radical Movement
  (*Mouvement des Radicauz de Gauche*, MRG)
Other Europe (*L'Autre Europe*, OE)
Social Democratic Center (*Centre des Démocrates Sociaux*, CDS)

ELECTION REVIEW

1995 Presidential Election Preview

In elections scheduled for May 7, Jacques Chirac of the Gaullist Rally for the Republic (RPR) party was expected to succeed in his third try to capture the French presidency. The two-time prime minister (1974-1976, 1986-1988) and mayor of Paris was predicted to benefit from the conservative victory in the 1993 legislative elections, when the center-right RPR and Union for French Democracy parties secured 80 percent of the seats in the National Assembly. Socialist Jacques Delors, the outgoing European Commission president, decided not to run for the position.

Socialist François Mitterrand has controlled the presidency for fourteen years. He defeated Chirac for the position in 1988. Chirac also lost in a bid in 1981. Mitterrand's term officially expires May 20, 1995.

1988 Presidential Elections:
Mitterrand Goes Middle of the Road

The election system mandated by a 1962 referendum requires a presidential candidate to win an absolute majority to win the elec-

1988 Presidential Election Results

Candidate	First Round (% Votes)	Runoff (% Votes)
François Mitterrand (PS)	34	54
Jacques Chirac (RPR)	20	46
Raymond Barre (UDF)	17	
Jean-Marie Le Pen (FN)	14	
André Lajoinie (PCF)	7	
Antoine Waechter (V)	4	
Others	3	

Note: Percentages may not add up to 100 due to rounding. PS = Socialist Party, RPR = Rally for the Republic, UDF = Union for French Democracy, FN = National Front, PCF = Communist Party, V = Greens.

tion. If needed, a second round of voting takes place between the top two vote-getters in the first round.

In the presidential elections of 1988, incumbent Socialist president François Mitterrand, seventy-two years old, sought and won a second seven-year term. His victory was not without irony.

A frequent and bitter opponent of Charles de Gaulle and the powerful presidency created by de Gaulle's Fifth Republic in 1958, Mitterrand adopted a shrewd and very Gaullist tactic in his reelection bid. Taking a page from the great general's book, Mitterrand positioned himself as the candidate for all of France. He portrayed himself as above petty partisanship and campaigned as a middle-of-the-road president.

In 1981, Mitterrand had offered French voters a bold leftist agenda that included sweeping nationalization of key industries. By 1988, however, Mitterrand seemed to eschew ideology in favor of becoming a reassuring figure, centrist in outlook and calming in demeanor. His success in downplaying issues and remaining above the fray has led many observers to proclaim the "end of ideology" in French politics.

Traditionally, the French have taken their politics very seriously, with nearly all voters identifying themselves as either "of the left" or "of the right." There has seldom been a safe middle ground, but that is exactly where Mitterrand found himself in

1988. His key campaign slogan, the brainchild of Socialist Party leader Michel Rocard, was *ouverture*, opening to the center and the opposition. It was a slogan well-suited to the times.

Mitterrand had already proved himself a formidable candidate and presence—much like former U.S. president Ronald Reagan. He was well suited to fit the mood of the people. Instead of a resurgence of ideological divisions and bold departures, France in 1988 seemed to be yearning for reassurance and calm.

Results. Mitterrand's strategy proved effective. In the first round of voting, the incumbent president received a respectable 34 percent of the vote. His closest rival, Prime Minister Jacques Chirac, garnered just under 20 percent. The other candidates, Raymond Barre (UDF) and Jean-Marie Le Pen (FN), received 17 and 14 percent, respectively. Mitterrand's margin in the runoff against Chirac was impressive: 54 percent to 46 percent.

That was a contrast to his slimmer margin of less than 4 percent over Valéry Giscard d'Estaing in 1981 (51.8 percent to 48.2 percent). Another contrast: in 1981 Mitterrand's presidential victory was followed by a Socialist landslide in the parliamentary elections that immediately followed. In 1988 there was no such landslide. Instead, the Socialists barely secured a plurality large enough to form a minority government—thanks more to the divisions of the right than the electoral strength of the left. Although a new round of cohabitation—the sharing of power between Mitterrand as president and Chirac as prime minister—was avoided, Mitterrand's political power was not fully restored to its pre-1986, pre-cohabitation luster.

The 1988 presidential race turned out to be more of a popularity contest than a campaign of substance. For years economic issues had been the major preoccupation of French voters, and in 1988 unemployment and job training were indeed concerns of the electorate. But France was experiencing an economic upturn, and so this was not a major area of contention between Mitterrand, Chirac, and Barre.

Jean-Marie Le Pen, the leader of the far-right National Front, was himself a key issue of the campaign. He was a major cause of the public bickering among the more moderate parties of the French right. The allied parties of the right were vocally divided as to whether to cooperate with Le Pen or to try to court his supporters. Le Pen made much tougher immigration controls and the repatriation of undesirable or illegal immigrants a centerpiece of his campaign. This forced all the presidential candidates to define their stance on immigration.

Mitterrand stated that he would not renationalize firms that had been privatized over the last two years by Chirac's government, although he would discontinue the prime minister's program and pursue a "mixed economy." Chirac, on the other hand, pledged to accelerate the transition toward a free market.

All three major candidates sought to strengthen the European pillar of the Atlantic Alliance. Mitterrand called for nothing less than an eventual "United States of Europe," but in the meantime supported a European confederation with a single currency, unified foreign policy and a common defense force. Barre supported Mitterrand's call for a European Central Bank, while Chirac believed "European construction" should be pursued along more nationalistic lines, providing the impetus for France to modernize.

Under the constitution of the so-called Fifth Republic, the president appoints the prime minister, who then must form a government that has the support of the National Assembly. Therefore, after his reelection, President Mitterrand dissolved the National Assembly and ordered new parliamentary elections to take place on June 5, 1988. He was eager to bring the uncomfortable power-sharing arrangement of cohabitation to an end.

1993 Parliamentary Elections: Cohabitation Part Deux

The legislative electoral system under the Fifth Republic has been a two-round, single-member constituency system. Effectively, this imposes a modified primary system on the left and the right because the two leading candidates who meet again in the second round usually represent parties from the right or left. The candidate must receive an absolute majority and at least one-quarter of the registered votes in order to be elected in the first round. If these conditions are not met, a second round of elections is held a week later for voters to choose between two candidates who received the support of at least 12.5 percent of the registered votes in the first round. The candidate receiving a simple majority in the second round is then elected.

Everything leading up to the 1993 National Assembly elections pointed to a major disaster for the Socialists. President François Mitterrand's popularity had plummeted to perhaps 30 percent in recent years. Within the ranks of the Socialist Party leadership there was a good deal of unseemly jockeying for position and finger pointing.

It had been a rocky road for the Socialists ever since Mitterrand won reelection in 1988. For starters, Mitterrand had to continually replace prime ministers. Michel Rocard lasted three years, longer than most. His minority Socialist government had a difficult time, since the Socialists did not command a majority in the National Assembly. Rocard survived as long as he did because most of his legislation tended to be fairly moderate.

Rocard's dismissal in 1991 was a response to growing social discontent within the country. Unemployment was higher in France than it was in most European nations. Outbreaks of violence were becoming common in some of the poorest suburbs. Since the Socialists wanted to appear as the champions of the underprivileged before the 1993 election, Mitterrand concluded that a change in prime ministers would convey the right message.

Mitterrand also had personal reasons for dismissing Rocard. The two were never friends and often rivals, and it was obvious that Rocard would be the strongest Socialist candidate for president in 1995. It is thought that Mitterrand released Rocard in order to hurt Rocard's chances for the presidency.

Enter Edith Cresson, depicted by the press as a leftist answer to Margaret Thatcher. She was appointed France's first female prime minister in May 1991. In contrast to the more centrist Rocard, Cresson had a clear left-wing bias. Her government found itself in a much more confrontational relationship with the conservative opposition. Importantly, she had to rely more directly on the Communists in the National Assembly.

In April 1992, following a disastrous showing for the Socialists (only 18.3 percent of the vote) in the March 1992 regional elections, Cresson resigned after serving just ten months. Many Socialists blamed Cresson for the Socialist debacle. She had made

1993 Parliamentary Election Results		
Party	*% Votes*	*Seats*
Rally for the Republic (RPR)	28	247
Union for French Democracy (UDF)	26	213
Socialist Party (PS)	28	54
Communist Party (PCF)	5	23
Left Radicals (MRG)	1	6
Others	12	34
Total Seats		577

Note: Percentages may not add up to 100 due to rounding.

some embarrassing comments during her brief tenure, such as likening the Japanese to ants and claiming that one-quarter of the men in Britain were homosexual. More importantly, however, were notable policy failures, including rising unemployment, labor strikes, and a protest by social workers, nurses, and artists who traditionally supported the Socialist Party.

Cresson's replacement was former finance minister Pierre Bérégovoy. Having won praise for stabilizing the franc and reducing inflation, Bérégovoy seemed to be a smart choice as prime minister, but the honeymoon did not last long. After only four months on the job, Bérégovoy's approval rating was even lower than Cresson's.

He was criticized for his poor handling of a lorry-drivers' strike, and numerous scandals rocked his government and shook the public's confidence in the Socialist Party. His minister for urban affairs resigned after being charged with fraud and forgery in a dispute with a former business partner. In addition, the president of the National Assembly was told he would be charged in connection with past irregularities in party finances. Laurent Fabius, a former prime minister and then first secretary of the Socialist Party, was attacked for failing to protect the country's emergency blood supply against HIV contamination.

Most damaging was the revelation of a scandal involving Bérégovoy himself. While professing his innocence, Bérégovoy admitted receiving a $180,000 interest-free loan in 1986 from a businessman friend named Roger-Patrice Pelat. The loan enabled Bérégovoy to buy an apartment in an upscale area of Paris.

Thus, leading up to the 1993 National Assembly elections, the Socialists were in the advanced stages of disarray. This prompted Michel Rocard to begin preparing for the 1995 presidential election by distancing himself from the party. He said the inevitable protest votes were against "Mitterrandism, not Socialism."

One month before the March parliamentary elections, Rocard created what he called a "Political Big Bang"—a center-left alliance with Socialists, environmentalists, human rights activists, and mainstream Communists that would effectively make the Socialist Party extinct.

The Big Bang idea was not new. It had been tried by Mitterrand and Laurent Fabius before to form a broad-based social democratic coalition. But coupled with the demise of the Socialist Party, Rocard's Big Bang was explosive, indeed.

Results. Even considering all the foreboding of disaster in the March elections, the scale of the defeat was unexpected. The party of the incumbent president won a mere 20 percent of the first-round vote and, following the second round, the Socialists and smaller allied parties managed to secure only 70 seats in the new National Assembly—one-quarter of their seat total in the outgoing parliament.

In contrast, the two center-right parties—the neo-Gaullist Rally for the Republic (RPR) and the Union for French Democracy (UDF)—together secured 80 percent of the National Assembly's seats (460 out of 577) on the strength of just 40 percent of the popular vote in the first round and 54 percent of the vote in the second round. The RPR is now the largest party in the National Assembly, which is why President Mitterrand called on former RPR finance minister Edouard Balladur to become the next prime minister.

Tragically, in the aftermath of the stunning Socialist electoral debacle, Prime Minister Pierre Bérégovoy committed suicide on May 1, 1993.

By all accounts, this cohabitation between a Socialist president and conservative prime minister ran much smoother than the pre-

Past Parliamentary Election Results

Party	1988 % Votes	1988 Seats	1986 % Votes	1986 Seats	1981 % Votes	1981 Seats
PS/MRG	49	277	33	209	38	283
RPR	23	129	21	148	22	83
UDF	21	130	18	129	19	66
PCF	3	27	10	35	16	44
FN	2	1	10	35	—	—
Others	2	13	8	21	4	15
Total Seats		**577**		**577**		**491**

Note: Percentages may not add up to 100 due to rounding. PS = Socialist Party, MRG = Left Radical Movement, RPR = Rally for the Republic, UDF = Union for French Democracy, PCF = French Communist Party, FN = National Front.

vious period from 1986 to 1988. The new government faced major problems, however, including the deficit, recession, and persistent unemployment.

Conservatives were not looking forward to another period of cohabitation with the Socialist president. RPR leader Jacques Chirac called on Mitterrand to step down, but Mitterrand, despite his poor health, stated repeatedly that he intended to serve out his full seven-year term.

1988 Parliamentary Elections: Cohabitation No More

The June elections took place just weeks after Mitterrand's triumphant reelection as president. The timing turned out to be propitious for the Socialist Party.

While Socialists and their leftist allies did not sweep to a resounding victory, they managed to win 277 seats—just short of the 289 they needed for an absolute majority in the National Assembly.

Together with the 27 seats won by the Communist Party, the Socialist-left grouping was able to form a government and put an end to the difficult period of left-right cohabitation.

European Parliament Election Results

Party	1994 % Votes	1994 Seats	1989 % Votes	1989 Seats	1984 % Votes	1984 Seats	1979 % Votes	1979 Seats
RPR/UDF	26	29	29	26	43	41	16	15
PS	15	16	24	22	21	20	24	22
OE	12	13	—	—	—	—	—	—
FN	11	10	12	10	11	10	1	0
PCF	7	6	8	7	11	10	21	19
Center	—	—	8	7	—	—	28	25
Greens	3	0	11	9	3	0	4	0
Others	26	13	8	0	11	0	6	0
Total Seats		**87**		**81**		**81**		**81**

Note: Percentages may not add up to 100 due to rounding. RPR = Rally for the Republic, UDF = Union for French Democracy, PS = Socialist Party, OE = Other Europe, FN = National Front, PCF = French Communist Party.

1994 European Parliament Elections: How to Lose and Win at the Same Time

The center-right RPR/UDF government lost some support from the voters but ended up winning 29 seats—3 more than it did in 1989. The National Front again captured 10 seats while also losing some voter support, and the French Communist Party won 6 seats, a 1-seat loss from its 1989 tally.

The biggest surprise was the strong showing by the anti-Maastricht group known as the Other Europe, which won 12.3 percent of the vote and 13 seats.

The Socialist Party, led by Michel Rocard, a potential presidential candidate in 1995, suffered its worst drubbing in a Euroelection. The Socialists received just 14.5 percent of the vote and 16 seats—a 6-seat loss. Rocard later resigned from the party leadership.

As usual, various minor parties were able to capture a few seats each, for a total of 13. Voter turnout was up from the previous Euro-election, totalling 53.5 percent of the populace.

ELECTION LEXICON

"Castle": Term for the presidential palace, the Elysée, intimating that its inhabitant may have regal pretensions.

Cohabitation: The French term for the sharing of power between a president of the opposition party and a government of the majority party, as occurred from 1986 to 1988. Cohabitation occurred again after the 1993 parliamentary elections that brought a new conservative government to power supported by a huge majority in the National Assembly.

Decade of renewal: Jacques Chirac's 1988 presidential campaign program, which promised a continuation of the policies of the previous two years, including accelerating privatization, as well as a promise to crack down on illegal immigrants.

ENA: The Ecole Nationale d'Administration, the prestigious school for public administration, is the training grounds for most of France's political elite. Graduating from ENA is a necessary—and almost sufficient—precondition for success in the French political and bureaucratic structure.

"Events of May": Protests in May 1968 shook the French political establishment, especially President de Gaulle, who announced a referendum on proposed constitutional reforms. In April 1969, voters rejected the proposals, forcing de Gaulle to resign.

Fifth Republic: These constitutional reforms, accepted by a national referendum in 1958, were developed by Charles de Gaulle. The Fifth Republic created a strong presidency and a National Assembly elected on the majoritarian principle.

La Force de Frappe: The French independent nuclear arsenal.

"La France aux français": "France for the French," Jean-Marie Le Pen's slogan in the 1988 presidential campaign, stressing his desire for tougher immigration controls and the repatriation of undesirable or illegal immigrants.

"La France unie pour la paix et le progres": "A united France for peace and progress," François Mitterrand's 1988 presidential campaign slogan.

l'Hexagone: A common geographic euphemism for France, referring to its vaguely hexagonal shape.

"Inaugurateur de chrysanthéme": Literally, "inaugurator of chrysanthemums." Refers to the functions of a purely ceremonial head of state, which Raymond Barre and others feared would befall the French presidency under "cohabitation," thus destroying the soul if not the existence of the Fifth Republic (see above).

"Leftist version of Margaret Thatcher": Description by the press of Edith Cresson, France's first female prime minister, who was in office for only ten months.

Letter to All the French People: Mitterrand's fifty-page electoral platform that stressed his commitment to European integration and social justice for all but was otherwise vague on most points.

"Little soldier": Term used by President Mitterrand to describe Edith Cresson.

Matignon: The prime minister's office.

"Mitterrandism, not Socialism": Slogan used by Michel Rocard prior to the 1993 National Assembly election, trying to persuade voters that the inevitable votes against the Socialist Party represented a failure of President Mitterrand, not socialism per se.

"Mon ambition: une France forte dans une Europe puissante": "My ambition: a strong France in a powerful Europe," Raymond Barre's 1988 presidential campaign slogan.

NATO's integrated command: In 1965, President de Gaulle announced the French decision to withdrawal from NATO's integrated military command while retaining French membership in NATO's political structure.

"Nous irons plus loin ensemble": "We'll go farther together," Jacques Chirac's 1988 presidential campaign slogan.

"Ouverture": Literally, "opening." This French version of Glasnost—opening to the center—was Michel Rocard's innovation, which dovetailed well with Mitterrand's desire to rule with a wider base of support than merely the Socialist Party. Mitterrand said it was not healthy for one party alone to govern.

Palais Bourbon: The National Assembly building.

Palais de Luxembourg: The Senate building in the Jardin de Luxembourg in Paris.

The Permanent Coup d'Etat: The title of Mitterrand's 1964 book criticizing the Fifth Republic's constitutional provisions— the strong presidency, the single-member districts, and centralized national power. Mitterrand thought this structure reduced the ability of the left to gain power. In office, Mitterrand introduced proportional representation in 1986 to prevent a massive victory for the right, but the system has since been changed back to single-member districts.

"Political Big Bang": A new center-left alliance urged by Michel Rocard after the 1993 parliamentary elections that would replace the Socialist Party with an alliance of Socialists, environmentalists, human rights activists, and mainstream Communists.

Quai d'Orsay: The foreign ministry, located on the Quai d'Orsay.

Rainbow Warrior: A major crisis erupted over the mysterious sinking in July 1985 of the *Rainbow Warrior*, the flagship of the environmental group Greenpeace. The ship and its crew were in New Zealand to monitor and protest French nuclear weapons testing in the South Pacific. One Greenpeace activist was killed in the explosion. The French defense minister and chief of intelligence operations were forced to resign.

Rapid Action Force (FAR): While officially eschewing foreign military adventures, President Mitterrand established in 1984 this 47,000-man mobile strike force that could be sent quickly to respond to trouble spots around the world.

"Ten years are enough": Slogan shouted by angry voters after Charles de Gaulle had been president for ten years. The same sentiment was expressed by voters in the 1992 regional elections, after President Mitterrand had been in office for ten years. The result was the Socialist Party's worst defeat in twenty years, presaging the disaster of the 1993 National Assembly elections.

HISTORICAL SYNOPSIS

In the fifteenth century, France began to unify its territory, but France's present borders were not established until the seventeenth century, when it became a great European power. After the French Revolution (1789) and the creation of the First Republic, a succession of republics mark the evolution of French history: Second Republic (1848), Third Republic (1875), Fourth Republic (1946), and the Fifth Republic (1958).

1936 The Popular Front, made up of Socialists and Radicals and supported by the Communists, comes to power.

1940 On May 10 Hitler's forces invade France. On June 22 France surrenders.

1944 Paris is liberated in August and the Vichy government of Nazi sympathizers and collaborators flees to Germany. Charles de Gaulle, leader of the French resistance movement, becomes interim French president.

1946 Fourth Republic. De Gaulle steps down because he is opposed to the unstable parliamentary system of the Fourth Republic and the relatively weak presidency. During the twelve years of the Fourth Republic (1946-1958), France has twenty-five governments.

1954 The end of France's colonial empire in Indochina. Rebellion erupts in Algeria. The ensuing war jolts France into political upheaval and begins the process that leads to the demise of the Fourth Republic.

1958 Fifth Republic. De Gaulle returns to power upon the establishment of the Fifth Republic.

1962 France grants Algeria independence. De Gaulle wins referendum to make the president directly elected by universal suffrage rather than by an electoral college.

1965 In the first direct presidential elections, de Gaulle defeats François Mitterrand for president.

1968 The "Events of May" rock the nation with riots and student unrest, triggering nationwide strikes.

1969 De Gaulle resigns from office after a relatively minor referendum is rejected by voters. Former prime minister Georges Pompidou is elected president.

1974	Valéry Giscard d'Estaing is elected president after Pompidou's death. Jacques Chirac is named prime minister.
1976	Chirac resigns and Raymond Barre is named new prime minister. Chirac forms the Rally for the Republic (RPR), a neo-Gaullist party.
1978	Socialist Party narrowly loses in National Assembly elections.
1981	Mitterrand becomes the first Socialist president of the Fifth Republic. The Socialist Party subsequently wins the National Assembly elections and Mitterrand forms a Socialist government.
1986	The Socialist Party loses the National Assembly elections and Socialist president Mitterrand names Gaullist leader Chirac as prime minister, ushering in first period of "cohabitation," in which the president and prime minister are from parties of the left and right.
1988	Mitterrand is reelected president and names Socialist Michel Rocard prime minister.
1993	In March, the Socialists suffer humiliating defeat in parliamentary elections. Center-right parties win 40 percent of the vote in the first round and, after the second round, win 80 percent of the 577 National Assembly seats. Neo-Gaullist Edouard Balladur becomes prime minister and a second period of "cohabitation" between a Socialist president and a conservative prime minister begins. On September 20 French voters narrowly approve (51 percent) the Maastricht Treaty on European Unity. A defeat in France would have doomed Maastricht, creating chaos in Europe's drive toward greater unity.
1994	Conservative parties continue to score well in March local elections and in the Euro-elections in June. The Socialists continue their downward trend.
1995	Socialist Jacques Delors, the outgoing European Commission president, decides not to run for the French presidency. Election to succeed President Mitterrand is held in May.

Germany

The Country in Brief

Official Name: Federal Republic of Germany (*Bundesrepublik Deutschland*)
Capital: Bonn (temporary; capital will move to Berlin by 2001)
Currency: Deutsche Mark
National Day: May 23 (Constitution Day)
Language: German
Religions: Protestant, Roman Catholic
Memberships: NATO and EU
Border Countries: Austria, Belgium, Czech Republic, Denmark, France, Luxembourg, Netherlands, Poland, Switzerland
Embassy in Washington, D.C.: 4645 Reservoir Road, N.W., 20007. Telephone: (202) 298-4000.

Political Profile

Government Type: Federal republic/parliamentary democracy
Head of State: President Roman Herzog
Political Party: Christian Democrat (CDU)
Assumed Office: 1994
Election Method: Elected by both chambers of parliament
Term of Office: Five years
Next Election: 1999
Head of Government: Federal Chancellor Helmut Kohl
Political Party: Christian Democrat (CDU)

Assumed Office: 1982
Reelected: 1983, 1987, 1990, 1994
Next Election: 1998
Legislature: Bicameral, Parliament (*Parlament*)
Upper Chamber: Bundesrat (Federal Council), 79 members
appointed from the 16 states (*Länder*). The Bundesrat must agree
with all measures touching Länder interests.
Lower Chamber: Bundestag (Federal Assembly), 656 members
(672 after 1994 elections due to "overhanging mandates"), elected
by direct voting and proportional representation. It is the only
branch of the federal government that is popularly elected. Because of the first-vote/second-vote system, there will occasionally
be extra members elected directly (overhanging mandates), increasing membership above the official number of seats.
Term of Office: Four years
Last Election: 1994
Next Election: 1998

Comparative Data

Population: 80 million
GDP: $1.6 trillion
GDP Per Capita: $23,600
Voting System: Mixed member proportional (5% threshold)
Per Capita Representation Rate: 123,000
Big Government Index: 44.9% (1989)
Women in Parliament: 21%
Voter Turnout Rate: 78%

MAJOR POLITICAL PARTIES

Christian Democratic Union
(*Christlich-Demokratische Union*, CDU)

Formed as a Catholic-Protestant alliance following the defeat of
Nazi Germany, the CDU has been a dominant force in German
politics. With the exception of the 1969-1982 period, the CDU and

allied CSU have participated, either alone or as the dominant coalition partner, in every government of postwar Germany. The CDU is committed to a socially responsible market economy and the full integration of Germany into the community of European and NATO democracies. Its politics have been pragmatic, placing less stress on doctrine than on responding to voter sentiment.

Christian Social Union (*Christlich-Soziale Union*, CSU)

Allied with the CDU, the CSU also favors the free market and democratic principles but is notably farther to the right on many issues. Led for many years by the late Franz Josef Strauss, the CSU has at times discomfited its coalition partners with hard-line positions on law and order, immigration restriction, and foreign policy.

Social Democratic Party of Germany (*Sozialdemokratische Partei Deutschlands*, SPD)

One of the oldest organized political parties in the world, the SPD was a force in Bismarck's Imperial Germany and in the interwar Weimar Republic. Driven underground during the Nazi era, it resurfaced as the primary opposition to the postwar CDU/CSU governments. In 1959, the party adopted the famous Bad Godesberg Program, renouncing Marxism and clearing the way to participation in government. Its first step was in a "Grand Coalition" with the CDU/CSU from 1966 to 1969 and then as the dominant partner in coalition with the Free Democratic Party. Dissension in the SPD left wing led to the collapse of the coalition in 1982. Since then the party has been torn by factional struggles between left and center in the search for an effective response to the SPD's fundamental problem. Prosperity and social change have eroded its traditional working-class base, while the rise of the Greens has attracted young voters who might otherwise have turned to the SPD.

Free Democratic Party (*Freie Demokratische Partei*, FDP)

Also known as the Liberals, the FDP occupies the pivotal center of the German political spectrum. With deep roots in the European liberal tradition, the FDP has a largely Protestant upper-middle-class base. Although weak at the local level and rarely polling more than 10 percent of the national vote (12.8 percent in 1961 was its best ever), the party has held a balance-of-power position since the establishment of the Federal Republic, participating in every government with the exception of the 1966-1969 Grand Coalition. The FDP has proved extremely adept at playing coalition politics, picking up more—and more important—ministries than its number of Bundestag seats might appear to warrant.

Greens (*Die Grünen*, GP)

Originating in the 1970s as an alliance of pro-environment, antinuclear, antimilitarist groups, the Greens attracted a wide range of antiestablishment support. This diversity of interests, with their rejection of politics as practiced by the traditional parties, has limited somewhat their parliamentary effectiveness. After scoring strongly on the local level, they entered the Bundestag in 1983. The Greens failed to gain the required 5 percent of the vote in 1987, so they were forced out of parliament and into a period of internal turmoil. Greens from the former East Germany won 8 seats in 1990. In 1994, Greens won 49 seats, reflecting the party's successful transition in projecting a more moderate image.

Party of Democratic Socialism
(*Partei der Demokratischen Sozialismus*, PDS)

This former Communist party of East Germany contested the December 1990 elections as part of a Left List (*Linke List*) and managed to win 17 seats. The PDS captured 30 seats following the 1994 elections, bringing the total "center-left" membership of the Bundestag very close to parity with the "center right" parties.

MINOR POLITICAL PARTIES

Instead Party (*Statt-Partei*, SP)
Republicans (*Die Republikaner*, DR)

ELECTION REVIEW

1994 Presidential Elections: Kohl Wins with Herzog

The Federal Convention (Bundesversammlung), which consists of both the upper (Bundesrat) and lower (Bundestag) houses of parliament, has one primary function: to elect a federal president once every five years. The presidency is largely a ceremonial office, although the president does represent the Federal Republic internationally, signs international agreements, and appoints the chancellor. On May 23, 1994, the Federal Assembly on a largely party-line vote, elected Roman Herzog, the head of the constitutional court and chosen candidate of Christian Democratic Chancellor Helmut Kohl, to succeed Richard von Weizsäcker as president.

Herzog's election, by a slender margin (only 696 votes of 1,320 possible), proved to be a good—and accurate—omen for Helmut Kohl's chances in the October general election. Both Herzog and Kohl (see "1994 Parliamentary Elections," below) managed to win by very slim margins.

In replacing the highly respected Richard von Weizsäcker (CDU), whose two terms as president won him wide praise both domestically and internationally, Herzog has some large shoes to fill.

1994 Parliamentary (Bundestag) Elections: Kohl's Coalition Continues . . . Barely

When the dust settled after Germany's Bundestag elections, held October 16, 1994, incumbent Chancellor Helmut Kohl and his Christian Democratic Union (CDU) emerged bruised and battered but victorious, holding onto power with a razor-thin majority of 10 seats. In contrast, after the 1990 elections Kohl and his coalition partners reigned with a whopping 134-seat majority.

The Bundestag is elected by a combination of direct constituency voting and proportional representation. Each voter has two votes, an *Erststimme* (first vote), which is cast for a specific candidate in a geographic district, and a *Zweitstimme* (second vote), which is cast for a party. Half of the members are elected by

1994 Parliamentary Election Results

Party	% Votes	Seats
Christian Democratic Union/ Christian Social Union (CDU/CSU)	42	294
Social Democratic Party (SPD)	36	252
Greens	7	49
Free Democratic Party (FDP)	7	47
Party of Democratic Socialism (PDS)	4	30
Total Seats		**672**

Note: Percentages may not add up to 100 due to rounding.

plurality of first votes; the remaining seats are divided among the parties according to their proportion of second votes and filled from party candidate lists. Only parties polling 5 percent or more of the second (party list) votes—or win three first vote seats—are eligible for a share of the proportional seats.

All things considered, Kohl's CDU party, together with its sister party, the Christian Social Union (CSU), did not fare too badly in the balloting. After all, a chancellor is expected to lose some luster after twelve straight years in power. The CDU/CSU won 41.5 percent of the vote, down just 2.3 percent from their result in 1990, yielding 294 seats compared with 319 four years earlier.

An important factor in the dwindling power base of Kohl's coalition was the poor showing of his coalition partner, the Free Democrats (FDP). The FDP dropped precipitously from 11 percent to 6.9 percent of the vote, which translated into just 47 seats—a steep decline of 32 FDP seats.

The surprisingly strong showing by the environmentalist Green party, which cleared the 5 percent vote threshold and returned to the Bundestag in 1994 with 7.3 percent of the vote, and a respectable if unspectacular improvement in support for the Social Democrats (SPD), helped to shift the parliamentary balance of power ever so tantalizingly close to a majority for the left. In the end, the SPD scored 36.4 percent of the vote, up from 33.5 percent in 1990, and won 252 seats, a gain of 13 seats over 1990. The Greens gathered 49 seats, two more than the FDP.

Also adding to the leftward swing in the Bundestag was the fact that the former Communists, the renamed Party of Democratic Socialism (PDS), managed to win four districts in Berlin, which entitled them to collect a total of 30 seats on the strength of receiving 4.4 percent of the national vote. (According to Germany's intricate electoral system, unless a party wins at least three districts outright, the normal threshold for earning seats in the Bundestag is 5 percent.)

Altogether, the three parties on the left won 331 seats, while the center-right Kohl coalition secured 341 seats in the 672-seat Bundestag. In terms of voting percentage, the combined left virtually split the vote with the ruling coalition, with 48.1 percent versus 48.4 percent. Thus, Germany's electorate seems to be evenly divided between right and left. Kohl remains in office with very few votes to spare in the Bundestag, and with an upper chamber, the Bundesrat, that the opposition SPD has begun to dominate. The CDU benefited from Germany's mixed member proportional voting system. The government's slim majority in the Bundestag was from 10 "overhanging mandates" (see Lexicon).

The message from voters seems to have been: You may continue in power, Mr. Kohl, but don't go beyond your promises to strengthen German unity and to guide integration within the European Union. In the end, the voters apparently decided to play it safe and retain the chancellor they knew rather than install an untried and largely unknown chancellor in the person of SPD leader Rudolf Scharping.

1990 Parliamentary Elections: Kohl's Coalition Continues

On October 3, 1990, the two countries known as West Germany and East Germany officially ceased to exist. The new, unified Germany retained West Germany's official name, the Federal Republic of Germany (FRG). Despite being relegated to the dustbin of history, the German Democratic Republic (East Germany) had a lingering impact on the all-German elections held December 2, 1990. The Federal Constitutional Court ruled that forcing East Germany's newly formed political parties to compete for representation on an all-German level under the West German voting system, especially the 5 percent threshold rule, would be unfair. The

Past Parliamentary Election Results

Party	1990 % Votes	1990 Seats	1987 % Votes	1987 Seats	1983 % Votes	1983 Seats	1980 % Votes	1980 Seats
CDU	37	268	34	174	38	191	34	174
CSU	7	51	10	49	11	53	10	52
SPD	33	239	37	186	38	193	43	218
Greens	5	0	8	42	6	27	2	0
FDP	11	79	9	46	7	34	11	53
PDS	2	17	—	—	—	—	—	—
Others	5	8	2	0	0	0	0	0
Total Seats		662		497		498		497

Note: Percentages may not add up to 100 due to rounding. CDU = Christian Democratic Union, CSU = Christian Social Union, SPD = Social Democratic Party, FDP = Free Democratic Party, PDS = Party of Democratic Socialism.

court ruled, therefore, that the 5 percent rule would apply to both parts of Germany separately.

Thus, just two short months after unification, the first all-German national elections in fifty-eight years were held under somewhat complicated circumstances. While the election results were generally unremarkable—West German Chancellor Helmut Kohl's ruling coalition retained power with 55 percent of the vote—the victory was seen in large part as a reward from a grateful nation for his leadership in bringing about a relatively painless reunification.

The decision to allow smaller parties in the former East Germany to win seats by achieving 5 percent of the East German vote did have significant consequences. For instance, a coalition of independent East German Green parties managed to win 5.1 percent of the vote and 8 seats. Meanwhile, the West German Green Party, which in 1987 had stunned the established parties by winning 8.3 percent of the vote and 42 seats in the Bundestag, won only 4.8 percent of the vote in West Germany and failed to win any seats.

Applying the 5 percent threshold separately clearly helped the former Communist Party in East Germany. Newly renamed the Party of Democratic Socialism (PDS), the "reformed" Communists managed to win 17 seats on the strength of winning 11.1 percent of the vote in Eastern Germany. Nationwide, PDS only won 2.4 percent of the vote and would have secured no seats under a uniform 5 percent rule.

While Kohl's coalition retained power, significant shifts occurred in the relative positions of the three parties within the coalition. Kohl's CDU/CSU group gained only marginally at the polls, winning 43.8 percent of the vote and 268 of the 656 Bundestag seats (increased from the 496 seats in the old West German Bundestag). The CDU's more conservative cousin, the Bavaria-based CSU, slid 3.2 percent, winning only 51 seats. Thus, the CDU and CSU together earned 319 seats, just shy of the 329 required for an absolute majority.

By contrast, the FDP (also known as the Liberals) gained considerably, reaching 11 percent nationwide and nearly 13 percent in Eastern Germany. The FDP secured 79 seats in the Bundestag, a showing that strengthened its hand in the CDU-led coalition. Together, the CDU and the FDP won a solid majority of 347 seats and thus could have formed a government without help from the CSU.

1994 European Parliament Elections

A few weeks after the May 23 victory of his candidate for preside%t, Helmut Kohl's CDU/CSU group scored well in the June 12 Euro-election, picking up 47 seats—a 15-seat increase compared with 1989. All was not rosy for the Kohl coalition, however. Kohl's coalition partner, the Free Democrats, fared poorly, getting only 4 percent of the vote and losing all 4 of their seats.

Meanwhile, voter support for the Social Democrats dropped off, some of it shifting to the environmentalist Greens. However, with the extra 18 seats allotted to Germany for this election, the SPD still managed to pick up 40 seats—an increase of 9 seats over its 1989 tally. Support for the environmental Green Party increased, giving them 12 seats, a 4-seat gain.

European Parliament Election Results

Party	1994 % Votes	1994 Seats	1989 % Votes	1989 Seats	1984 % Votes	1984 Seats	1979 % Votes	1979 Seats
SPD	32	40	37	31	37	33	41	35
CDU	32	39	30	25	38	34	39	34
Greens	10	12	8	8	9	7	3	0
CSU	7	8	8	7	9	7	10	8
FDP	4	0	6	4	5	0	6	4
DR	4	0	7	6	—	—	—	—
Others	10	0	4	0	2	0	0	0
Total Seats		99		81		81		81

Note: Percentages may not add up to 100 due to rounding. SPD = Social Democratic Party, CDU = Christian Democratic Union, CSU = Christian Social Union, FDP = Free Democratic Party, DR = Republican Party.

Minor parties, including the Republicans and former Communists, captured approximately 10 percent of the vote but no seats.

ELECTION LEXICON

Alternative List: Another name for the Green Party.

"Ampul coalition": *Ampul* is the German word for traffic light. The phrase refers to a possible red-yellow-green coalition government after the December 1990 elections, made up of Social Democrats (red), Free Democrats (yellow), and Greens.

Anschluss: Literally, "joining." Refers to the union of Austria and Germany after Hitler absorbed Austria in 1938.

Berlin or Bonn: The issue of returning the capital to Berlin became very heated immediately after unification. After a long debate, the Bundestag voted narrowly on June 20, 1991, in favor of making Berlin the capital but to do so over a ten-year period.

Bundeskanzler: Literally, "federal chancellor."

Bundesversammlung: Joint meeting of the Bundestag and representatives of the various Länder; the sole purpose this meeting is to
elect the federal president.

"Bunte listen": Literally, "colorful list," yet another name used
for the Greens.

Constructive censure: The Bundestag can bring down the government by a motion of censure or "no confidence," but it must
be "positive" by simultaneously proposing an alternative government. This tends to increase the stability of the governments.

Erststimme/zweitstimme: The "first-vote/second-vote" election
system. The first vote is used for a specific candidate to represent
a geographic district and the second vote is for a particular party.
Half of the Bundestag membership is elected by a plurality of the
first votes and the other half is elected by proportional representation based on the second (party) votes.

Five percent rule: Parties must poll at least 5 percent of the total
national vote list in order to win seats in the Bundestag.

Fraktion: Term used for political party organizations in parliament.

"Fundis": "Fundamentalist" faction within the Green Party that
rejects any compromise on basic principles, even if it means sacri-
ficing political power.

Gästarbeiter: Literally, "guest workers"—people who were allowed into Germany to meet the labor shortage during the economic boom years in the 1960s and 1970s. Many have remained in
Germany. The largest group is Turkish.

Grand Coalition: Between 1966 and 1969, the Social Democratic
Party (SPD) and the Christian Democratic Union formed a government, giving the SPD its first experience in government. The
SPD used that experience to advantage, forming a coalition with
the Free Democratic Party in 1969 and ruling for the next thirteen
years.

Grundgesetz: Germany's basic law, or constitution, which came
into force in 1949.

"Let Justice Reign and Not Social Coldness": Social Democratic
Party slogan during the 1987 campaign, protesting the social and
economic policies of the Christian Democratic Union.

Liberals: The Free Democrats are popularly known as "Liberals" *(Die Liberalen)*, referring to their ties to European liberalism, which emphasizes free market solutions to social problems.

November 9: This has been a fateful day in German history. On November 9, 1918, Kaiser Wilhelm II abdicated, ending the rule of the Hohenzollern dynasty. On November 9, 1923, Adolf Hitler attempted to seize power in the infamous "beer hall putsch." Fifteen years later, on the night of November 8-9, 1938 (which became known as Kristallnacht, for "night of broken glass"), a tragic series of riots and looting directed against the Jewish community took place. Finally, November 9, 1989, marked the dramatic opening of the Berlin Wall, which catapulted East and West Germany toward reunification within a year.

Overhanging mandate (Uberhang mandat): This is a peculiar result of Germany's complicated voting system. Because of the first-vote/second-vote system, there will occasionally be a few extra members elected directly to the Bundestag, increasing the total membership over the official number. Following unification there were officially 656 Bundestag members, but the 1990 election resulted in 662 members being seated. The 1994 election ended with 672 members winning seats. These extra seats, called "overhang mandates," occur when a party wins more district-based (first vote) seats than it should receive given the party's share of the proportional (second vote) seats. In effect, the district (first) vote takes precedence over the proportional (second) vote in those rare instances when a party succeeds in winning "extra" district seats.

Ostpolitik: The Federal Republic's "Eastern policy" was initiated by former Chancellor Willy Brandt in the early 1970s. A series of treaties regularized relations with the Soviet Union, Poland, Czechoslovakia, and the German Democratic Republic.

"Realos": "Realist" faction of the Greens that would agree to compromise and cooperate with traditional parties to further the aims of the Greens.

"Rot-grön": Term referring to a possible coalition of the "red" Social Democratic Party and the Greens, a prospect that has some support in both parties but is also a bitterly divisive issue in each.

The concept was first tried out on the local level in West Berlin, where a "red-green" coalition took control after the Christian Democratic Union lost its dominant position in 1988 city elections.

Skinheads: Term for members of right-wing, openly Nazi youth groups that spread violence against minorities, especially Turks and Jews. Thousands of attacks took place leading up to the 1992 outlawing of the neo-Nazi German Alternative Party.

Sozialmarktwirtschaft: The Christian Democratic vision of a socially responsible market economy.

Volkspartei: Literally, "people's party," which is how the Christian Democratic Union sees itself.

Weimar Republic: Democratic German republic (1919-1933) that was toppled by Hitler after the Reichstag (parliament) fire in February 1933.

Wende: "A change of direction." This was the promise of Chancellor Helmut Kohl upon taking office in 1982. Specifically, he proposed reducing the state's role in the economy and encouraging greater private initiative.

Wirtschaftswunder: Term for the German postwar economic miracle.

"Yes to Germany": Nationalistic slogan of the Republicans.

HISTORICAL SYNOPSIS

Germany's march toward unity did not begin until the Napoleonic Wars helped to sweep away the fragmented Germany of the Middle Ages.

1862   Prussian aristocrat Otto von Bismarck becomes chancellor.

1871   The German Empire is proclaimed at Versailles, and King Wilhelm I of Prussia becomes emperor. Bismarck, having secured the unification of all German states, begins enacting some of the most progressive social legislation of the time.

1914–	World War I. Germany is defeated by the Allies. Revolution overthrows the monarchy. A republic is proclaimed in the university town of Weimar.
1918	
1932	In elections, the Nazis emerge as the largest party in the Reichstag, although short of an absolute majority.
1933	Adolph Hitler is appointed chancellor. The Reichstag building is destroyed by fire. Hitler rules by decree. All parties except the Nazis are abolished. Germany begins to rearm.
1936	German troops enter the demilitarized Rhineland, unopposed by the Allies.
1938	German troops occupy Austria (the *Anschluss*). At a conference in Munich, Britain and France agree to cede German-speaking areas of Czechoslovakia to Germany.
1939–	Germany occupies all of Czechoslovakia, signs a non-aggression pact with the Soviet Union, and attacks Poland, launching World War II, which ends with Germany's unconditional surrender. Germany is partitioned among the victorious powers: the United States, the United Kingdom, France, and the Soviet Union.
1945	
1948	The three Western Allies relinquish governing powers in their occupation zones and the Federal Republic of Germany is established.
1949	First election to the Bundestag, producing a center-right majority. Konrad Adenauer (CDU) becomes chancellor. Theodor Heuss (FDP) is elected federal president. A Soviet blockade of Berlin is neutralized by U.S. airlift.
1954	The Federal Republic becomes a member of NATO.
1963	Konrad Adenauer resigns as chancellor and Ludwig Erhard succeeds him.
1966	Erhard government falls when FDP withdraws from the coalition. SPD enters "Grand Coalition" under Chancellor Kurt Georg Kiesinger (CDU).
1969	Bundestag election yields gains for SPD, which forms new coalition government with the FDP. Chancellor Willy Brandt initiates *Ostpolitik* to improve relations with Eastern Europe.

1974	Espionage scandal involving Brandt's personal secretary leads to Brandt's resignation. Helmut Schmidt (SPD) takes over as chancellor.
1976	SPD-FDP coalition wins narrow victory in Bundestag election.
1982	SPD left-wing opposition to economic and defense policies causes FDP to pull out of coalition. FDP joins CDU/CSU in new center-right government.
1983	Bundestag election returns center-right coalition to power.
1987	Bundestag election returns CDU/CSU-FDP coalition, with reduced majority.
1989	Berlin Wall is opened and revolutionary change sweeps through East Germany and Eastern Europe. German reunification becomes distinct probability.
1990	German Economic and Monetary Union (GEMU) takes effect July 1. Unification takes place October 3. On December 2, first all-German elections in fifty-eight years return CDU-led coalition to power.
1991	The Bundestag votes (338-320) on June 20 to move the capital from Bonn to Berlin, but to do so over a ten-year period.
1992	Germany ratifies Maastricht Treaty on European Union.
1992	Kohl's government outlaws neo-Nazi German Alternative Party after "skinhead"-instigated violence reaches frightening levels. A total of 4,600 acts of violence, resulting in fourteen deaths, take place.
1994	Chancellor Helmut Kohl narrowly wins reelection on October 15. Earlier, on May 23, Kohl's candidate for president wins the support of a slim majority of Bundestag and Bundesrat members.

Greece

The Country in Brief

Official Name: Hellenic Republic (*Elliniki Dimokratia*)
Capital: Athens
Currency: Drachma
National Day: March 25 (Independence Day)
Language: Greek
Religion: Greek Orthodox
Memberships: NATO and EU
Border Countries: Albania, Bulgaria, Macedonia, Turkey
Embassy in Washington, D.C.: 2221 Massachusetts Avenue, N.W., 20008. Telephone: (202) 667-3168.

Political Profile

Government Type: Presidential/parliamentary democracy
Head of State: President Constantine Karamanlis (until March 1995)
Political Party: New Democracy (Conservative)
Assumed Office: 1990 (previously served as president 1980-1985)
Election Method: Indirectly elected by two-thirds of parliament; limited powers.
Term of Office: Five years
Next Election: 1995

Head of Government: Prime Minister Andreas Papandreou
Political Party: Socialist
Assumed Office: 1993 (previously served as prime minister 1981-1989)
Next Election: 1997
Legislature: Unicameral assembly. Vouli, 300 members, elected by proportional representation.
Term of Office: Four years
Last Election: 1993
Next Election: 1997

Comparative Data

Population: 10.2 million
GDP: $69 billion
GDP Per Capita: $6,500
Voting System: Party list proportional (3% threshold)
Per Capita Representation Rate: 33,000
Big Government Index: 31.9%
Women in Parliament: 5%
Voter Turnout Rate: 77%

Major Political Parties

Pan-Hellenic Socialist Movement (*Panellenio Sosialistiko Kinema*, PASOK)

Founded in 1974 by Andreas Papandreou, PASOK advocates traditional Socialist policies and promotes a strong national identity. While in power from 1981 to 1989, PASOK nationalized certain industries and strengthened the social welfare system. It has not supported membership in NATO or the EU.

New Democracy Party (*Nea Democratia*, ND)

This center-right party was founded in 1974 by Constantine Karamanlis, the former prime minister and president. The party supports Greek membership in NATO and the EU and emphasizes cultural ties and a foreign policy favoring the West. It advocates free market economic policies.

Communist Party of Greece
(*Kommuistiko Komma Ellados*, KKE)

The Communist Party had to deal with turmoil within its ranks in the last decade, but it returned to some measure of prominence in 1993 when it captured 9 seats. Although Stalinists seemed to have control of the the Central Committee in 1991, reformist Harilaos Florakis was elected president of the Central Committee.

Political Spring (*Politiki Anixi*, POLA)

A conservative splinter group comprised of some powerful ex-New Democracy members, Political Spring was founded in 1993 by former foreign minister Antonis Samaras. The party was instrumental in toppling the government of Prime Minister Constantine Mitsotakis.

MINOR POLITICAL PARTIES

Greek Communist Party-Interior
(*Kommunistiko Komma Ellados-Esoterikou*, KKES)
Left Alliance/Alliance of Progressive and Left-Wing Forces
(*Symmachia Proodeftikon kai Aristeron Dinameron*, LA)
Union of the Democratic Center
(*Enose Demokratikon Kentrou*, EDK)

ELECTION REVIEW

1993 Parliamentary Elections: Play It Again, Andreas

After enduring nearly four years of painful austerity dished out by the conservative New Democracy government, Greek voters sent a message in the October 1993 elections. Stated briefly,

1993 Parliamentary Election Results

Party	% Votes	Seats
Pan-Hellenic Socialist Party (PASOK)	47	170
New Democracy (ND)	39	111
Political Spring (POLA)	5	10
Communist Party (KKE)	5	9
Others	4	0
Total Seats		**300**

Note: Percentages may not add up to 100 due to rounding.

the message said: "Play it again, Andreas. Socialism isn't so bad, after all."

As in France, it was a bit like "déjà vu all over again," but instead of installing a conservative government to "cohabit" with a Socialist president, the Greek election brought in a Socialist government to cohabit with President Constantine Karamanlis, the conservative who had been elected to a five-year term in 1990. It is lucky for the Greek Socialists that the Greek presidency is not as powerful as its French counterpart. Andreas Papandreou rejoined Spain's Felipe González as the EU's only two Socialist prime ministers at that time.

Despite poor health and the humiliation of being driven from office in 1990, Papandreou staged a dramatic political comeback in the 1993 elections. Because of the hardships imposed during the three-and-a-half years of conservative Constantine Mitsotakis's tenure as prime minister, Papandreou's Socialists (also known as the Pan-Hellenic Socialist Movement, PASOK) were widely expected to win the 1993 elections. Mitsotakis had pursued a tight-fisted fiscal policy to bring down Greece's overblown public sector debt. He also pushed aggressive privatization and anti-inflation programs that Papandreou promised to amend significantly.

Although a Socialist win was expected, the scale of the victory came as a surprise. PASOK drew 46.9 percent of the vote and won 170 seats in the 300-seat parliament. The ruling New Democracy party secured just 39.3 percent of the vote and 111 seats. Political Spring, a breakaway conservative party founded by former foreign minister Antonis Samaras, garnered 4.9 percent of the vote and 10 seats, just ahead of the unreformed Greek Communists, who garnered 4.5 percent of the vote and 9 seats.

Campaign promises notwithstanding, changing course dramatically proved to be a difficult chore for Papandreou. In order to stay in compliance with the requirements of the Maastricht Treaty on European Unity, Greece would have to continue reforming its economy in the direction of privatization, lower debt, and less inflation (which had been running at close to 13 percent).

The newly independent republic of Macedonia was another point of contention for Papandreou. When Macedonia, a province in neighboring Yugoslavia, declared its independence in 1992, Greece was concerned that the new country of Macedonia would try to unite with the Greek province of Macedonia to create a greater Macedonian state. For that reason, Athens steadfastly opposed use of the name, claiming that Greece alone had exclusive right to it. Papandreou stated that the Greek government would not recognize any government that used the name of Macedonia, arguing that this would cause confusion about the status of the Greek province of Macedonia.

In February 1993, Greece announced that it would accept UN arbitration on the matter and that the name of Macedonia could be used if it was done in such a way as to distinguish it from the Greek province. The compromise creation was FYROM—the former Yugoslav Republic of Macedonia.

1989, 1990 Parliamentary Elections: To the Polls, Again!

On April 8, 1990, ballot-weary Greek voters dragged themselves to the polls for the third time in ten months to try to elect a stable government. While much of the pre-election polling suggested yet more Greek gridlock, the conservative New Democracy Party won 47 percent of the vote and managed to eke out a 1-seat parliamentary majority and form a government, naming Constantine Mitsotakis prime minister. New Democracy captured 150 seats—one short of majority in the 300-seat parliament—but the Democratic Renewal Party aligned its 1 seat in support of the ND, thus forming the majority. Support for the Socialist Party slipped from 128 to 123 seats.

Past Parliamentary Election Results

Party	1990 % Votes	1990 Seats	Nov. 1989 % Votes	Nov. 1989 Seats	June 1989 % Votes	June 1989 Seats	1985 % Votes	1985 Seats
PASOK	37	123	41	128	39	125	46	161
ND	47	150	46	148	44	145	41	126
LA/KKE	10	19	11	21	13	28	12	13
Others	5	8	2	3	3	2	0	0
Total Seats		**300**		**300**		**300**		**300**

Note: Percentages may not add up to 100 due to rounding. PASOK = Pan-Hellenic Socialist Party, ND = New Democracy, LA = Left Alliance, KKE = Greek Communist Party.

Mitsotakis initiated a program of severe fiscal austerity, which was developed in order to meet conditions imposed by the then European Community (EC). The EC (now the European Union) had informed Greece that it must lower its inflation rate to 7 percent before it could participate in the European Monetary System. The EC also said that, within the next three years, Greece had to sharply reduce government borrowing to 1.5 percent of GDP, cut public sector employment by 10 percent, curb public sector pay rises, and radically broaden the tax base.

Within three weeks of taking office in 1990, Mitsotakis launched his economic austerity program. Taxes were raised, costs for government services increased, and the indexing of wages to inflation was abolished. But despite significant progress in curtailing the debt problem, the government was only able to reduce the rate of increase in the debt.

Background. The 1990 election really got started on June 18, 1989, when Prime Minister Andreas Papandreou's eight-year reign came to an end. Papandreou's Pan-Hellenic Socialist Party (PASOK) failed to win a majority of votes cast in the election held that day. The same fate befell PASOK's main opposition, the center-right New Democracy Party.

In an unusual move, New Democracy and the Left Alliance (Communists) joined forces to form an interim coalition government until new elections could be held in November. The Left Alliance emerged as a power broker after the June election, thanks to the election reforms that introduced a purer form of proportional representation, making it possible for smaller parties to win more seats in parliament.

Papandreou, in a gambit reminiscent of French President Mitterand's switch to proportional representation in 1986, knew he could not win under the old rules and sought to make it more difficult for any other party to garner a majority. As a result, the relatively small Left Alliance more than doubled its yield of seats from 13 in 1985 to 28 in June 1989.

A caretaker coalition government was formed under the leadership of New Democrat Tzannis Tannetakis for the explicit purpose of launching a process of "catharsis" by punishing the corruption-plagued Papandreou regime and then holding new elections.

On November 5, 1989, the second of three elections was held, again producing stalemate (*adiexodos*). New Democracy increased its share of the vote from 44.3 percent in June to 46.2 percent in November, a gain of 3 seats, but PASOK also increased its vote share from 39.2 percent to 40.7 percent, adding 3 seats. After a two-week political crisis, the three major parties agreed to form an all-party coalition government under the leadership of eighty-five-year-old economist and elder statesman Xenophon Zolotas. The main goals of this interim government were to address the economic crisis and somehow hold the country together until the April 1990 election. It managed to accomplish the latter objective, but did poorly on the former.

Papandreou's political problems were manifold leading up to the June 1989 elections. The amazing thing was not that Papandreou was voted out of office after eight years of Socialist rule, but that he and his party retained so much political clout, keeping New Democracy from winning a solid majority of seats in three separate attempts. Papandreou's shrewd electoral reform before the election saw to that.

Prior to the June 1989 elections, resentment and distrust of PASOK had grown. Allegations of widespread nepotism, cronyism, graft, and corruption tainted Papandreou's government. PASOK exercised strict controls over state television, virtually silencing the voices of any opposition to PASOK.

Even Papandreou's personal life became an issue. There were revelations about Papandreou's extramarital affair with Dimitra Liani, who was about half Papandreou's age. Many Greeks found it difficult to forgive this blatant flaunting of traditional Greek family values.

A number of financial scandals seemed ultimately to seal Papandreou's political doom. Just prior to the elections, allegations involving misuse of EU agricultural subsidies came to public attention. The so-called Koskotas Affair badly hurt Papandreou's standing. George Koskotas, the thirty-four-year-old owner of the Bank of Crete, was charged with embezzling $252 million in government funds, money that allegedly ended up in the hands of Papandreou's closest associates and friends.

1994 European Parliament Elections

Prime Minister Andreas Papandreou's Socialist Party (PASOK) emerged as the largest vote-getter, winning 10 seats and 37.6 percent of the vote—a 1-seat gain over the 1989 Euro-vote totals in

European Parliament Results

	1990		1989		1984		1981	
Party	% Votes	Seats	% Votes	Seats	% Votes	Seats	% Votes	Seats
PASOK	38	10	36	9	42	10	40	10
ND	33	9	41	10	38	9	31	8
LA/KKE	13	4	14	4	12	3	13	3
POLA	9	2	—	—	—	—	—	—
Others	7	0	9	1	8	2	16	3
Total Seats		25		24		24		24

Note: Percentages may not add up to 100 due to rounding. PASOK = Pan-Hellenic Socialist Party, ND = New Democracy, LA = Left Alliance, KKE = Greek Communist Party, POLA = Political Spring.

which PASOK was bested by the New Democracy forces. In this balloting, New Democracy dropped 1 seat, emerging with 9 seats and 32.7 percent of the vote. Both PASOK and New Democracy declined substantially against their results in the 1993 general elections.

The Communists and the ex-Communist Left Alliance won 2 seats each and a combined 13.1 percent of the vote, maintaining the spots they had held in the previous European Parliament. Political Spring, a new right-wing nationalist party, garnered 8.7 percent of the vote and 2 seats.

ELECTION LEXICON

Adiexodos: "Stalemate," a familiar expression in Greece to describe the elections of June 1989 and April 1990.

Allaghi: "Change," the campaign slogan of Andreas Papandreou's Pan-Hellenic Socialist Movement (PASOK) in 1981 and 1985. Papandreou promised "Socialist change."

Amphylios: The Greek civil war (1946-1949) between the political left and right. Forty years later, the coalition government of June 1989 was charged with the responsibility of abolishing the final remnants of that period by ending discrimination in the workplace and in pension rights and by burning thousands of police files on left-wing activists.

Antistasi: "Resistance," a term referring to the resistance of the Greek people to the totalitarianism of Nazi Germany and to the military junta of 1967-1974.

Atallaghi: "Get rid of change," the anti-PASOK campaign slogan of the New Democracy Party in 1989.

Catharsis: While prime minister, Constantine Mitsotakis sought a political "catharsis" by cleansing and purging the government of PASOK-era corruption and scandal.

"Colonels": Period from 1967 to 1974 when the military "colonels" ruled Greece, persecuting political opponents and violating democratic principles.

Davos process: The attempt at Greek-Turkish dialogue and rapprochement on the Cyprus and Agean issues. The process was initiated by the prime ministers of both countries at the World Economic Forum meeting in January 1988 at Davos, Switzerland.

Enosis: Longtime goal of bringing Cyprus—the population of which is 80 percent Greek—under Greek authority.

FYROM: Former Yugoslav Republic of Macedonia. Greece opposed the recently independent country's desire to use the name of Macedonia, claiming use of the name implied a scheme to create a greater Macedonian state that would include the Greek province of Macedonia. The UN admitted FYROM on April 8, 1993.

Junta: The former military dictatorship (1967-1974).

Koskotas Affair: The scandal named after George Koskotas, a thirty-four-year-old banker charged with embezzling $200 million from the Bank of Crete.

Liani Affair: Papandreou's very public extramarital affair with Dimitra Liani, a former airline stewardess.

Marshall Plan: U.S. economic aid after World War II was crucial in helping Greece recover from years of war and civil war.

Mitso-Thatcherism: Derisive term used by the Socialists for the economic austerity program of Mitsotakis's New Democracy party.

Ochi Day: "No" Day. October 28 is a holiday commemorating Greece's refusal to surrender to Italy's fascist government and Greece's entry into the alliance against Germany and the Axis powers.

"Out with the Bases of Death": One of Papandreou's anti-American slogans that helped him win the 1981 election. Later in his administration the Socialist leader began to cool down his anti-American and anti-EU rhetoric.

Polytechneio: The 1973 student uprising against the military junta.

Rogers' Plan: Named after former NATO commander General Bernard Rogers, this key agreement provided for two NATO bases to patrol the Aegean Sea.

Rousfeti: "Influence peddling" or "patronage." The traditional practice in Greek politics of giving out jobs and other political favors to partisan supporters.

Stephanopoulos, Constantine: The single elected member of parliament from the rightist Democratic Renewal party who pledged to support the New Democracy government of Mitsotakis, thus giving Mitsotakis a total of 151 votes in the 300-seat parliament. Mitsotakis was sworn in as prime minister on April 11, 1990.

"The Tall One": Term of endearment for former prime minister Mitsotakis, who at 6'3" towered above Greeks of average height.

Truman Doctrine: U.S. policy that supplied desperately needed military assistance to Greece and Turkey to help them defeat communist insurrections supported by the Soviet Union.

"Uncrowned Democracy": On December 8, 1974, 69.2 percent of the Greek electorate voted against the monarchy and in favor of an "uncrowned democracy."

Vouli: The unicameral Greek parliament with 300 members.

HISTORICAL SYNOPSIS

It is impossible to do justice to modern Greek history, let alone ancient, with a short list of key dates. The modern period began when Greece won independence from the Ottoman Empire in 1827. The monarchy began in 1831. Beginning in 1912, Greece expanded its territory to include Crete and Macedonia.

1941-1944	Axis forces occupy Greece during World War II.
1946	In a referendum, 68 percent of voters support restoration of the monarchy.
1946-1949	Civil War: Communists, supported by the Soviet Union, pursue armed insurrection in an attempt to topple Greek government. U.S. military aid to Greece and Turkey under the Truman Doctrine is instrumental in defeating the Communists. Economic assistance under

the Marshall Plan helps the Greek economy recover from the ravages of war.

1952 Greece and Turkey join NATO.

1967 Army officers, led by Colonel George Papadopoulos, seize the government and suspend the constitution.

1973 Prime Minister George Papadopoulos abolishes the monarchy and proclaims Greece a republic. Military leaders overthrow the Papadopoulos government.

1974 "Colonels" are overthrown and democracy restored. Greece holds its first parliamentary election in more than ten years, and a civilian government is formed by Constantine Karamanlis's New Democracy Party.

1981 Greece becomes a member of the EC. Andreas Papandreou becomes first Socialist prime minister. Although Papandreou threatens to withdraw from both the EC and NATO, he never carries this out.

1990 Conservative New Democracy Party, led by Constantine Mitsotakis, wins 1-seat majority in parliament and forms government. Karamanlis is reelected president. Austerity and privatization programs begin to bring down national debt and reduce inflation.

1993 October elections return Papandreou's Socialists to power. Future of economic reforms in doubt.

1995 In March, the five-year term of President Karamanlis ends and the parliament elects a successor.

Iceland

The Country in Brief

Official Name: Republic of Iceland (*Lydveldid Island*)
Capital: Reykjavík
Currency: Króna
National Day: June 17 (birthday of national hero)
Language: Icelandic
Religion: Evangelical Lutheran
Memberships: NATO
Border Countries: Island in North Atlantic Ocean. Scotland lies 335 miles southeast and Norway 425 miles east.
Embassy in Washington, D.C.: 2022 Connecticut Avenue, N.W., 20008. Telephone: (202) 265-6653.

Political Profile

Government Type: Presidential/parliamentary democracy
Head of State: President Vigdís Finnbogadóttir
Political Party: Nonpartisan
Assumed Office: 1980
Election Method: Directly elected
Reelected: 1984, 1988, 1992
Term of Office: Four years
Next Election: 1996
Head of Government: Prime Minister David Oddsson

Political Party: Independence (Conservatives)
Assumed Office: 1991
Next Election: 1995
Legislature: Unicameral. Althing, 63 members, elected by proportional representation.
Term of Office: Four years
Last Election: 1991
Next Election: 1995

Comparative Data

Population: 260,000
GDP: $6.3 billion
GDP Per Capita: $22,900
Voting System (Lower Chamber): Party list proportional
Per Capita Representation Rate: 4,100
Big Government Index: 34.9%
Women in Parliament: 24%
Voter Turnout Rate: 86%

MAJOR POLITICAL PARTIES

Independence Party (*Sjalfstaedisflokkurinn*, IP)

Founded in 1929 by a merger of the Conservative and Liberal parties, the IP has been the largest party in the country, usually attracting around 40 percent of the vote and supplying most prime ministers. During the postwar period, the IP had increasingly accepted the welfare state, but in recent years greater emphasis has been placed on the free market. The IP has been a consistent supporter of NATO and the NATO base at Keflavík.

Progressive Party (*Framsóknarflokkurinn*, PP)

The PP was founded in 1916 almost exclusively as an agrarian party. It has recently tried to appeal to urban voters by presenting a "middle ground" image. Until 1991, the PP had been in government continuously since 1971. It emphasizes rural development in which the state plays a major role. Traditionally, the PP has supported membership in NATO.

Social Democratic Party (*Althyduflokkurinn*, SDP)

The SDP was formed in 1916 as the political arm of the labor movement. It was tied organizationally to the Icelandic Federation of Labor until 1942. The Icelandic SDP is smaller and less influential than similar parties in the rest of the Nordic countries. It has a long tradition of cooperation with the IP and has supported membership in NATO and the NATO base in Keflavík.

People's Alliance (*Althydubandalagid*, PA)

In 1956, the PA was established as a loose electoral alliance between the United Socialist Party (USP) and breakaway groups from the Social Democratic Party. The Communist Party was a part of the USP. The PA is the most stridently leftist party in Iceland. PA favors neutrality and opposes membership in NATO and the NATO base at Keflavík.

Women's Alliance (*Samtok um Kvennalista*, WA)

Founded in 1983, the WA focuses on women's issues as a separate political movement. The WA's social and economic policies can be termed left-of-center and the party advocates a pacifist foreign policy.

Citizen's Party (*Borgariflokkurinn*, CP)

The CP was founded in 1987 when members broke from the IP. The CP won 7 legislative seats that year. It lost all its seats in 1991.

ELECTION REVIEW

1992 Presidential Elections:
Finnbogadóttir Wins Fourth Term

In 1992, Vigdís Finnbogadóttir, the nonpartisan, popular president of Iceland, was handed a fourth consecutive term without a fight. Since she was unchallenged for reelection, formal balloting was unnecessary. In her previous reelection bids (1984, 1988), Finnbogadóttir had been either unopposed or has won overwhelmingly.

While the presidency can be a high-profile position, the office has almost no governmental power beyond that of appointing the prime minister, who then must win and maintain majority support in parliament.

1991 Parliamentary Elections:
From Mayor to Prime Minister in Sixty Days

It was an extraordinary couple of months for Reykjavík mayor David Oddsson. First, he became leader of the Independence Party (IP). Then, just six weeks later, he led the party to an electoral victory on April 20, 1991. Ten days after the election, he became prime minister of Iceland.

The IP needed a change at the top. Iceland's largest party, the IP had suffered its worst outing in the 1987 elections when a party split resulted in the creation of the breakaway Citizen's Party (CP). The IP lost 5 of its 23 seats to the upstart CP. Strong leadership was needed to regain the lost seats in 1991, so the party turned to Oddsson. The IP regained all the seats it had lost to the CP in 1987 plus 3 more.

For the first time in many years, inflation was not the top issue in the campaign. At 7.3 percent, inflation was at its lowest point in two decades. The Progressive Party (PP), a member of the ruling coalition at the time, attempted to stir up some controversy by trying to make membership in the European Commission (EC) a major issue. Progressive leader Steingrímur Hermannsson argued that the election should be seen as a referendum on EC membership. Though none of the major parties favors immediate membership, the IP and the Social Democrats have not ruled out membership at some future date.

The IP won 38.6 percent of the vote and 26 of the 63 seats. While it had the best showing of all the parties, it fell 6 seats short of the absolute majority the polls had indicated might be possible in the early stages of the campaign. The PP, with 18.9 percent of the vote, held onto its 13 seats, while the Social Democrats, with

1991 Parliamentary Election Results		
Party	*% Votes*	*Seats*
Independence Party (IP)	39	26
Progressive Party (PP)	19	13
Social Democratic Party (SDP)	16	10
People's Alliance (PA)	14	9
Women's Alliance (WA)	8	5
Others	3	0
Total Seats		63

Note: Percentages may not add up to 100 due to rounding.

15.5 percent, maintained its 10 seats. The People's Alliance increased slightly to 14.4 percent of the vote and gained an additional seat, bringing its total to 9. The Citizen's Party, which had won 7 seats in 1987, split into yet another party—the Liberals—and now ceases to exist. The Women's Alliance, meanwhile, suffered a 1-seat loss, garnering just 5 seats.

In total, the former coalition government (PA, SDP, and CP), which excluded the IP, won 32 seats, giving it a 1-seat majority in parliament. Despite this, the government resigned on April 23, following the announcement by Social Democratic leader Jon Baldvin Hannibalsson that he did not foresee being able to obtain a working majority on major policy issues.

The SDP decided to join the IP in a two-party coalition since both were in relative agreement over key issues, such as the European Economic Area and economic rationalization. They both also were in agreement on negotiations for the planned Atlantal aluminum plant. The coalition was established in a record ten days after the election—the fastest ever since proportional representation was introduced in 1959.

1987 Parliamentary Elections: Icelandic Hot Springs

The 1980s were not kind to the established political order in Iceland, and the election of 1987 served to underscore just how volatile Icelandic politics had become.

Three reforms altered the political landscape. The voting age was lowered from twenty to eighteen. Parliamentary seats were redistributed from the rural areas to urban centers. The number of seats in the parliament (called the Althing) increased from 60 to 63.

In a country with fewer than 260,000 people, those reforms were bound to have some fallout. In addition, Iceland had been straining under severe economic problems—particularly inflation and budget and trade deficits. These all combined to create a situation of considerable volatility.

This volatility was reflected in the emergence of the Citizen's Party (CP) and the Women's Alliance (WA)—two new political parties that showed potential for becoming power brokers in Icelandic politics.

The creation of the Citizen's Party (CP) was a real blow to the dominant Independence Party (IP). The CP was established from a breakaway IP faction led by Albert Gudmundsson, a charismatic former industry minister who would be appointed ambassador to France in 1989. In 1987, the CP won 10.9 percent of the vote and 7 seats in the Althing. This growth resulted in a sharp reduction of the Independence Party's political clout.

In addition, the WA, which had been formed in 1983, doubled its electoral strength from 5.5 percent in the 1983 election to 10.1 percent in 1987. With 6 seats, the Women's Alliance became a political force to be reckoned with.

Because of this shifting political ground, the Independence-Progressive coalition captured only 31 of the 63 available seats—not enough to continue in office. The coalition was broadened to include the Social Democratic Party. Thorstein Palsson, leader of the Independence Party, replaced the Progressive Party's Steingrímur Hermannsson as prime minister, but his coalition proved to be short-lived. After only fifteen months in office, the coalition broke apart because it could not agree on urgent matters of economic policy.

In September 1988, Progressive leader Hermannsson formed a new government in coalition with the Social Democrats, the left-leaning People's Alliance, and the sole member of parliament from the Regional Equality Party. Together this coali-

Past Parliamentary Election Results

Party	1987 % Votes	1987 Seats	1983 % Votes	1983 Seats	1979 % Votes	1979 Seats	1978 % Votes	1978 Seats
IP	27	18	39	23	36	21	33	20
PP	19	13	19	14	25	17	17	12
SDP	15	10	12	6	17	10	22	14
PA	13	8	17	10	20	11	23	14
WA	10	6	6	3	—	—	—	—
CP	11	7	—	—	—	—	—	—
NSD	0	0	7	4	—	—	—	—
Others	4	1	1	0	2	1	—	—
Total Seats		**63**		**60**		**60**		**60**

Note: Percentages may not add up to 100 due to rounding. IP = Independence Party, PP = Progressive Party, SDP = Social Democratic Party, PA = People's Alliance, WA = Women's Alliance, CP = Citizens' Party, NSD = New Social Democrats.

tion could muster only 32 of the 63 seats, the slimmest possible majority.

Hermannsson's first act as prime minister was to impose a tough economic program: a 3 percent devaluation of the Króna, a freeze on prices and wages until February 15, 1989, and establishment of two public funds to subsidize exports.

Hermannsson subsequently had to reshuffle his government. In September 1989, Hermannsson included the Citizen's Party as a coalition partner to broaden the government's base of support in the Althing.

Among the most divisive and pressing issues in Icelandic politics were the economy, fishing policy, relations between the European Free Trade Association and the European Community, and NATO, especially those questions related to nuclear weapons and the U.S.-manned air and naval base at Keflavík. The country faced a severe economic strain, as inflation had been running at about 20 percent while real GDP had actually been declining. The biggest concern, however, was the sharp drop in the cod catch.

ELECTION LEXICON

Act of Union: This 1918 agreement between Iceland and Denmark granted Iceland full independence but maintained a "Union." Iceland continued to recognize the Danish king as sovereign until independence in 1944.

Althing: The 63-member unicameral parliament, founded in the year 930.

"Cod Wars": Disputes with Britain in the 1960s and 1970s over fishing rights and Iceland's claim to an exclusive economic zone, which in 1975 was extended to 200 miles around Iceland. The most serious "war" took place in 1976, when diplomatic relations were briefly suspended.

Eternal neutrality: Iceland had intended to remain neutral after independence from Denmark and World War II but in 1949 opted instead to become a founding member of NATO.

IDF: The Iceland Defense Force, a contingent of 3,000 U.S. troops at the Keflavík NATO base. Iceland does not have its own military.

Keflavík: Stategically important U.S.-staffed NATO air and naval base on Iceland.

"Male privilege": Though 80 percent of Iceland's women work, they receive only 40 percent of the pay of men. To protest this "male privilege," tens of thousands of women staged a twenty-four-hour strike in 1985.

National Accord: Voluntary wage and price controls agreed to by employers and unions in February 1990. This action helped to bring inflation down to its lowest level in twenty years.

"Natural party of government": Term describing the Independence Party, which has held a dominant position in Icelandic politics (similar to that of the Christian Democratic Party in Italy). Until 1978, the IP had supplied all post-World War II prime ministers.

Nordic Council: An organization created in 1952, consisting of the parliaments and cabinets of Denmark, Finland, Iceland, Norway, and Sweden. Its goal is to coordinate policy on economics, foreign affairs, social welfare, and cultural affairs. It has succeeded in facilitating substantial uniformity in the legislation of these countries.

Nuclear-free zone: In 1985, the Althing declared the Icelandic coast to be a "nuclear-free zone," banning all nuclear devices.

Reykjavík: Iceland's capital city. It gained worldwide prominence as the site of the controversial 1986 superpower summit between U.S. president Ronald Reagan and Soviet general secretary Mikhail Gorbachev. At the summit, the two leaders took the world by surprise when they almost agreed to a radical plan for nuclear arms reduction.

Sea Shepherds: In 1986, saboteurs from this environmental group attacked Iceland's only whale-oil processing plant and sunk two of its four whaling ships.

Thingvellir: The original site of the Icelandic Althing, the oldest parliament in the world, where annual sessions were held from 930 to 1800.

Viking Squad: A crack team of twenty heavily armed and well-trained anti-terrorist commandos—the Icelandic equivalent of the U.S. Delta Force.

Women's Alliance: Formed in 1983, this women's political party has received between 8 and 10 percent of the vote in the past three parliamentary elections. It is one of the only women's parties in the world.

HISTORICAL SYNOPSIS

Settled by Norsemen in the ninth century, Iceland was a free state until it lost its sovereignty to Norway in 1262. After the Danes conquered it in the following century, Iceland would not know independence for another 500 years.

1904	Iceland wins home rule and an Icelandic minister responsible to the Althing.
1918	The Act of Union restores Icelandic independence, but Iceland continues to recognize the Danish king.
1944	On July 17, the Icelandic Republic is proclaimed at Thingvellir. Sveinn Björnsson is elected the first president, and a new constitution is adopted.
1949	Iceland abandons its "eternal neutrality" policy by becoming a founding member of NATO.
1975	After years of dispute with Britain over fishing rights, Iceland declares an exclusive economic zone extending 200 miles from its shores.
1980	Vigdís Finnbogadóttir becomes Iceland's first female head of state elected by popular vote.
1983	Women's Alliance wins 3 seats in the Althing, becoming the first party with a feminist platform to enter parliament.
1987	Citizens' Party is formed and wins 7 seats in the Althing, denying the ruling Independence-led coalition a majority of seats. A Progressive-led coalition is established, headed by former prime minister Hermannsson.
1991	David Oddsson, mayor of Reykjavík, becomes prime minister, heading an Independence-led coalition with the Social Democrats.
1992	Vigdís Finnbogadóttir is reelected (unopposed) to a fourth term as president.

Ireland

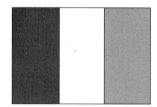

The Country in Brief

Official Name: Republic of Ireland (*Eire*)
Capital: Dublin
Currency: Irish Pound (*punt Eireannach*)
National Day: March 17 (St. Patrick's Day)
Languages: Irish (Gaelic), English
Religions: Roman Catholic, Protestant
Memberships: Non-NATO, EU
Border Countries: Northern Ireland. Great Britain lies across the Irish Sea to the East.
Embassy in Washington, D.C.: 2234 Massachusetts Avenue, N.W., 20008. Telephone: (202) 462-3939.

Political Profile

Government Type: Presidential/parliamentary democracy
Head of State: President Mary Robinson
Political Party: Nonpartisan, endorsed by Labour Party
Assumed Office: 1990
Election Method: Directly elected, majority preferential system
Term of Office: Seven years
Next Election: 1997
Head of Government: Prime Minister John Bruton
Political Party: Fine Gael

Assumed Office: 1994 (following November 1994
resignation of Albert Reynolds's government)
Next Election: 1997
Legislature: Bicameral, National Parliament (*Oireachtas*)
Upper Chamber: Senate (*Seanad*), 60 members, 11
nominated by the prime minister, 6 by the universities, and 43
from five vocational organizations.
Lower Chamber: House of Representatives (*Dáil*), 166 mem-
bers, directly elected by the proportional system, utilizing the
single transferable vote.
Term of Office: Five years
Last Election: 1992
Next Election: 1997

Comparative Data

Population: 3.5 million
GDP: $43 billion
GDP Per Capita: $12,100
Voting System (Lower Chamber): Proportional
representation (single transferable vote)
Per Capita Representation Rate: 21,000
Big Government Index: 40.1%
Women in Parliament: 12%
Voter Turnout Rate: 69%

MAJOR POLITICAL PARTIES

Ireland's two largest political parties, Fianna Fáil and Fine Gael,
do not fall neatly onto a typical right/left ideological continuum.
They both tend to be rather centrist in approach, although Fine
Gael, being the smaller of the two, has tended to line up politically
with the Labour Party or the Progressive Democrats in the hope
of forming a coalition.

These two large parties came into being in response to the
Anglo-Irish Treaty, which created the Irish Free State from
twenty-six counties of Ireland, leaving six counties in the northeast

in British hands. Fianna Fáil vehemently opposed the treaty. Fine Gael, on the other hand, endorsed it. Fine Gael formed the first government of the Irish Free State.

Fianna Fáil (*Republican Party*, FF)

Fianna Fáil ("soldiers of destiny") was founded in 1926. Often called a center-right party, Fianna Fáil has pursued a "no frills" economic program. The party supports Irish membership in the European Union but has also staked out a strong environmental stance. Fianna Fáil supports making Ireland a "nuclear-free zone"—not exactly a position associated with a "rightist" party. Fianna Fáil had been in government most of the time since 1932, but until 1989 it had not ruled as part of a coalition.

Fine Gael (*United Ireland Party*, FG)

Fine Gael ("family of the Irish") was created in 1933 from the Cosgrave Party (*Cumann na nGaedheal Party*), the Center Party, and the National Guard, which formed the first government of the Irish Free State. A Christian Democratic party, Fine Gael favors a political solution to the situation in Northern Ireland, preferring compromise and dialogue, but the party's ultimate goal is union. Fine Gael has joined other parties, especially Labour, to form coalition governments in the 1950s, the mid-1970s and again, in the mid-1980s. In 1985, the Fine Gael-Labour government signed the Anglo-Irish Agreement.

Labour Party (*Páirtí Lucht Oibre*, LP)

The Labour Party is a traditional European Democratic Socialist party committed to creating a socialist republic through democratic means. The party has called for higher taxes on capital, public works projects, and worker participation in management. Labour strongly opposed Ireland's entry into the EU and advocates a strict neutrality for Ireland. The LP has entered government occasionally in coalition with Fine Gael and other parties.

Progressive Democrats (PD)

The PD was founded in 1985 by Desmond O'Malley, a prominent member of Fianna Fáil who led a breakaway faction out of frustration with Fianna Fáil's reluctance to endorse the 1985 Anglo-Irish Agreement. The PD's first showing in 1987 was impressive, capturing 14 seats and becoming the country's third largest party. The PD's fortunes worsened dramatically in 1989, when they won only 6 seats in the new Dáil. The PD was forced to cooperate with Fianna Fáil to form a coalition government.

Sinn Féin (SF)

The original Sinn Féin ("ourselves alone") was formed in 1905 to bring about Irish independence from the United Kingdom. It worked in conjunction with the Irish Republican Army (IRA), a guerrilla-type organization formed in 1919 to actively fight against British forces on Irish territory and the partitioning of the country. They were instrumental in promoting the revolutionary movement that let to the formation of the Irish Free State in 1921. Many members then left Sinn Féin and the IRA and aligned with the more moderate Fianna Fáil and Fine Gael parties. Over the years, Sinn Féin has been a radical, anti-British party with various factions, some more radical and militant than others. In 1969, in response to a policy dispute, the IRA split into two main factions. The traditional nationalists formed the "provisional" (provos) wing, while the Marxist-leaning members committed to nonviolence formed the "official" wing, which emerged as the Workers' Party (see below). Sinn Féin functions as the political wing of the outlawed Provisional IRA. The party has had no representation in the Dáil, but it appears poised to seek seats in upcoming elections.

The Workers' Party (*Pairtí na nOibri*, WP)

This party was aligned with Sinn Féin until 1977, when it broke off as a separate faction and changed its name to Sinn Féin—The Workers' Party. In 1982 it gave up all ties to the Sinn Féin name and became known simply as the Workers' Party. The party has a Marxist tilt and promotes the notion of a united, socialist Ireland. The party supports Irish neutrality, a nuclear-free Europe, and nuclear arms control. The Workers' Party is the only party represented in the Dáil that is also organized in Northern Ireland.

MINOR POLITICAL PARTIES

Communist Party of Ireland (CPI)
Democratic Left (DLP)
Green Alliance *(Comhaontás Glas)*
Irish Republican Socialist Party (IRSP)
Republican Sinn Féin

ELECTION REVIEW

1990 Presidential Elections:
Second-Choice Candidate Wins Majority

The November 7, 1990, election of Mary Robinson as Ireland's first female president was a turning point in Irish politics. Backed by the relatively small Labour Party, Robinson defeated the pre-election favorite, Fianna Fáil candidate Brian Lenihan, and Austin Currie of the Fine Gael party.

Although an underdog through most of the campaign, Robinson's chances brightened just a few weeks before the election when Lenihan's name became entangled in a old controversy stemming from 1982, when Lenihan was alleged to have suggested that the president at that time appoint a Fianna Fáil government, without authorizing the proper election. Fianna Fáil's coalition partner, the Progressive Democrats, forced Lenihan from his position as deputy prime minister and minister of defense. This embarrassment so close to the election clearly damaged Lenihan's cause.

Robinson campaigned on a platform of making the presidency less of a ceremonial job. A lawyer with leftist tendencies, Robinson also promoted a number of strong and controversial positions, such as more liberal or permissive policies on contraception, divorce, abortion, and homosexuality.

The election was held using the majority preferential voting method. After the tally of first-preference votes, Lenihan led with 44 percent, followed by Robinson with 39 percent, and Currie with 17 percent. Since no candidate won the required majority of first-preference votes, Currie was dropped from the race and his

1990 Presidential Election Results		
Candidate	First Ballot (% Votes)	Runoff (% Votes)
Mary Robinson (I)	39	53
Brian Lenihan (FF)	44	47
Austin Currie (FG)	17	

Note: Percentages may not add up to 100 due to rounding. I = Independent, FF = Fianna Fáil (Republican Party), FG = Fine Gael (United Ireland Party).

supporters' ballots were distributed to their second-choice candidates. In this "runoff," Robinson picked up the lion's share of Currie's second-choice ballots, receiving a total of 53 percent of the vote against Lenihan's 47 percent.

Had the plurality, winner-take-all method of voting been used, Lenihan would have been elected outright. The transferable vote mechanism enabled Irish voters to vote for their second-choice candidate, and that made all the difference.

Upon gaining the presidency, Robinson indeed did enhance the role of that office. In July 1992, she addressed both houses of the parliament on a major matter of state, something that had never been done before. Her speech dealt with Ireland's place in Europe. She made it clear that she considered the presidency as a way to lead Ireland at home and in the world. She also visited Northern Ireland a number of times and publicly condemned the ongoing violence.

1995 Parliamentary Update

Ireland started 1995 with a new government headed by a new prime minister, Fine Gael (Conservative) leader John Bruton. This was the first change of government in Ireland without an election. It occurred after the unexpected resignation in October 1994 of Prime Minister Albert Reynolds, who had assumed the position in 1992 from within the Fianna Fáil Party. An unusual coalition, dubbed the Rainbow Coalition, formed among three unlikely allies—Fine Gael, Labour, and the

1992 Parliamentary Election Results		
Party	% Votes	Seats
Fianna Fáil (FF)	39	68
Fine Gael (FG)	24	45
Labour	19	33
Progressive Democrats (PD)	5	10
Democratic Left (DL)	3	4
Others	10	6
Total Seats		166

Note: Percentages may not add up to 100 due to rounding.

Democratic Left—and forced Fianna Fáil and Albert Reynolds into the opposition.

While new elections have been averted for the time being, it remains to be seen whether Bruton's government will be able to survive sharp ideological differences among the three coalition partners.

1992 Parliamentary Elections: Controversy and Crisis

Like 1990, 1992 was an eventful year in Irish politics. Highlights included the resignation of a prime minister, a cabinet shakeup, a referendum on abortion, and snap general elections called after the prime minister denounced his own commerce minister as "dishonest."

This series of events started when the government of longtime Prime Minister (*Taoiseach*) Charles J. Haughey was shaken in February. In fact, he was forced to resign following revelations that he had known about police wiretaps of two journalists' telephones. His successor was Albert Reynolds, a fellow Fianna Fáil member and the finance minister. Reynolds immediately launched a massive cabinet shake-up, replacing three-quarters of the sitting ministers.

Soon after taking office, Reynolds was faced with an ethical and constitutional crisis involving one of the most controversial issues in Ireland—abortion. With abortions illegal in Ireland, the government received a court order preventing a fourteen-year-old rape victim from traveling to Britain for an abortion. After widespread international criticism, she was finally allowed to go to Britain for the procedure, but the controversy did not subside. It would result in balloting on a referendum later in the year.

In November, snap parliamentary elections were scheduled after Reynolds called Desmond O'Malley—his own coalition partner, the leader of the Progressive Democrats, and minister of industry and commerce—"dishonest." During an inquiry concerning the selling of EU-subsidized beef, Reynolds asserted that O'Malley was being "dishonest" in his recollections about what Reynolds did for beef traders in the late 1980s as minister of commerce. The elections were not kind to the coalition.

Although Fianna Fáil remained the largest party in parliament with 68 seats, it suffered a major election setback, winning less that 40 percent of the vote. The Labour Party was the big winner, doubling its parliamentary representation to 33 seats. Labour attracted voters from the middle class in Dublin's suburbs and received significant support from women voters. Political pundits on all sides agreed that the election result represented a major realignment of the country's politics.

With Fine Gael, the government's junior coalition partner, also losing seats (capturing only 45 seats, down from 55 in 1989), the Labour Party was now poised to dictate the composition of the new government. In a surprising move, Labour and Fianna Fáil, with 101 of the 166 seats in the Dáil, decided to join in a coalition government, with Reynolds as prime minister and Labour leader Dick Spring as foreign minister.

Balloting also took place that November on a constitutional referendum on abortion. Voters rejected a measure to make abortions legal in Ireland, but they approved amendments enabling women to obtain information about abortion and guaranteeing their right to travel outside the country to receive abortions.

1989 Parliamentary Elections: "Fáiled" Again

Charles Haughey, known as the "Great Survivor," made a career of not winning a clear majority in parliament while serving

Past Parliamentary Election Results

Party	1989 % Votes	1989 Seats	1987 % Votes	1987 Seats	Nov. 1982 % Votes	Nov. 1982 Seats	Feb. 1982 % Votes	Feb. 1982 Seats
FF	44	77	44	81	45	75	47	81
FG	29	55	27	51	39	70	37	63
Labour	9	15	6	12	9	16	9	15
PD	5	6	12	14	—	—	—	—
WP	5	7	4	4	3	2	2	3
Greens	0	1	—	—	—	—	—	—
Others	7	5	7	4	3	3	4	4
Total Seats		**166**		**166**		**166**		**166**

Note: Percentages may not add up to 100 due to rounding. FF = Fianna Fáil (Republican Party), FG = Fine Gael (United Ireland Party), PD = Progressive Democrats, WP = Workers' Party.

as prime minister. Before the 1989 elections, which he called early with the specific goal of winning a solid majority from the voters, he had led his party into general elections four times and come up short each time. Even though his Fianna Fáil party fell short again in 1989, Haughey emerged again as prime minister—the most powerful man in Ireland.

Calling a general election for June 15, 1989—nearly three years ahead of schedule—was not a popular move, but Haughey was irritated at the thought that his minority government relied for its existence on the opposition. He had been defeated in the Dáil on minor issues six times since his election in 1987, and on the sixth defeat he decided on the "snap" election strategy, hoping to catch the opposition unaware and take advantage of high public approval ratings for his government.

After the 1987 elections, Fianna Fáil held 81 seats in the Dáil, only 3 short of an absolute majority. Haughey must have hoped to improve on that already strong position and finally grasp the majority support he thought he needed from parliament.

It was not to be. The public seemed content with a government that had to negotiate and deal with the opposition. Haughey's minority government seemed to be working just fine. As a result of Haughey's austerity measures—which included drastic reductions in public spending and higher taxation—inflation had dropped from 20 percent to 3 percent, the GDP was predicted to grow, and the deficit had shrunk from 13 percent to 6 percent of GDP. Moreover, the major opposition party, Fine Gael, had backed Haughey's economic austerity program. So why call a new election? As it turned out, the public did not want an election, and they showed their irritation at the polls.

The backlash against Haughey came primarily from the rural areas, where voters were deeply disgruntled about the cutbacks in health care funding. The imposition of a fishing license fee had also caused serious disaffection in western Ireland.

In the end, Fianna Fáil garnered 44 percent of the vote and lost 4 seats in the Dáil. Fine Gael, with 29 percent of the vote, gained 4 seats. The Progressive Democrats won a mere 5 percent, down from 12 percent in 1987, and dropped from 14 seats to 6. The major gains went to the leftist parties. The Labour Party and the Workers' Party (Sinn Féin) each won an additional 3 seats, giving them 15 and 7, respectively. The environmental Greens captured their first and only seat in the Dáil.

Given those results, Fianna Fáil—which had gone from 2 votes short of a majority to 6 votes short—was forced to reach out to the Progressive Democrats (with exactly 6 seats) to form a coalition government—the very "multiparty chaos" Haughey had warned against. Fianna Fáil had never before joined a coalition with another party, relying instead on the support of smaller parties or independents to stay in power. While Haughey managed to cling to power, Fine Gael leader Alan Dukes called Haughey a "five-times loser" for having failed to win a majority in his fifth attempt.

1994 European Parliament Elections

In the 1994 Euro-election, Prime Minister Albert Reynolds's Fianna Fáil party came out ahead with 35 percent of the vote and 7 seats, one more than in 1989. Fine Gael held steady with 4 seats, while increasing its percentage of the vote.

European Parliament Election Results

Party	1994 % Votes	1994 Seats	1989 % Votes	1989 Seats	1984 % Votes	1984 Seats	1979 % Votes	1979 Seats
FF	35	7	32	6	39	8	35	5
FG	27	4	22	4	32	6	33	4
Independents	10	1	12	2	10	1	14	2
Labour	8	1	10	1	8	0	15	4
Others	20	2	24	2	11	0	3	0
Total Seats		**15**		**15**		**15**		**15**

Note: Percentages may not add up to 100 due to rounding. FF = Fianna Fáil (Republican Party), FG = Fine Gael (United Ireland Party).

Surprisingly, the Green party captured 2 seats—the first Green seats in the European Parliament from Ireland. Labour and independents each won 1 seat.

The Progressive Democrats dropped from 12 percent of the vote and 1 seat in 1989 to just 7 percent, which was not enough to capture a seat. The Workers' Party also was forced to give up the only seat it held in the previous EP allotment.

ELECTION LEXICON

Abortion: Ireland is the only country in Western Europe in which abortion is strictly illegal. In a 1983 referendum, two-thirds of the electorate supported a constitutional amendment protecting the "unborn child's" right to life. In November 1992, voters approved amendments to allow women to receive information about abortion and to travel abroad for the procedure.

Anglo-Irish Agreement of 1985: Established the Inter-governmental Conference, a forum by which the Irish government may make recommendations regarding the affairs of Northern Ireland. The agreement seeks peace and stability in Northern Ireland by creating a political environment whereby the minority Catholic community will gain confidence in existing lawful governmental structures.

"The Boss": Nickname for Charles Haughey, a four-time prime minister, who survived many political setbacks during his career, which began in the early 1950s. He was known for having an autocratic streak.

Dáil: Pronounced "Doyle," the 166-member lower house of parliament.

"Dishonest": In 1992, Prime Minister Albert Reynolds called Desmond O'Malley, a leader of the Progressive Democrats and Reynold's coalition partner, "dishonest" in his recollections over a beef trade inquiry. Reynolds then lost a "no confidence" vote in parliament, leading to early parliamentary elections in November 1992.

Divorce: A 1986 referendum—passed with 63.5 percent of the vote—established a constitutional prohibition against any divorce legislation.

Downing Street Declaration: The joint peace initiative on Northern Ireland issued on December 15, 1993, by John Major and Albert Reynolds, the British and Irish prime ministers.

Easter Rebellion: Easter Monday, 1916, Irish rebels captured parts of Dublin and proclaimed the creation of the Irish Republic. The British reacted swiftly to what they considered treason (*see* "The Troubles," below).

Fianna Fáil: Pronounced "Feena Fall," this is the largest party in the parliament. The name literally means "soldiers of destiny."

Fine Gael: Pronounced "Finna Gwale," this is the second largest party in the parliament. The name literally means "family of the Irish."

Gaelic: The Irish language. One of the two official languages of Ireland. Its use was outlawed during British rule of Ireland.

Gaeltacht: A native Irish-speaking district. The state provides government support for a broad range of economic and cultural programs to these areas, including industrial development and housing improvement grants to individual households, in order to promote and preserve the Irish language and authentic Irish heritage of the people.

Great Potato Famine: Between 1846 and 1848, starvation and emigration because of potato shortages caused the Irish population to drop dramatically, from 8 million to just over 4 million around the turn of the century.

"Great Survivor": Another nickname for Charles Haughey (*see* "The Boss," above).

Harp: The official symbol or coat of arms of Ireland. It is often depicted as a gold harp with silver strings on a blue field.

"Houdini of Irish Politics": Another nickname for Charles Haughey (*see* The Boss, above).

Majority Preferential Voting: A variation of the single transferable vote (*see* below) used for single-winner races, such as the Irish presidency. As with STV, voters rank candidates in order of preference; if no candidate receives a majority, first-choice votes for eliminated candidates are then transferred to the second-ranked candidates, etc., until one candidate wins a majority of the votes cast.

Nationalist: Someone who favors the unification of Northern Ireland and the Republic of Ireland.

New Ireland Forum: A consultative group established in 1983 that was open to all democratic parties with members in the Irish Parliament (*Oireachtas*) or the Northern Ireland Assembly who opposed violence as a means of settling the Northern Ireland issue. Its recommendations were reflected in the Anglo-Irish Agreement of 1985.

The North: Northern Ireland.

Oireachtas: The National Parliament.

Rainbow Coalition: After the resignation in 1994 of Fianna Fáil prime minister Albert Reynolds, the Labour Party managed to establish a coalition with Fine Gael and the Progressive Democrats, forcing the largest party, Fianna Fáil, into opposition. Fine Gael leader John Bruton became prime minister.

Seanad: Pronounced "Say-Nod," this is the 60-member upper house of parliament.

Single Transferable Vote (STV): A variation on the typical European system of party list proportional representation. The STV system is complex to count but fairly simple for voters to execute. Within each district, the voter is given a ballot listing all the candidates and their party affiliations. Beside each name, the voter indicates a "preference" by writing a number (1 for first choice, 2 for second choice, etc.). Some candidates will be elected outright by reaching the mathematical threshold of first-preference votes needed to win a seat. Any surplus votes are passed along to other candidates in descending order of preference. After all surplus votes for elected candidates are distributed, the candidate with the fewest number of votes is eliminated, and that candidate's ballots are distributed to other candidates according to the voters' second choices. This process of candidate elimination and vote distribution continues until the seats from that district are filled. STV ensures that very few votes are wasted on losing candidates.

Sinn Féin: Pronounced "Shin Fain," it is the political wing of the Irish Republican Army. The name means "we ourselves."

Taoiseach: Pronounced "Tee-such," this term for the Irish prime minister literally means "chieftain."

"The Troubles": Three-year period (1916-1919) of violence and strife between Irish and British. It started with the Easter Rebellion of 1916, when Irish rebels proclaimed the formation of the Irish Republic. The British, engaged in World War I at the time, treated the rebellion as treasonous. The term is often used to generally describe the violence in the North.

Unionist: Someone who favors maintaining Northern Ireland's "union" with Great Britain.

HISTORICAL SYNOPSIS

Ireland had over 8 million citizens when it joined with England to become the United Kingdom of Great Britain and Ireland in

1801; by 1921 the population had dwindled to 4.3 million. The reasons were starvation, emigration, and violent struggles for national sovereignty.

1916-
1919 "The Troubles" begin after the Easter Rebellion fails to secure Irish independence. Three years of murders, lootings, and other violence between British and Irish.

1922 On December 6, the Irish Free State—which includes twenty-six counties of Ireland but not six counties of Northern Ireland—is established following a brief, bitter civil war about whether to accept the Anglo-Irish Treaty. Universal adult suffrage is adopted.

1937 Ireland adopts a new constitution declaring Ireland to be a "sovereign, independent, and democratic state."

1940-
1945 Ireland remains officially neutral during World War II, but the island serves as an important refueling site for the British war effort.

1949 Republic of Ireland is proclaimed. Ireland withdraws from the British Commonwealth.

1955 Ireland joins the United Nations.

1973 Ireland joins the European Community, along with United Kingdom and Denmark.

1981 Garret FitzGerald, leader of Fine Gael, becomes prime minister and leads a coalition with the Labour Party.

1982 In January FitzGerald resigns and Charles Haughey becomes prime minister. By December, following November elections, FitzGerald is again sworn in as prime minister.

1985 Fianna Fáil member Desmond O'Malley leads breakaway group and forms Progressive Democrats.

1987 Fianna Fáil wins 81 seats in the Dáil and Haughey becomes prime minister again. Progressive Democrats win 14 seats in their first election.

1989 Haughey calls snap election in June hoping to win a majority of seats. He fails and is forced to form a coalition government with his rival Desmond O'Malley's Progressive Democrats, although both Fianna Fáil and PD lose a combined total of 12 seats in the election.

1990	Mary Robinson becomes Ireland's first female president.
1992	Haughey resigns in February and is succeeded by Albert Reynolds, of Fianna Fáil. Reynolds forms a coalition government with the Labour Party after snap elections that November.
1994	Albert Reynolds resigns and his Fianna Fáil-Labour coalition government falls. Fine Gael leader John Bruton becomes prime minister of a Fine Gael-Labour-Progressive Democratic "Rainbow Coalition."

Italy

The Country in Brief

Official Name: Italian Republic (*Repubblica Italiana*)
Capital: Rome
Currency: Lira
National Day: June 2 (anniversary of the proclamation of the republic)
Language: Italian
Religion: Roman Catholic
Memberships: NATO and EU
Border Countries: Austria, Croatia, France, Slovenia, Switzerland, Vatican City
Embassy in Washington, D.C.: 1601 Fuller Street, N.W., 20009. Telephone: (202) 328-5500.

Political Profile

Government Type: Republic/parliamentary democracy
Head of State: President Oscar Luigi Scalfaro
Political Party: Italian Popular (formerly Christian Democratic) Party
Assumed Office: 1992
Election Method: Elected by both chambers of parliament
Term of Office: Seven years
Next Election: 1999
Head of Government: Prime Minister Lamberto Dini (a care-

taker government replaced the Forza Italia-led government of Silvio Berlusconi on January 17, 1995)
Political Party: Independent
Assumed Office: 1995
Legislature: Bicameral, Parliament (*Parlemento*)
Upper Chamber: Senate (*Senata*), 315 senators elected by a mixed member proportional system (232 from single-member districts and 83 by proportional representation), 5 appointed for life by head of state, former presidents are ex officio.
Lower Chamber: Chamber of Deputies (*Camera dei Deputati*), 630 members, elected by mixed member proportional representation (475 from single-member districts and 155 by proportional representation); this body elects the government.
Term of Office: Five years
Last Election: 1994
Next Election: 1999 (due to government instability, a new election is likely to occur in 1995 or 1996)

Comparative Data

Population: 57.7 million
GDP: $1.1 trillion
GDP Per Capita: $18,900
Voting System: Modified in 1993 for both chambers of parliament from party list proportional to mixed member proportional. Beginning in 1994, three-quarters of both chambers are elected by plurality from single-member districts, one-quarter via party list proportional (4% threshold)
Per Capita Representation Rate: 92,000
Big Government Index: 42.1%
Women in Parliament: 13%
Voter Turnout: 89%

MAJOR POLITICAL PARTIES

The Italian political landscape has changed dramatically since 1993. A whole new array of political parties has emerged. Every major party has changed its name and/or leadership in an effort to survive following widespread corruption scandals and a new electoral law adopted in 1993 (see "Corruption Scandals" and "1993 Election Reforms," below).

The political upheaval leading up to the March 27-28, 1994, parliamentary elections was so extensive and widespread that this period is being referred to as the dawn of the "Second Italian Republic."

The three large party alliances outlined below (Freedom Alliance, Progressive Alliance, and Pact for Italy) were the main contestants in the March elections, together receiving more than 90 percent of the national vote and all but a handful of seats in parliament.

FREEDOM ALLIANCE (*Pollo delle Liberta*, PL). A group of center-right and right-wing parties banded together to form this new alliance, which brings three main groups together: Forza Italia, the Northern League in the north, and the Good Governance Alliance (which is comprised of the National Alliance and the Christian Democratic Center) in the south. These, plus the Radical Party, campaigned under the name Freedom Alliance. The three main forces in the alliance are discussed below.

Forza Italia (*Go, Italy*, FI)

Founded and led by communications mogul Silvio Berlusconi, Forza Italia is Italy's newest party, and it arrived on the political scene in a big way. FI is a right-of-center upstart that forged a shaky alliance to field joint candidates in the 1994 elections with two other major rightist parties: the Northern League and the National Alliance (formerly called the Italian Social Movement or MSI). Forza Italia's main issues involve speeding up free market reforms, cutting taxes, and trying to stimulate the economy.

Northern League (*La Lega Nord*, NL)

Led by Umberto Bossi and concentrated in the north, this grouping of parties champions local and regional autonomy versus the central government. The league opposes the fact that the relatively wealthy northern part of Italy has been taxed heavily in order to subsidize the poorer southern areas of the country. The league also opposes the favors-and-patronage habits that have been ingrained for so long in the establishment parties.

National Alliance (*Alleanza Nazionale*, NA)

Led by Gianfranco Fini, the National Alliance—formerly the Italian Social Movement, MSI—is often called a neofascist party. It has done surprisingly well in recent local elections and made a real breakthrough in the 1994 parliamentary elections. The party's strength is centered in the southern sections of the country. Following the March 1994 parliamentary elections, Fini created a major flap when he described Italy's former fascist dictator, Benito Mussolini, as "the greatest statesman" of the century.

PROGRESSIVE ALLIANCE (*Alleanza Progressiste*, AP). This alliance was created prior to the 1994 election. It is comprised of the Democratic Party of the Left (formerly the Communist Party) and various smaller parties, including the Italian Socialist Party, the Communist Refoundation Party, the Democratic Alliance (which includes the Italian Republican Party), the Socialist Renewal, La Rete (The Network, an antimafia party), and the Greens.

Democratic Party of the Left
  (*Partito Democratico della Sinistra*, PDS)

The PDS, led by Achille Occhetto, is the renamed Communist Party (PCI), which was originally formed from a split in the Socialist Party in 1921. The Communists owe their enduring strength, at least in part, to their struggle against fascism during the Mussolini period. PCI took part in the first post-World War II government, but has been excluded since 1947. PCI had been Italy's second largest party, winning as much as 35 percent of the vote in the mid-1970s. PCI for years showed greater independence from Moscow than other West

European Communist parties, advocating a moderate form of Marxism known as "Eurocommunism." The renamed party has moved even further toward democratic principles and moderation.

Italian Socialist Party (*Partito Socialista Italiano*, PSI)

All but decimated in the wake of Italy's corruption scandals, PSI deserves mention here since it was one of the key parties in Italian politics for many years. Founded in 1892, PSI split and regrouped a number of times throughout its history. The Communists split away in 1921, then the Social Democrats split in 1947. Until 1992, PSI had steadily increased its strength at the polls. Together with the Social Democrats, the PSI forged what it called a "third force" between the former Christian Democrats and the PCI. The party believes in achieving socialist goals while recognizing democracy and individual freedom. The PSI has been a strong supporter of NATO and the European Union (EU).

PACT FOR ITALY (*Patto per l'Italia*, PI). This is a centrist alliance of the Italian Popular Party and the Segni Pact, urging reform of the Italian political system.

Italian Popular Party (*Partito Populare Italiano*, PPI)

The PPI emerged in 1994 from the remains of the once-dominant Christian Democratic Party (CD). Heir to the Catholic Popular Party (Partido Popolare), the former Christian Democrats had dominated Italian politics since 1945, being part of every government and providing most of the prime ministers in the postwar period. The party is a strongly anti-Communist party of the center, pro-EU, and pro-NATO in orientation.

Segni Pact (*Patto Segni*, PS)

The Segni Pact is named after its leader, Mario Segni, the former Christian Democrat who led the movement in 1993 for electoral reform. Ironically, in the March 1994 elections Segni failed to win election from any of the 475 single-member districts created as a result of his reforms. Instead, his parliamentary seat came from one of the remaining 155 party list proportional seats.

MINOR POLITICAL PARTIES

Christian Democratic Center
  (*Centro Cristiana Democratico*, CCD)
Democratic Alliance (*Alleanza Democratic*, AD)
Greens
Italian Republican Party (*Partito Repubblicano Italiano*, PRI)
Italian Social Democratic Party
  (*Partito Socialista Democratico Italiano*, PSDI)
Radical Party (*Partito Radicale*, PR)
Reformed Communist Party
  (*Partito della Rifondazione Communista*, RC)
La Rete (The Network)
Socialist Renewal (*Rinascita Socialista*, RS)
Union of the Democratic Center
  (*Union delle Centro Democratico*, UCD)

ELECTION REVIEW

Parliamentary Elections 1994:
Forza Italia, A New Force to be Reckoned With

Businessman-turned-politician Silvio Berlusconi led his new party, Forza Italia, and the multiparty Freedom Alliance to a decisive victory in Italy's first election held under its revamped electoral system (see "Corruption Scandals" and "1993 Election Reforms," below).

The Freedom Alliance, comprised principally of Forza Italia, the federalist-minded Northern League, and the neofascist National Alliance, won a total of 43 percent of the vote and a disproportionate 366 seats, for a comfortable majority in the 630-seat Chamber of Deputies. In the Senate, the Freedom Alliance captured 155 seats—just short of a majority in the 315-member upper chamber, while the Progressive Alliance won 122, and Pact for Italy, 31.

After extensive negotiations with his Freedom Alliance partners on forming a government, Berlusconi was finally sworn in May 11,

1994 Parliamentary Election Results		
Party	*% Votes*	*Seats*
Freedom Alliance	43	366
Progressive Alliance	32	213
Pact for Italy	16	46
Others	9	5
Total Seats		**630**

1994, as head of Italy's fifty-third post-World War II government. All previous post-war governments were led by the Christian Democrats (CD).

The CD had little impact on the 1994 results. The reformed and renamed CD, now called the Italian Popular Party (PPI), won just 11.1 percent of the vote. The PPI campaigned as part of an alliance with the Segni Pact called the Pact for Italy, which won a combined total of 15.7 percent of the vote and 46 seats.

On the left, the former Communist Party reemerged as the Democratic Party of the Left (PDS), capturing 20.4 percent of the vote and making it Italy's second largest party. They formed an electoral alliance known as the Progressive Alliance with other leftist groups and secured a total of 213 seats, with a collective 32.2 percent of the vote.

Parties with less than 4 percent of the party-list vote did not qualify for a share of the 155 seats (25 percent) distributed under the party list proportional system. About 9 percent of the total vote went to parties that failed to clear the 4 percent threshold.

Time for a Change. After a grueling two years of unrelenting revelations about scandals and government corruption, Italian voters embraced Berlusconi's promise of change and stability. With the Christian Democrats and the Socialists completely discredited and virtually defunct, Italian voters were ready for a major change—even if that meant a billionaire political novice like Berlusconi, who had burst onto the national scene just a few months before the elections.

While voters desperately wanted a change, they were not ready for a wholesale shift to the parties on the left if that meant a government led by the former Communist PDS. Although the electorate did not want to see PDS leader Achille Occhetto elected prime minister, they did vote for the PDS in sufficient numbers to make it the second largest party.

Until Berlusconi appeared out of nowhere, it was conceivable that Occhetto might be elected prime minister. The old Communist Party, after all, was the only major political party to emerge virtually untainted by the corruption scandals that had so dramatically changed the political landscape in Italy. Berlusconi's meteoric rise was a terrible blow to Occhetto's dream of becoming prime minister, which would have made him the first leader of a reformed Communist party to ascend to that office in Western Europe.

1992 Parliamentary Elections: A Political Earthquake

Beginning with the 1991 arrest of a Socialist Party official in Milan, official investigations (known as Operation Clean Hands) into the workings of hundreds of prominent politicians and all of the ruling political parties uncovered a nationwide network of embezzlement, bribes, and kickbacks in return for public works contracts.

Leading up to the 1992 parliamentary elections, the investigations enlarged from the *tangentopolis* (bribe city) of Milan to *tangentopoli* (bribe cities) throughout Italy. Oddly enough, given this background of impending crisis, the outgoing Chamber of Deputies had been one of the longest-lived parliaments in recent Italian history, surviving just five months short of its full five-year term. Such longevity between elections was almost unprecedented in Italian politics.

Italian voters sent the political establishment a message of warning in 1992: "We're mad as hell and we're not going to take it anymore." That warning turned into political upheaval in the national referendum of 1993, which resulted in the adoption of far-reaching electoral reforms.

A number of factors lead to this watershed political crisis. The fall of Soviet communism had eroded the foundations of Italy's post-World War II political establishment. The dominant Chris-

Past Parliamentary Election Results

Party	1992 % Votes	1992 Seats	1987 % Votes	1987 Seats	1983 % Votes	1983 Seats	1979 % Votes	1979 Seats
DC	30	206	34	234	33	225	38	261
PCI	16	107	27	177	30	198	30	207
PSI	14	92	14	94	11	73	10	62
NL	9	55	—	—	—	—	—	—
CRF	6	35	—	—	—	—	—	—
MSI	5	34	6	35	7	42	5	31
PSDI	3	16	3	17	4	23	4	21
PRI	4	27	4	21	5	29	3	15
PLI	3	17	2	11	3	16	2	9
PR	1	0	3	13	2	11	4	18
Others	10	41	6	28	4	13	3	6
Total Seats		630		630		630		630

Note: Percentages may not add up to 100 due to rounding. DC = Christian Democratic Party, PCI = Communist Party, PSI = Italian Socialist Party, NL = Northern League, CRF = Communist Refoundation Party, MSI = Italian Social Movement, PSDI = Italian Social Democratic Party, PRI = Italian Republican Party, PLI = Liberals, PR = Radical Party.

tian Democrats (which later became the Italian Popular Party in 1994), the leading coalition partner in every postwar government, had a virtual lock on political power by positioning itself as the only bulwark against the huge Italian Communist Party (renamed the Democratic Party of the Left in 1991).

To keep the Communists at bay, the public voted time after time for the Christian Democrats and its allies. This continued despite the fact that the voters were aware of the widespread corruption that existed throughout the political establishment. In effect, the fall of Soviet communism made it safe for the public to express its anger and frustration about the culture of bribes and favors that for many years had characterized Italian politics.

Voter frustration also found expression in the growth of new parties, most notably the Northern League and its sister parties and the neofascist Italian Social Movement (MSI), which changed its name in 1994 to the National Alliance.

Results. In Italy's first post-Cold War elections, the Northern League, with nearly 9 percent of the vote, won 55 seats by siphoning votes away from the ruling Christian Democrats (DC). The DC, meanwhile, continued to slide, falling to a record low of 29.7 percent, with only 206 seats—down from 34.3 percent and 234 seats in the 1987 election.

The DC-led four-party coalition partners—including the Socialists (PSI), Social Democrats (PSDI), and Liberals (PLI)—received 48.8 percent of the vote, for a combined seat total of 331, down from its pre-election 356 seats. In particular, the Socialists dropped from 14.3 percent to 13.6 percent, winning 92 seats compared with 94 in the previous parliament. The Liberals won 17 seats and the Social Democrats 16.

In opposition, the Democratic Party of the Left (the former Communist Party) remained Italy's second largest party, but declined sharply from 26.6 percent of the vote and 177 seats to 16.1 percent and with 107 seats. The Communist Refoundation Party (CRF), a hard-line faction, won 5.6 percent of the vote and 35 seats. The neofascist Italian Social Movement (MSI) took 5.4 percent and 34 seats, down slightly from the 5.9 percent tally it recorded in 1987. Alessandra Mussolini, the former Italian dictator's granddaughter won a seat from Naples, running on the neofascist ticket.

Among even smaller parties, the Republicans increased to their vote from 3.7 percent to 4.4 percent, winning 27 seats; the Greens gained slightly from 2.5 percent to 2.8 percent, securing 16 seats; and the antimafia La Rete (Network) won 1.9 percent of the vote and 12 seats, becoming the biggest party in Palermo, Sicily.

In all, sixteen parties won seats, but only three received more than 10 percent of the vote.

Following the election, Socialist Giuliano Amato became the prime minister, as head of the continuing four-party coalition. He lasted a little more than a year in office and was replaced in May 1993 by Carlo Azeglio Ciampi, the former governor of the Bank of Italy. Ciampi was the first nonpolitician to become Italian prime minister in this century. Given the political upheaval underway at

European Parliament Election Results

Party	1994 % Votes	1994 Seats	1989 % Votes	1989 Seats	1984 % Votes	1984 Seats	1979 % Votes	1979 Seats
FI	31	27	—	—	—	—	—	—
PCI/PDS	19	16	28	22	33	27	31	25
NA/MSI	13	11	6	4	7	5	5	4
PPI	10	8	33	26	33	26	36	30
NL	7	6	2	2	—	—	—	—
PSI	2	2	15	12	11	9	11	9
PSDI	1	1	3	2	4	3	4	4
Others	17	16	12	13	12	11	12	9
Total Seats		**87**		**81**		**81**		**81**

Note: Percentages may not add up to 100 due to rounding. FI = Forza Italia, PCI = Communist Party, PDS = Democratic Party of the Left, NA = National Alliance, MSI = Italian Social Movement, PPI = Italian Popular Party, NL = Northern League, PSI = Italian Socialist Party, PSDI = Italian Social Democratic Party.

that time, a nonpolitician was perhaps the only leader acceptable to the parliament and the public.

1994 European Parliament Elections

Newly elected Prime Minister Silvio Berlusconi's Forza Italia built upon its momentum from the March parliamentary elections in Italy, winning 30.6 percent of the European Parliament vote (and 27 seats). The former Christian Democrats (now known as the Italian Popular Party, PPI) won only 10 percent of the vote and 8 seats, a stunning 18-seat decline versus the 1989 results.

The Socialists (PSI) continued their dramatic slide into near political oblivion, winning only 2 seats, down from 12 seats in 1989. Italy's second largest party continued to be the Democratic Party of the Left (PDS, the renamed Italian Communist Party). The PDS won 19.1 percent of the vote and 16 seats—a 6-seat loss.

The National Alliance claimed 11 seats—a 7-seat increase. The Northern League also saw its numbers rise, securing 6 seats versus 2 in 1989. The Communist Refoundation Party, Greens, and a smattering of smaller parties won the remaining 17 seats.

CORRUPTION SCANDALS

President Francesco Cossiga's term of office ended in 1992, and he was succeeded by fellow Christian Democrat Oscar Luigi Scalfaro. Cossiga had spent the first five years of his seven-year term filling the traditional ceremonial role of previous Italian presidents. In 1990, however, Cossiga began attacking the political establishment, winning praise from angry and dissatisfied voters. He came out against the waste, corruption, and inefficiency that had slowed the state sector and caused so much despair. He feuded with political leaders and even severed his forty-five-year relation with the Christian Democrats. The establishment parties blamed Cossiga for inspiring the large number of candidates running in 1992 with the battle cry of "Let's throw the rascals out."

The upheaval started almost accidentally. A Socialist functionary was caught receiving a kickback for a cleaning contract at a retirement home. This discovery led to the "Milan Corruption Scandal" and resulted in the arrest, conviction, and even the suicides of numerous cabinet members, party leaders, and business leaders.

One of the politicians caught in the Operation Clean Hands investigation was Bettino Craxi, the former Socialist prime minister who had hoped to become the president or prime minister after the 1992 elections. Instead, Craxi faced charges of receiving illegal contributions to his party. He denied any wrongdoing and accused the magistrates of waging a personal vendetta against him. He said all parties had benefited from illegal payments.

Others tainted by scandal included Antonio Cariglia, chairman of the Social Democratic party, Republican Giorgio La Malfa, Socialist Claudio Martelli, and Francesco Paolo Mattioli, who was the director of an insurance group controlled by Fiat. One-quarter of the members of the sitting Chamber of Deputies became caught up in various corruption inquiries, mostly connected with party financing.

The leaders of five political parties had to step down. The Socialists changed leadership twice. The government went through five finance ministers and three foreign ministers in just two years.

1993 ELECTION REFORMS

Italy's post-World War II constitution sought to atone for dictatorial fascism by embracing a pure form of proportional representation, but the result has been a much criticized political fragmentation and governmental instability—with more than fifty governments in the last half century. Ironically, despite this legendary instability, the protracted continuity of the ruling parties, especially the Christian Democrats, seems to have bred widespread corruption throughout the political establishment. In many ways, once Soviet communism collapsed, it could be argued that proportional representation itself gave rise to new parties and new political forces that opposed the old culture of corruption.

Whatever the actual effects of Italy's pure form of party list proportional representation, the public and many leading politicians argued that this voting system was a large part of the problem and needed to be changed. Enter Mario Segni, a breakaway Christian Democrat who led the successful campaign for electoral reform in Italy.

The new electoral system was first endorsed by more than 80 percent of voters in the April 1993 referendum and applied only to the Senate. In August the same reform was extended to the Chamber of Deputies.

The 1994 elections marked the first time that the new mixed member proportional system was used for both chambers. Under this system, 75 percent of the seats are chosen by the plurality or "first-past-the-post" system. The remaining 25 percent of the seats are allocated by the party list proportional method. A 4 percent threshold applies only to the Chamber of Deputies.

By adopting this "mixed" system, Italy did not completely repudiate proportional representation. In fact, Italy joined a long list of countries (including Germany, Hungary, Bulgaria, Russia, Japan, and Mexico) that have moved or are moving toward this kind of mixed system.

ELECTION LEXICON

Apertura a sinistra: "Opening to the left," a plan devised in 1963 that enabled the ruling Christian Democrats (CD) and the Socialist Party to enter CD-led coalition governments. This opening changed the dynamics of Italian post-World War II politics by splitting the democratic leftist parties away from the Communists.

I Barabari: "The Barbarians," Italians use this term to refer to the Northern League (*see Lega Nord, below*).

Caretaker government: Caretaker governments exist only to hold elections so other governments can take power. This follows a planned parliamentary defeat that is constitutionally necessary to dissolve parliament before the end of its term.

Cicciolina: "Little Fleshy One," the porno star elected to the Italian parliament in 1987.

Compromesso storico: "Historic compromise," a resolution the Communist Party (PCI) advocated for many years to bring the PCI into a coalition government with the Christian Democratic Party. The CD always balked at the idea. The PCI later advocated a "left alternative."

"Converging parallels": A phrase coined during the 1960s when the Christian Democrats did the unthinkable and joined a coalition with the Socialists. It is now used to describe situations that had previously been considered unthinkable.

Craxi a la Mussolini: In cartoons, former prime minister Bettino Craxi was often portrayed in the high boots favored by the former fascist leader Benito Mussolini.

Il Duce: "The Leader," the nickname Mussolini gave himself.

Franci tiratori: "Sharp shooters," party members who do not vote as instructed by their party in the secret ballots of parliament. These "sharp shooters" often are blamed for toppling governments and creating unexpected voting results.

Grande riforma: "Great institutional reform," the major theme of the 1979 and 1983 elections, which has faded out since. It was supposed to render Italy more "governable" and reduce governmental instability.

Left alternative: In the 1987 elections, the Communists, Socialists, and Social Democrats garnered 44 percent of the national vote—much higher than the 34 percent picked up by the Christian Democrats—but these leftist parties were not able to agree on a common program.

Lega Nord: "Northern League," a regional alliance that includes the Lombard League and other related parties. It was the fourth largest party in Italy after the 1992 national elections.

Lottizzazione: The spoils system that doles out jobs and other government benefits to family, friends, and supporters. This system has been an integral part of Italian political life.

Operation Clean Hands: Name for investigations into political corruption throughout Italy.

P-2: Name for the secret Masonic Lodge in which many of the country's leading politicians, industrialists, and tax officials were linked in a major influence-peddling scandal.

Passing the baton (la staffetta): In 1983, Christian Democrat Ciriaco de Mita agreed to Socialist Bettino Craxi becoming prime minister on the condition that Craxi would "pass the baton" in early 1987. In 1987, Craxi denied that he had made such a pledge and said that his government needed to meet its democratic responsibility and govern. In retaliation, de Mita created major confrontations between the Christian Democrats and the Socialists to force an election.

Peones: Term to describe politicians who never rise to any position of authority in their party or the government.

La Pergola Law: At the start of each year, the Italian government reviews what unfulfilled EU legal obligations are left over from the previous years. The legislative backlog is then either bundled into an omnibus statute or passed by decree.

"Piove, governo ladro": Literally, "the government rains thieves." This colloquial phrase hints at the perennial corruption in Italy's government.

Scala Mobile: Indexing wages to inflation was a pet program of the trade unions—and a major reason for high inflation. Bettino Craxi was able to roll back this program while prime minister and bring inflation down from 16 percent to 4 percent.

Stivale: "Boot," how Italians describe the shape of their country.

Tangentopolis: Literally, "bribe city." This term refers to Milan, where the corruption scandals started in 1991, but has broadened into *Tangentopoli*, "bribe cities."

Transatlantico: "Transatlantic," a large rectangular room outside the parliament's voting chamber where members wait to vote. It resembles a ship.

"White Semester": In the final six months of a presidential term, the constitutional power to dissolve parliament is suspended to avoid possible abuses of power. This restriction is a kind of an enforced political "purity."

HISTORICAL SYNOPSIS

A land divided and ruled by outsiders, ranging from Germany to France to Austria, Italy did not know sovereignty and unification until Victor Emmanuel II became king in 1861. Venetia became part of Italy in 1866. Rome joined four years later and became the capital city the following year.

1915-1918	Italy fights on Allies' side in World War I.
1919	First election in which all adult males are allowed to vote. Two new mass parties, the Popular Party—which later developed into the Christian Democratic Party—and the Socialist Party, emerge as the domi-

nant parties in Italy. They oppose each other, making it difficult to form an effective government.

1922 Fascists march on Rome, and King Victor Emmanuel III names Benito Mussolini premier of Italy. By 1925 Mussolini rules Italy as a dictator.

1935 Italy invades and annexes Ethiopia.

1936 Mussolini and Hitler form Rome-Berlin Axis.

1940 Italy enters World War II on Germany's side.

1943 Italy surrenders to the Allies.

1945 On April 28, Mussolini is executed.

1946 On June 2, Italy holds its first free election in twenty years. Italians choose a republic to replace the monarchy. They elect a Constituent Assembly to prepare a new democratic constitution.

1948 On January 1, the new constitution goes into effect.

1949 Italy becomes a founding member of NATO.

1957 Italy becomes one of six original signatories to the Treaty of Rome, which establishes the European Economic Community.

1963 The first Christian Democratic-led coalition government is established.

1973 Communist Party leader Enrico Berlinguer articulates "historic compromise," in which he proposes alliances with progressive forces in Italian society. This pluralistic approach (also known as Euro-communism) is seen as less threatening to democratic principles than Soviet-backed Communist parties elsewhere.

1976 Communist Party wins 34.4 percent of the vote, compared with 38.7 percent for the Christian Democrats, but is kept out of government.

1981 On May 26, the P-2 scandal forces Christian Democratic prime minister Amintore Forlani to resign. The resignation leads to Giovanni Spadolini of the Republican Party becoming the first non-Christian Democrat prime minister in the post-World War II era.

1983 Bettino Craxi, leader of the rejuvenated Socialist Party, becomes prime minister even though his party wins only 11.4 percent of the 1983 vote compared with

32.9 percent and 29.9 percent for the Christian Democrats and the Communists, respectively.

1987 Craxi hangs on as prime minister for a postwar record of four years, but he is forced to resign, leading to the 1987 elections. The Socialists and the Christian Democrats both improve on their 1983 vote. Christian Democrat Giovanni Goria becomes prime minister.

1988 Secret voting in parliament is abolished. Goria is succeeded as prime minister by Ciriaco de Mita.

1991 The Operation Clean Hands investigation into political corruption begins in Milan.

1992 "Earthquake" elections take place, resulting in a surge for the Lombard League and drop in support for the ruling Christian Democratic coalition.

1993 April referendum results in sweeping changes in Italy's electoral system. A mixed member proportional system replaces the pure party list proportional system.

1994 Parliamentary elections under the new mixed member proportional voting system gives the Freedom Alliance a commanding majority in the Chamber of Deputies.

Luxembourg

The Country in Brief

Official Name: Grand Duchy of Luxembourg (*Grand-Duché de Luxembourg*)
Capital: Luxembourg
Currency: Luxembourg franc
National Day: June 23 (birthday of Grand Duke Jean)
Languages: Luxembourgish (*Letzeburgish*); French and German used for business and government
Religion: Roman Catholic
Memberships: NATO and EU
Border Countries: Belgium, France, Germany
Embassy in Washington, D.C.: 2200 Massachusetts Avenue, N.W., 20008. Telephone: (202) 265-4171.

Political Profile

Government Type: Constitutional monarchy/parliamentary democracy
Head of State: Grand Duke Jean
Succeeded to Throne: 1964
Head of Government: Prime Minister Jean-Claude Juncker
Political Party: Christian Social Party
Assumed Office: 1994 (replaced Jacques Santer, who became president of the European Commission)

Next Election: 1999
Legislature: Unicameral. Chamber of Deputies, 60 members, elected by proportional representation.
Term of Office: Five years
Last Election: 1994
Next Election: 1999

Comparative Data

Population: 382,000
GDP: $8.9 billion
GDP Per Capita: $22,900
Voting System: Modified party list proportional/preference voting for individual candidates
Per Capita Representation Rate: 6,400
Big Government Index: 53%
Women in Parliament: 13%
Voter Turnout Rate: 90%

MAJOR POLITICAL PARTIES

Christian Social Party (*Parti Chrétien Social*, PCS)

Founded in 1914, the PCS has much in common with the European Christian Democratic parties. The PCS is Luxembourg's leading party, having been a member of nearly every government coalition since 1914. It is pro-monarchy and pro-church (Roman Catholic). It supports NATO and EU membership, as well as a planned expansion of the economy.

Socialist Workers' Party
(*Parti Ouvrier Socialiste Luxembourgeios*, POSL)

Founded in 1902 as the Luxembourg Social Democratic Party, the POSL is only slightly leftist in orientation. It has participated in coalition governments with both the Christian Social and Democratic parties.

Democratic Party (*Parti Démocratique*, PD)

Also known as the Liberals, the PD occupies the ideological middle ground and has been a frequent partner in governing coalitions, most often with the Christian Social Party, but also with the Socialists (1974-1979). The PD supports a free enterprise economy and opposes excessive government interference. It strongly supports the EU and NATO. Anti-cleric, the party draws its support mainly from the middle class and professionals.

MINOR POLITICAL PARTIES

Action Committee for Democracy and Pension Rights/Five-Sixths
    Action Committee (*Aktiounskomitee fir Demokratie an
    Rentengerechtegkeet*, ADR)
Communist Party (*Parti Communiste Luxembourgeios*, PCL)
Green Alternative Party (*Gréng Alternativ*, GAP)
Green Ecologist Initiative List
    (*Gréng Lëscht Ekologesch Initiativ*, GEI)

ELECTION REVIEW

1995 Parliamentary Update

The Grand Duchy started 1995 with a new prime minister, even though the previous one, Jacques Santer, had been reelected in the June 1994 election. Santer went on to become president of the European Commission and was replaced as prime minister by his fellow Christian Democrat, thirty-nine-year-old Jean-Claude Juncker, Luxembourg's former finance minister.

1994 Parliamentary Elections:
Not Much Changes in the Grand Duchy

A total of twelve parties—a record number—vied for the support of the Grand Duchy's 200,000 voters in the June 12, 1994, general

1994 Parliamentary Election Results

Party	% Votes	Seats
Christian Social Party (PCS)	31	21
Socialist Party (POSL)	24	17
Democratic Party (PD)	21	12
Greens	10	5
Action Committee for Democracy and Pension Rights (ADR)	9	5
Others	5	0
Total Seats		60

Note: Percentages may not add up to 100 due to rounding.

elections. To nobody's surprise, Prime Minister Jacques Santer of the Christian Social Party (PCS) emerged victorious from the elections and was sworn in on July 13 for his third term as prime minister.

Santer's party remained the country's largest party, with 21 seats in the 60-seat parliament. The Christian Social's coalition partner, the Socialist Party, remained the second largest party with 17 seats. The ruling Christian Social-Socialist coalition thus garnered 38 seats, more than enough support in parliament to stay in office for another five years. The opposition Democratic Party, known as the Liberals, won 12 seats.

The campaign was relatively unsuspenseful, despite the presence of twelve parties on the ballot. Opposition parties tried to make an issue of the unemployment rate, which was approaching 3 percent. This was considered painfully high by many in the country, although most other European countries would be very happy with such a low unemployment rate.

Two smaller parties campaigned on issues of special interest to their voters. The pro-pensioner Action Committee for Democracy and Pension Rights (ADR, formerly known as the Five-Sixths Action Committee), whose leader, Fernand Rau, was killed in an automobile accident a week before the election, campaigned on the issue of maintaining adequate funding for pensions. The party won 5 seats, a 1-seat increase over 1989.

Two Green parties, the Green Alternative and Green Ecologist Initiative List, having formed a pact for the elections, ran together as one party and managed to win 5 seats, an improvement of 1 seat over 1989.

EU Selects Santer. On July 15, just a few weeks after claiming victory in the parliamentary elections, Jacques Santer was selected by the European Union's Council of Ministers to succeed Jacques Delors as the next president of the European Commission. On July 21, the newly elected European Parliament voted narrowly to approve Santer's elevation to the commission presidency.

1989 Parliamentary Election: Santer's Close Call

When the votes were counted in the June 18, 1989, national elections, Prime Minister Jacques Santer had managed to keep his Christian Social-Socialist coalition in power, although each partner lost 3 seats in the 60-seat Chamber of Deputies.

	1989		1984		1979		1974	
Party	% Votes	Seats	% Votes	Seats	% Votes	Seats	% Votes	Seats
PCS	32	22	35	25	36	24	30	18
POSL	27	18	34	21	23	14	27	17
PD	16	11	19	14	22	15	23	14
Greens	8	4	5	2	—	—	—	—
ADR	8	4	—	—	—	—	—	—
PCL	5	1	5	2	5	2	9	5
Others	4	0	2	0	13	4	10	5
Total Seats		60		64		59		59

Past Parliamentary Election Results

Note: Percentages may not add up to 100 due to rounding. PCS = Christian Social Party, POSL = Socialist Party, PD = Democratic Party (Liberals), ADR = Action Committee for Democracy and Pension Rights, PCL = Communist Party.

European Parliament Election Results

Party	1994 % Votes	1994 Seats	1989 % Votes	1989 Seats	1984 % Votes	1984 Seats	1979 % Votes	1979 Seats
PCS	31	2	35	3	35	3	36	3
POSL	25	2	25	2	30	2	22	1
PD	19	1	20	1	22	1	28	2
Greens	11	1	4	0	—	—	—	—
Others	14	0	16	0	13	0	14	0
Total Seats		6		6		6		6

Note: Percentages may not add up to 100 due to rounding. PCS = Christian Social Party, POSL = Socialist Party, PD = Democratic Party (Liberals).

The Christian Socials emerged with 22 seats and the Socialists took 18.

After the 1984 elections, Santer's coalition held 46 seats—72 percent of the chamber's 64 seats. (A constitutional reform subsequently lowered the number of seats to 60, effective 1989.) After the 1989 elections, the coalition government held 40 seats—exactly two-thirds of the chamber's seats—still a commanding percentage.

The third-largest party, the Democrats, captured 11 seats, a drop of 3 seats. The biggest gains in the election were recorded by the environmentalist Greens, who jumped from 2 seats to 4, and by a new, single-issue party called the Five-Sixths Action Committee, which took 4 seats. The latter advocated that every retiree should receive a pension worth five-sixths of the worker's final salary. That generous pension formula had only applied to retired civil servants.

The final seat in the chamber went to the Communist Party, constituting a 1-seat loss.

1994 European Parliament Elections

Once the balloting was complete, the only real surprise was that the Greens had won 11 percent of the vote (up from only 4 percent in 1989) and 1 seat. This seat—the party's first in the EP—came at the expense of the ruling Christian Democrats, who fell to just 2 seats, having captured 31 percent of the vote (as compared with 35 percent in 1989).

The Socialists held steady with their tallies from the last election, retaining their 2 seats and winning 25 percent of the vote. The Democratic Party (Liberals) also remained at their 1989 levels, winning the last of Luxembourg's 6 seats.

ELECTION LEXICON

Arbed: Luxembourg's leading steel producer and the fourth-largest steel production company in Europe. Arbed employs nearly 10 percent of the workforce.

BENELUX: The Belgium, Netherlands, and Luxembourg economic union, founded in 1948.

BLEU: The Belgium-Luxembourg Economic Union, established in 1922. Expanded in 1948 to include the Netherlands (*see* BENELUX).

"A capital city": Nickname for Luxembourg, the headquarters of many European Union institutions: the European Court of Justice, the European Investment Bank, the Court of Auditors, and the Secretariat for the European Parliament. Luxembourg has proposed that it should be the EU's "capital"—a kind of Washington, D.C., of Europe; the EU has not adopted the proposal.

"Dirty money": Reference to the allegation that Luxembourg is a tax haven or that its banks have been used for money laundering. Luxembourg enacted a law in 1989 making money laundering illegal, but the Duchy insists on keeping banking matters confidential unless there is evidence of criminality.

Foreign workers: Luxembourg, with more than 25 percent, has the highest percentage of foreign workers of any country in the world. That percentage is projected to grow to more than 30 percent by the year 2000. This reliance on foreign workers results in large part because of Luxembourg's low birth rate, which is one of the lowest in the world.

Frontaliers: Term for the roughly 30,000 Belgians, French, and Germans who cross into Luxembourg each day to work.

"Gibraltar of the North": In 963 A.D., Siegfried, the Count of Ardennes, constructed a virtually impregnable fortress on the steep cliffs of what is now Luxembourg's capital city of Luxembourg. *Luxembourg* means "little fortress."

Linguistic pluralism: Luxembourgish—a Moselle Franconian German dialect with many French words added—is the vernacular of natives. French and German are the official languages for business and government. Children are taught German beginning at age six and French at age seven.

Luxembourg Model: In response to the economic downturn in 1975-1976, Luxembourg launched extensive public works projects and introduced a part-time work program to keep unemployment to a minimum.

Luxembourg Stock Exchange: A major European stock exchange that quotes over half of all Euro-bonds issued on the Eurobond market. Financial services account for about 20 percent of Luxembourg's economic output.

National Credit and Investment Company: A state-funded financial institution established to support investments and exports by offering credits, loans, and government joint-equity participation.

HISTORICAL SYNOPSIS

Luxembourg was dominated by foreigners until 1815, when the Congress of Vienna established it as a grand duchy within the kingdom of the Netherlands. In 1867 the London Conference recognized Luxembourg as an independent state with perpetual neutrality, and a constitution was adopted the following year.

1914   Germany violates Luxembourg's neutrality.
1922   The Belgium-Luxembourg Economic Union (BLEU) is formed.

1948	Belgium, the Netherlands, and Luxembourg form the BENELUX economic union.
1949	After occupation in both world wars, Luxembourg abandons neutrality and joins NATO.
1952	Luxembourg becomes an original member of the European Coal and Steel Community, precursor of the European Community.
1957	Luxembourg is among the original six countries signing the Treaty of Rome and establishing the European Economic Community, effective January 1, 1958.
1964	Crown Prince Jean becomes grand duke upon abdication of his mother, Grand Duchess Charlotte.
1974	Christian Social-Democratic (Liberal) coalition is replaced by Socialist-Democratic government. This marks the first time since 1919 that the Christian Social Party had not been part of the governing coalition.
1975	Government responds to economic crisis with program of public investments and part-time employment to keep unemployment down.
1979	Christian Social Party returns to power in coalition with the Liberals.
1982	Belgium devalues its currency—which is linked with Luxembourg's—without consultation with the Luxembourg government. Christian Social-Liberal coalition adopts austerity measures, including abolition of automatic wage indexation, to fight inflation.
1984	Socialists rebound and become second largest party, joining with Christian Social Party to form ruling coalition with Jacques Santer as prime minister.
1989	Santer's coalition retains control of parliament following election.
1992	Luxembourg ratifies Maastricht Treaty on European Union in July.
1994	Santer is reelected prime minister but moves on to become president of the European Commission. His finance minister, thirty-nine-year-old Jean-Claude Juncker, becomes prime minister.

Netherlands

The Country in Brief

Official Name: Kingdom of the Netherlands (*Koninkrijk der Nederlanden*)
Capital: Amsterdam
Seat of Government: The Hague
Currency: Guilder
National Day: May 5 (Liberation Day)
Language: Dutch
Religions: Roman Catholic, Dutch Reformed Lutheran
Memberships: NATO and EU
Border Countries: Belgium, Germany
Embassy in Washington, D.C.: 4200 Linnean Avenue, N.W., 20008. Telephone: (202) 244-5300.

Political Profile

Government Type: Constitutional monarchy/parliamentary democracy
Head of State: Queen Beatrix Wilhelmina Armgard
Succeeded to Throne: May 1, 1980
Head of Government: Prime Minister Willem (Wim) Kok
Political Party: Labor Party
Assumed Office: 1994
Next Election: 1998
Legislature: Bicameral, parliament (*Staten Generaal*)

Upper Chamber: First Chamber (*Eerste Kamer*), 75 members, indirectly elected by members of provincial councils.
Term of Office: Four years
Lower Chamber: Second Chamber (*Tweede Kamer*), 150 members, directly elected by proportional representation.
Term of Office: Four years
Next Election: 1998

Comparative Data

Population: 15 million
GDP: $285 billion
GDP Per Capita: $18,700
Voting System: Party list proportional
Per Capita Representation Rate: 100,000
Big Government Index: 50%
Women in Parliament: 29%
Voter Turnout Rate: 80%

MAJOR POLITICAL PARTIES

Labor Party (*Partij van de Arbeid*, PvdA)

The Labor party was founded in 1946 and remains a typical European Social Democratic party. In the opposition throughout most of its history, Labor seeks greater social, political, and economic equality for all citizens. It supports Dutch membership in NATO but opposes many of NATO's nuclear weapons programs, including the deployment of cruise missiles. Labor supports legalization of euthanasia, abolition of nuclear power, and increased taxes to pay for social welfare programs.

Christian Democratic Appeal (*Christen Democratisch Appel*, CDA)

The CDA was formed in the late 1970s through a merger of the Catholic People's Party (KVP) and two Protestant parties, the Anti-Revolutionary Party (ARP) and the Christian-Historical

Union (CHU). A center-right party, CDA has supported deployment of cruise missiles, opposes legalization of voluntary euthanasia, supports nuclear power production and further European integration, stresses the free enterprise system, but also recognizes the need for state intervention and welfare programs.

People's Party for Freedom and Democracy (*Volkspartij Voor Vrijheid en Democratie*, VVD)

Founded in 1948, the VVD is commonly known as the Liberals. It supports individual initiative against state intervention. A bit to the right of the CDA, the VVD favors NATO membership (although some members voiced opposition to the deployment of cruise missiles), opposes voluntary euthanasia, and wants to spend more on environmental protection. VVD has expressed concern about rising crime and supports profit-sharing plans for workers. Party support has declined markedly in recent elections. The party's image was not improved when some party members posed nude in the parliament chamber for the Dutch edition of *Playboy*.

Democrats 66 (*Democraten '66*, D66)

A center-left party founded in 1966, D66 wants to do away with proportional representation and favors the direct election of the prime minister. D66 refused Prime Minister Ruud Lubbers's invitation to join his CDA/VVD coalition after the 1989 elections, forcing Lubbers to form a coalition with Labor.

Green Left Alliance (*Groen Links*, GL)

This disparate alliance of leftist and environmentalist parties— Pacifists, Radicals, Evangelical People's, and Communists— banded together prior to the 1989 election and became a permanent party in 1991 when the constituent groups voted to disband.

MINOR POLITICAL PARTIES

Center Democrats (*Centrumdemocraten*, CD)
55+ Union (*Unie 55+*)

General Union of the Elderly (*Algemeen Ouderen Verbond*, AOV)
Political Reformed Party
  (*Staatkundig Gereformeerde Partij*, SGP)
Reformational Political Federation
  (*Reformatorische Politieke Federatie*, RPF)
Reformed Political Union (*Gereformeerd Politiek Verbond*, GPV)
Socialist Party (*Socialistische Partij*, SP)

ELECTION REVIEW

1994 Parliamentary Elections: Brinkman on the Brink

Christian Democratic prime minister Ruud Lubbers's chosen successor, Elco Brinkman, led the long-ruling party to an embarrassing defeat in the parliamentary elections on May 3. The Christian
Democratic Appeal (CDA) suffered a stunning drop in voter support, declining from 35.3 percent of the vote in 1989 to 22.2 percent in 1994. This translated into a loss of 20 seats, from 54 to 34
seats in the 150-seat parliament.

This precipitous slide for the CDA meant that the Labor Party
(PvdA) emerged as the largest party in parliament, having cap-
tured 37 seats. However, the PvdA also suffered at the hands of
voters, dropping 12 seats from its previous 49. The right-leaning
People's Party for Freedom and Democracy (VVD), known as the
Liberals, gained 9 seats, growing from 22 to 31, and the center-left
Democrats 66 (D66) doubled their seat total from 12 to 24.

As a result of these shifting fortunes, a "purple coalition"—
combining the traditional red color of Labor with the blue of the
Liberals, together with the D66—began to take shape. But it took
a while. The first attempt at forming a government failed in June.
It took Labor leader Willem (Wim) Kok until August 18, more
than 100 days after the election, to finally cobble together the new
three-party coalition government (with a combined 92 seats in
parliament). With this, the Christian Democratic Appeal was
forced into opposition for the first time since the party was formed
in a merger of three different parties in the late 1970s. Moreover,
this was the first time in more than seventy-five years that the

1994 Parliamentary Election Results

Party	% Votes	Seats
Labor Party (PvdA)	24	37
Christian Democratic Appeal (CDA)	22	34
People's Party for Freedom and Democracy (VVD)	20	31
Democrats 66 (D66)	16	24
General Union of the Elderly (AOV)	4	6
Greens	4	5
Center Democrats (CD)	3	3
Reformational Political Federation (RPF)	2	3
Political Reformed Party (SGP)	2	2
Reformed Political Union (GPV)	1	2
Socialist Party (SP)	1	2
55+ Union (55+)	1	1
Total Seats		**150**

Note: Percentages may not add up to 100 due to rounding.

CDA or one of its predecessors had not dominated the government.

Wim Kok's government consisted of five ministers from the PvdA, five from the VVD, and four from D66. Gerrit Zalm of the VVD claimed one of the key ministerial posts, that of finance minister. With Joris Voorhoeve's appointment as defense minister, the VVD also claimed this important position. Hans van Mierlo of D66 was named foreign affairs minister.

The "purple" coalition brings together some pretty strange political bedfellows. One can only wonder how long the VVD and the PvdA will be able to stay united since the two parties do not agree on many issues, most notably public spending. The VVD is a champion of sharp budget cuts, while the PvdA generally advocates greater spending on such things as health, pensions, and education.

In fact, CDA leader Brinkman seems to have been hurt politically because he proposed a freeze on pension payments. The VVD also supports major reforms in the pension program, but the PvdA and D66 do not. With sharp policy differences dividing the

Past Parliamentary Election Results

Party	1989 % Votes	1989 Seats	1986 % Votes	1986 Seats	1982 % Votes	1982 Seats	1981 % Votes	1981 Seats
PvdA	32	49	33	52	30	47	28	44
CDA	35	54	35	54	30	45	31	48
VVD	15	22	17	27	23	36	17	26
D66	8	12	6	9	4	6	11	17
Greens	4	6	—	—	—	—	—	—
Others	5	7	9	8	13	16	12	15
Total Seats		150		150		150		150

Note: Percentages may not add up to 100 due to rounding. PvdA = Labor Party, CDA = Christian Democratic Appeal, VVD = People's Party for Freedom and Democracy (Liberals), D66 = Democrats 66.

new government, the future may not be all that rosy for the "purple" coalition.

The 1989 Parliamentary Elections: Holland Is for Lubbers

Other issues may have been discussed during this campaign, but the big issue on everyone's agenda was the environment. This issue had brought down Christian Democratic prime minister Ruud Lubbers' coalition government, forcing an election a year earlier than scheduled.

The government crisis occurred in May 1989, over a relatively minor point. Feeling taken for granted by Lubbers, his coalition partners, the Liberals, rejected his proposal to help finance his sweeping environmental cleanup plan by abolishing existing tax breaks for automobile commuters and using the proceeds to pay for modernizing the public transportation system.

There was not much disagreement within the coalition—or among the various parties generally—about whether to implement strong environmental protection. The Dutch, whose cramped country lies at the mouth of the polluted Rhine river and on the banks of the dirty North Sea, take environmental protection very seriously. The question has always been how to pay for it.

Lubbers had proposed a far-reaching, twenty-year plan, called the National Environment Plan, that would have cost an estimated $6 billion by 1994 and as much as 3.5 percent of the nation's gross domestic product by 2010. The plan was expected to reduce water, air, and soil pollution by 90 percent. During the 1989 campaign, most parties pledged to spend even more money cleaning up the environment, a reflection of just how powerful the environmental issue is in Holland.

The Christian Democratic Appeal campaigned under the slogan "Further with Lubbers," seeking to capitalize on their popular prime minister's seven-year record of reducing inflation, chopping unemployment, and slicing the trade deficit. These gains came at a heavy price, however. Seven years of austerity was taking its toll. Recognizing that voters were suffering from "austerity fatigue," Lubbers pledged to spend more on the environment, education, and medical care.

Lubbers went into the campaign the heavy favorite. He had led the Netherlands through tough economic times and most voters seemed ready to "stay the course" with a proven leader. The election was never about whether Lubbers would win reelection. It was about which party would be the Christian Democrat's next coalition partner.

Results. The elections resulted in a strong vote of confidence in Lubbers. The CDA increased its percentage of the vote slightly and retained all of its 54 seats (out of parliament's 150), remaining the strongest party in the Netherlands. The rightist Liberal Party (VVD) lost 5 of its 27 seats, while the Labor Party (PvdA) lost 3 of its 52 seats. The new Green Left Alliance—which included the Communist Party of the Netherlands—captured 6 seats and the center-left Democrats 66 party won 12 seats—a gain of 3 for each. Thus, the small leftist parties made slight gains, shifting Dutch politics cautiously leftward.

In light of this subtle shift, Lubbers opted to change coalition partners, dropping the declining Liberals and forming a coalition government with Labor. Lubbers had little choice. His coalition with the Liberals would have had a hard time governing

European Parliament Election Results

Party	1994 % Votes	1994 Seats	1989 % Votes	1989 Seats	1984 % Votes	1984 Seats	1979 % Votes	1979 Seats
CDA	31	10	35	10	30	8	37	10
PvdA	23	8	31	8	34	9	30	9
VVD	18	6	14	3	19	5	16	4
D66	12	4	6	1	2	0	9	2
Greens	4	1	6	2	6	2	—	—
Others	11	2	7	1	9	1	7	0
Total Seats		31		25		25		25

Note: Percentages may not add up to 100 due to rounding. CDA = Christian Democratic Appeal, PvdA = Labor Party, VVD = People's Party for Freedom and Democracy (Liberals), D66 = Democrats 66.

with a mere 1-seat majority of 76 in the 150-seat parliament. In cooperation with Labor, on the other hand, Lubbers's government enjoyed a comfortable two-thirds majority, controlling 103 of the 150 seats.

1994 European Parliament Election

In the June 1994 Euro-election, the Netherlands had 31 seats to fill, a 6-seat increase over the 1989 allocation. The Christian Democratic Appeal (CDA) again captured 10 seats, which was a remarkable comeback from their dismal general election showing in May, where they had polled only 22 percent of the vote. The CDA won 31 percent of the Euro-vote, enough to finish at the top of the balloting. Second place went to the Labor Party (PvdA), which took 23 percent of the vote and 8 seats. The PvdA had outpolled the CDA just a month before in the parliamentary elections.

Two parties gained 3 seats each to capture the 6 new seats. The Liberals (VVD) won 18 percent and 6 seats, while the D66 tallied 12 percent and 4 seats. The Political Reformed Party accounted for 8 percent and 2 seats, while the Greens garnered 4 percent and 1 seat.

ELECTION LEXICON

BENELUX: The Belgium, Netherlands, and Luxembourg economic union, founded in 1948.

Binnenhof: The inner court in the Hague where the parliament meets. The term is used to refer to the parliament.

Compartmentalization: Dutch term for the coexistence of organizations with similar goals, even though they may have different ideologies. This is reflected in various political alliances (the CDA and the Green Left) that bring groups with differing philosophies together to achieve common objectives.

Delta Project: Project to form lakes by closing off all estuaries in the southwestern part of the country. Through desalinization, these lakes can be used for recreational purposes.

Equal Rights Policy Plan: Adopted in 1985, this plan committed the Netherlands to equal rights for women.

Euthanasia: Polls show that about two-thirds of the Dutch favor voluntary euthanasia (mercy killings) for terminal patients who expressly request that their life be ended by a fatal injection. Efforts to legalize this practice have been a hot political topic. Most courts have stopped imprisoning doctors who perform such mercy killings.

"Front-door sharers": Term for unmarried couples with two incomes who live together, sharing a "front door."

"Further with Lubbers": 1989 campaign slogan used by the Christian Democratic Appeal to take advantage of Prime Minister Lubbers's popularity.

Gateway to Europe: Reference to the Netherlands' role as a major trading center with a convenient location in Northern Europe and modern port and airport facilities.

Holland: Common name for the Netherlands, taken from the name of one of the country's principal provinces.

Informateur/formateur: The Dutch monarch's role in the formation of governments is a delicate but essential one. After an election, the sovereign appoints an *informateur*—usually a leading politician—to offer advice about the best formula for a governing coalition. The monarch names a *formateur* to form and lead a government as prime minister.

Maastricht: Small Dutch town in the southern part of the country near the Belgian border. Site of the European Community meeting at which the Maastricht Treaty on European Union was first signed. The Netherlands ratified the treaty in December 1992.

Press Fund: A government fund designed to aid failing periodicals and thereby ensure the widest range of journalistic expression.

Randstad Conurbation: Term referring to Amsterdam, the Hague, Rotterdam, and Utrecht, the most densely populated area of the Netherlands.

Schiphol: The Netherlands' major airport, which is reputed to be the best run in Europe.

South Flevoland: Reclaimed (drained) land area near the Randstad Conurbation being used to relieve population congestion. More than 20 percent of the Netherlands consists of reclaimed land.

Staten Generaal: "States General," the Dutch name for the bicameral legislature, comprised of the 75-member First Chamber and the 150-member Second Chamber.

Tweede Kamer: The Second Chamber in the parliament. The Dutch government is formed by the party or parties that commands a majority of this body's 150 seats.

Water control boards: Local government bodies responsible for protecting the land against flooding. One-third of the Netherlands lies below sea level. Board members are elected by local property owners.

Zoertemeer: A new, model town located near the Hague that epitomizes the Dutch desire to engineer living space in harmony with the environment. The government worked in conjunction with artists, designers, and sociologists to plan it.

HISTORICAL SYNOPSIS

Once the Netherlands won independence from Spain in 1648, the country was ruled by hereditary governors of the House of Orange. The tradition continued (surviving twenty years of control by Napoleon) until 1848, when the present constitutional monarchy system was adopted.

1914–1918	The Netherlands remains neutral throughout World War I.
1919	Women are granted the right to vote.
1940–1945	The Netherlands is occupied by Germany. Queen Wilhelmina heads a Dutch government-in-exile in London.
1943	The Netherlands joins BENELUX economic union.
1949	The Netherlands joins NATO as founding member. The East Indies, later known as the Republic of Indonesia, is granted its independence from the Netherlands.
1957	The Netherlands is among the original six countries signing the Treaty of Rome and establishing the European Economic Community, effective January 1, 1958.
1980	Princess Beatrix sworn in as Queen of the Netherlands.
1981	Prime Minister Van Agt loses his majority in parliament over the issue of deployment of U.S. cruise missiles on Dutch soil.
1982	Ruud Lubbers succeeds Van Agt as prime minister.
1985	Lubbers accepts the deployment of U.S. cruise missiles.
1989	Lubbers is elected to fourth term as prime minister.
1992	In December, Holland ratifies Maastricht Treaty on European Union.
1994	Lubbers decides not to seek reelection as prime minister. His chosen successor as head of the CDA party, Elco Brinkman, leads his party to a disastrous election defeat in May. CDA goes into opposition and a "purple coalition" of Labor, Liberals, and D66 forms a government with Labor leader Wim Kok as prime minister.

Norway

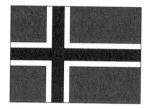

The Country in Brief

Official Name: Kingdom of Norway (*Kongeriket Norge*)
Capital: Oslo
Currency: Krone
National Day: May 17 (Constitution Day)
Language: Norwegian
Religion: Evangelical Lutheran
Memberships: NATO (1994 referendum on proposed membership in EU defeated 52.8% to 47.2%)
Border Countries: Finland, Russia, Sweden
Embassy in Washington, D.C.: 2720 34th Street, N.W., 20008. Telephone: (202) 388-6000.

Political Profile

Government Type: Constitutional monarchy/parliamentary democracy
Head of State: King Harald V
Succeeded to Throne: 1991
Head of Government: Prime Minister Gro Harlem Brundtland
Political Party: Labor Party
Assumed Office: 1993
Term of Office: Four years
Next Election: 1997

Legislature: Modified unicameral parliament. Storting, 165 members, elected by universal suffrage and proportional representation. The upper chamber (*Lagting*) is composed of one-quarter of the members of the Storting; the lower chamber (*Odelsting*) is composed of remaining three-quarters of the Storting members.
Term of Office: Four years
Last Election: 1993
Next Election: 1997

Comparative Data

Population: 4.2 million
GDP: $108 billion
GDP Per Capita: $25,000
Voting System: Party list proportional (4% threshold)
Per Capita Representation Rate: 26,000
Big Government Index: 55%
Women in Parliament: 36%
Voter Turnout Rate: 83%

MAJOR POLITICAL PARTIES

Norwegian Labor Party (*Det Norske Arbeiderparti*, DNA)

Founded in 1887, the Labor Party remains similar in outlook to other Scandinavian Social Democratic parties. The DNA helped establish the welfare system in Norway; is closely connected to the national labor unions; and has emphasized the need for equality in health, housing, and education. The party favors a mixed economy that combines private enterprise, economic democracy, and state interventionism in strategic sectors. A strong supporter of the NATO alliance, the Labor Party also favors creating a nuclear-free zone for the Nordic area. Its constituency is primarily the working class, with some elements of the urban middle class. The Labor government supports Norway's application to join the European Union.

Center Party (*Senterpartiet*, SP)

The Center Party is Norway's agrarian party. Founded in 1920, its primary concern is protecting the interests of Norway's small farmers, which means strong support for agricultural subsidies and a government effort to maintain a balance between urban and rural populations. The SP is slightly right of center and generally votes with the Conservatives. It is stridently anti-EU and just as stridently pro-environmental protection.

Conservative Party (*Hoyre*, H)

Founded in 1884, the Conservative Party is business-oriented, favoring the deregulation of the economy and tax breaks to encourage investment and economic expansion. The party name *Hoyre* literally means "right." The Conservatives' economic program has called for limited wage increases, devaluation of the Krone, cutting the government's budget, and raising excise taxes. Generally, the party has been staunchly pro-NATO, supporting the NATO deployment of Pershing and cruise missiles in the early 1980s, and very much in support of Norway joining the EU. After the 1993 elections, this staunchly pro-EU outlook has been challenged by some Conservatives members of parliament.

Christian People's Party (*Kristelig Folkeparti*, KFP)

The KFP supports an expanded private sector and increased incentives for investment, but it is less doctrinaire in this area and more tolerant of the welfare state system than the Conservatives. Founded in 1933, the party has two main concerns: environmental policy and matters affecting religion. The party derives its support from the Pietist Protestant movement, predominantly on the west coast. The KFP strongly opposes abortion, pornography, and alcoholic beverages.

Progress Party (*Fremskrittspartiet*, FP)

The Progress Party is the most right-wing party in the Norwegian parliament. Founded in 1973, it strongly favors supply-side economics and deregulation of the public sector. The party is hostile to the welfare system, pointing to the success of privatization in

Britain as an example of what it would like to see in Norway. Lower taxation and anti-immigration measures are among the FP's main campaign issues. In the 1989 campaign, the FP attacked the abuse of the welfare state, the breakdown of law and order, and the decline in moral standards. Much of its support has come from protest voters in the countryside and among the urban working classes, with some middle-class support as well. However, its support declined sharply in the 1993 elections.

Socialist Left Party (*Sosialistisk Venstreparti*, SVP)

The SVP is the most left-wing party in parliament. Founded in 1975, it opposes Norway's membership in NATO and supports a neutral Norway instead. It also opposes EU membership for Norway. On most domestic matters, the SVP supports policies similar to those of the Labor Party.

MINOR POLITICAL PARTIES

Liberal Party (*Venstre*, V)
Norwegian Communist Party
   (*Norges Kommunistiske Parti*, NKP)
Red Electoral Alliance (*Red Valgalianse*, RV)

ELECTION REVIEW

1993 Parliamentary Elections: Labor Support "GROs"

Prime Minister Gro Harlem Brundtland led her Labor Party to an expected showing in Norway's September 13, 1993, parliamentary (Storting) elections. The Labor Party improved on its 1989 results, winning 37 percent of the vote and 67 seats. It had captured 34.3 percent of the vote and 63 seats in 1989. Labor emerged from the elections with nearly twice the seats of its nearest rival, the Center Party.

1993 Parliamentary Election Results

Party	% Votes	Seats
Norwegian Labor Party (DNA)	37	67
Center Party (SP)	17	32
Conservative Party (H)	17	28
Socialist Left Party (SVP)	8	13
Christian People's Party (KFP)	8	13
Progress Party (FP)	6	10
Others	7	2
Total Seats		**165**

Note: Percentages may not add up to 100 due to rounding.

Even though Labor scored well in 1993, the most dramatic gains were made by the anti-EU Center Party, which nearly tripled its share of the vote from 6.5 percent to 17 percent, securing 32 seats in 1993 compared with just 11 four years earlier. The Center Party is now Norway's leading opposition party.

On the losing side, the pro-EU Conservatives declined markedly from 22.2 percent of the vote and 37 seats in 1989 to 17 percent and 28 seats in 1993. The Progress Party also stumbled, dropping from 13 percent of the vote and 22 seats in 1989 to only 6 percent and 10 seats in 1993. Support for the Christian People's Party (KFP) and the Socialist Left (SVP) also declined somewhat, with the KFP winning 13 seats compared with 14 in 1989 and the SVP winning 13 seats compared with 17 in 1989.

One seat each went to the Liberals and the Red Electoral Alliance. Neither party had captured any seats in 1989.

With these results, the incumbent minority Labor government continued to rule with the tacit support of other smaller parties on an issue-by-issue basis. The bad news for the Labor Party was that the nonsocialist parties continued to hold a majority of parliamentary seats. On the issue of Norway's membership in the EU, the surge in support of the anti-EU Center Party did not bode well for Prime Minister Brundtland's desire to join the EU by 1995. Recent opinion polls suggest growing public opposition to EU membership.

Political Background. Following the collapse of Conservative prime minister Jan Syse's minority coalition government on October 29, 1990, Labor's Gro Harlem Brundtland was once again named prime minister, returning her to the position she had held briefly in 1981 and again from 1986 to 1989. Syse's alliance with the Christian People's Party and the Center Party had dissolved over disagreements about the proposed signing of the European Economic Area agreement and about joining the EU.

Norway has consistently had a high percentage of women in top government positions. Brundtland's 1990 cabinet had women occupying nine of the nineteen ministerial positions. In addition, 59 of the 165 Storting members—or 36 percent—were women.

At one time or another, women have assumed leadership positions in all the country's major political parties. After 1990, the Labor, Conservative, and Center parties—which represented 70 percent of the voters—were headed by Gro Harlem Brundtland, Kaci Kullmann Five, and Anne Inger Lahnstein, respectively. Brundtland has been at the helm of the Labor Party, Norway's largest, since 1981. Five replaced Syse as head of the Conservatives in April 1991 after Syse's government collapsed, but she has since been replaced. Lahnstein has guided the Center Party since March 1991.

A New King. On January 17, 1991, Norway's longstanding monarch, King Olav V, died of a heart attack. After serving as monarch since 1957, King Olav was succeeded by his third oldest child, Harald, because the law at the time favored male succession to the throne. The law has since been changed.

1989 Parliamentary Elections: When Losing Means Winning

Norwegian voters in 1989 were tough on the establishment parties of the center-right and center-left. The ruling Labor Party and the opposition Conservatives both took a drubbing at the polls, while the parties on the extremes surged.

Up to that time, Norwegian politics had been fairly predictable and consensus-oriented. Domestically, the Welfare State had become establishment dogma for most parties, and in foreign policy

Past Parliamentary Election Results

	1989		1985		1981		1977	
	% Votes	Seats	% Votes	Seats	% Votes	Seats	% Votes	Seats
DNA	34	63	41	71	37	66	42	76
SP	7	11	7	12	4	11	8	12
H	22	37	30	50	32	53	25	41
SVP	10	17	6	6	5	4	4	2
KFP	9	14	8	16	9	15	10	22
FP	13	22	4	2	4	4	2	0
Others	5	1	2	0	9	2	9	2
Total Seats		165		157		155		155

Note: Percentages may not add up to 100 due to rounding. DNA = Norwegian Labor Party, SP = Center Party, H = Conservative Party, SVP = Socialist Left Party, KFP = Christian People's Party, FP = Progress Party.

NATO served as a solid anchor. As the 1980s ended, however, the consensus seemed to be fraying around the edges. Norwegian politics was becoming increasingly fragmented. Parties espousing nationalistic issues and opposing "big government" policies were gaining greater support at the polls.

In 1989, Labor had its worst showing since 1930, declining from 41 percent of the vote in 1985 to 34 percent in 1989. The Conservatives did even worse. Their share of the vote dropped more than 8 percent, down from 30 percent in 1985 to 22 percent in 1989.

Despite that miserable showing, the Conservatives were able to muster sufficient active and passive support from enough parties elected to the Storting to unseat the incumbent Labor-led coalition and assume power. The nonsocialist bloc eked out a fragile 3-seat majority in the 165-seat Storting, but it was forced to rely uncomfortably on support from Carl Hagen's extreme-right Progress Party. The Progress Party more than tripled its share of the vote from 1985 to 1989, climbing from less than 4 percent to 13 percent and from 2 seats to 22.

While the fringe right was siphoning support from the center-right, the fringe left was doing the same to the center-left. The

Socialist Left doubled its share of the vote and almost tripled its harvest of seats, jumping from 6 to 17.

After weeks of negotiations, the new Conservative prime minister, Jan Syse, managed to form a three-party minority coalition that directly controlled a mere 62 seats of the 165-member Storting. While keeping Hagen's Progress Party out of the government, the coalition of the Conservatives, the Christian People's Party, and the Center Party depended on the Progress Party's 22 votes to stay in power.

The Campaign. The 1989 campaign centered on two main issues—immigration policy and whether Norway should reconsider joining the European Community (EC). On both issues, the Progress Party's Carl Hagen set the agenda and the tone of the campaign, forcing other parties to respond to his pointed opposition.

The two issues were actually related. At the time, only 2.5 percent of the Norwegian population was foreign-born. Should the parliament decide to reverse the 1972 referendum against joining the EC, this would very likely encourage a greater influx of "foreigners" into Norway. This created an emotional debate about the anticipated free flow of workers from Spain, Portugal, and Greece—all EC-member countries with relatively high unemployment and comparatively lower standards of living than Norway.

The political forces opposed to EC membership were strengthened considerably by the election results. The Social Left, Progress, and Center parties were staunchly anti-EC. Despite the support of the Conservative Party for Norway's eventual membership in the EC, Prime Minister Syse had to appease his coalition partners by not moving forward with any plans in that direction. Eventually, differences over EC policy led to the fall of the Syse government.

ELECTION LEXICON

Arctic Gibraltar: British term for Spitsbergen, an island on an arctic Norwegian colony, because the area is very close to the sea lanes connecting the former Soviet Union's northern ports and the Atlantic Ocean.

Ballyhoo entertainer: Popular description of the campaign style of Carl Hagen, chairman of the Progress Party.

Bible belt: The southwest coast line of Norway, where the residents are religious and politically conservative. This is an area of growing support for the Progress Party.

"Conservative Party of Progress": How the Conservative Party defines itself. It wants to project an image of being a modern, forward-thinking party.

Fixed term: A constitutional provision that prevents the king from dissolving the parliament before the end of its four-year term. This enables minority governments to be quite stable and long-lived, unless parliament itself opts to pass a "no-confidence" measure.

Free grasp: Reference to the lack of a tight economic policy during the government of Conservative Kaare Willoch from 1984 to 1986.

Ghetto schools: The schools predominantly attended by immigrant children. The term is used to point out one of the problems that result from concentrating immigrants in one area of a city.

"The Green Goddess": Nickname given to Prime Minister Gro Harlem Brundtland when she was a minister for the environment. She passionately sought protection of the Norwegian forests.

"De gronne vaerdier": "The green values," a slogan of the Center Party, reflecting the party's environmental sensitivity.

Hoyre: Literally, "right." Reference to the Conservative Party, often known simply by the initial "H."

"Hoyre taler for dig": "The right speaks for you," a slogan of the Conservative Party.

Landsmodern: Literally, "The mother of her country." Prime Minister Brundtland's nickname in Labor Party circles.

Lillehammer: Host city for the 1994 Winter Olympics.

"Nej til Formynderstaten": "No to the guardian state," a slogan of the Progress Party.

Nordic Council: An organization created in 1952, consisting of the parliaments and cabinets of Denmark, Finland, Iceland, Norway, and Sweden. Its goal is to coordinate policy on economics, foreign affairs, social welfare, and cultural affairs. It has succeeded in facilitating substantial uniformity in the legislation of these countries.

Nuclear-free zone: A proposal, supported by the parties on the left, that Norway should join with the other Scandinavian countries to establish a zone that would be devoid of nuclear weapons.

Nynorsk: "New Norwegian," a dialect spoken in the rural areas. It is associated with the language of the common, country person as opposed to that of the inhabitants of Oslo and other urban centers. Nynorsk speakers tend to support traditional Norwegian values, are religious, favor prohibition of alcohol, and are anti-EU.

Quisling: Major Vidkun Quisling's name has become synonymous with *"traitor"* because he collaborated with the Nazis during their occupation of Norway in World War II. Prime Minister Quisling was executed in 1945.

Storting: The 165-seat bicameral Norwegian parliament.

"Tryghed i hjem, skole og samfund": "Security in the home, school, and community," a slogan of the Christian People's Party.

"Work shy": Carl Hagen's expression for many unemployed people who stay on welfare and take advantage of Norwegian generosity.

HISTORICAL SYNOPSIS

After centuries of battle for autonomy from Denmark and Sweden, the Norwegians achieved a parliamentary government in 1884 and independence from Sweden in 1905. Norway, Denmark, and Sweden remained neutral during World War I.

1940-1945	Norway is occupied by Germany.
1942	Major Vidkun Quisling becomes prime minister.
1945	Labor Party wins absolute majority of seats in parliament and forms government under the leadership of Prime Minister Einar Gerhardsen.
1949	After two years of failing to create a Nordic Defense Union, Norway enters NATO as a founding member.
1961	Labor Party loses its majority in the Storting.
1963	A "no confidence" vote replaces Labor with a Conservative government.
1971	Conservative coalition is defeated largely over the question of whether Norway should apply for membership in the EC.
1972	In a referendum on EC membership, 53 percent of the Norwegian voters vote against joining.
1990	King Olav V has a stroke and his son Harald assumes most of the king's obligations. A law is passed that states that the oldest child of the king, regardless of sex, is next in line for the throne. This applies only to children born after 1990. Jan Syse's nonsocialist coalition government collapses. Gro Harlem Brundtland becomes prime minister for the third time.
1991	King Harald V becomes king after King Olav V dies of a heart attack in January.
1993	Brundtland's Labor government gains ground in elections and retains power, but the anti-EU Center Party surges past Conservatives to become largest opposition party in parliament.
1994	In November referendum, voters defeat (52.8 percent to 47.2 percent) Norway's proposed entry into the European Union.

Portugal

The Country in Brief

Official Name: Republic of Portugal (*República Portuguesa*)
Capital: Lisbon
Currency: Escudo
National Day: June 10 (birthday of Luis de Camoes)
Language: Portuguese
Religion: Roman Catholic
Memberships: NATO and EU
Border Country: Spain
Embassy in Washington, D.C.: 2125 Kalorama Road, N.W., 20008. Telephone: (202) 328-8610.

Political Profile

Government Type: Presidential/parliamentary democracy
Head of State: President Mário Soares
Political Party: Socialist Party
Assumed Office: February 1986
Election Method: Majoritarian/second ballot
Term of Office: Five years
Reelected: 1991
Next Election: 1996
Head of Government: Prime Minister Anibal Cavaco Silva
(announced he will not seek reelection in 1995)

Political Party: Social Democratic Party
Assumed Office: 1985
Reelected: 1987, 1991
Legislature: Unicameral. Assembly of the Republic, 230 members (deputies), elected by proportional representation.
Term of Office: Four years
Last Election: 1991
Next Election: 1995

Comparative Data

Population: 9.9 million
GDP: $68.9 billion
GDP Per Capita: $6,100
Voting System: Party list proportional (no threshold)
Per Capita Representation Rate: 43,000
Big Government Index: 38.7%
Women in Parliament: 9%
Voter Turnout Rate: 68%

MAJOR POLITICAL PARTIES

Social Democratic Party
(*Partido Social Democrata*, PSD)

The PSD is a moderate, reformist, Social Democratic party, founded in 1974 as the Popular Democratic Party. The PSD leader since 1985 has been Prime Minister Anibal Cavaco Silva, who has enjoyed majority support in parliament since 1987 and has pursued a pro-private enterprise economic policy designed to boost productivity and investment.

Portuguese Socialist Party
(*Partido Socialista Português*, PSP)

Founded in 1875, the PSP has been one of the two largest parties in Portugal since the evolution toward democracy in 1974. The

PSP emphasizes the need for greater social justice and effective cooperation between government and the private sector.

Portuguese Communist Party
(Partido Comunista Português, **PCP)**

A hardline Stalinist party, the PCP was declared illegal until 1974, when it became a major force in the military and government. The PCP's share of the vote declined steadily throughout the 1980s.

MINOR POLITICAL PARTIES

Democratic Renewal Party
(Partido Renovador Democrático, PRD)
National Solidarity Party (*Partido Solidariedade Nacional*, PSN)
Popular Democratic Union (*União Democrático Popular*, UDP)
Popular Monarchist Party (*Partido Popular Monárquico*, PPM)
Portuguese Democratic Movement
(Movimento Democrático Português, MDP)
Social Democratic Center Party
(Partido do Centro Democrático Social, CDS)
Unified Democratic Coalition
(Coligação Democrático Unitária, CDU)
United Workers' Organization
(Organização Unida de Trabalhadores, OUT)

ELECTION REVIEW

1991 Presidential Election:
Cohabitation, Portuguese Style

On January 13, 1991, Socialist Mário Soares was easily reelected to a second five-year term as president. On October 6, Prime Minister Anibal Cavaco Silva, a Social Democrat, also coasted to victory in the parliamentary elections. Thus, the two leaders—Soares on the center-left and Cavaco Silva on the center-right—

1991 Presidential Election Results

Candidate	First Round (% Votes)
Mário Lopes Soares (PSP)	70
Basilio Horta da Franca (CDS)	14
Carlos Gomes Carvalhos (PCP)	13
Carlos Marques da Silva (UDP)	3

Note: Percentages may not add up to 100 due to rounding. PSP = Socialist Party, CDS = Social Democratic Center Party, PCP = Communist Party, UDP = Popular Democratic Union.

were forced to "cohabit," at least until new parliamentary elections in 1995. From all accounts, cohabitation Portuguese style has worked fairly well.

From the start of the campaign, Soares was the clear favorite—so much so that the Social Democrats (PSD), the majority party in parliament, did not even bother to field a presidential candidate. They decided, wisely, to concentrate on the October parliamentary elections.

The Communist Party (PCP) ran Carlos Gomes Carvalhos, while the more extreme Popular Democratic Union (UDP) nominated Carlos Marques da Silva in the hopes that a good showing would increase its bargaining clout with the PCP for joint lists in the October general election. The Social Democratic Center Party (CDS) sought to profit from the PSD's absence by running Basilio Horta da Franca, a founding member of the CDS. Horta campaigned against government corruption and pointed a finger directly at Soares.

Despite the large lineup of candidates, Soares commanded 70 percent of the vote in the first round of balloting, thus making a runoff unnecessary.

In the presidential election of 1986, Soares became Portugal's first civilian president in sixty years when he defeated Freitas do Amaral (51 percent to 49 percent) in the February 16 runoff. Soares united the left and center-left vote but, abandoning his Socialist Party label, declared himself to be "president of all the Portuguese."

1991 Parliamentary Election Results

Party	% Votes	Seats
PSD	50	135
PSP	29	72
CDU	9	17
CDS	4	5
PSN	2	1
Others	6	0
Total Seats		**230**

Note: Percentages may not add up to 100 due to rounding. PSD = Social Democratic Party, PSP = Socialist Party, CDU = Unified Democratic Coalition, CDS = Social Democratic Center Party, PSN = National Solidarity Party.

1991 Parliamentary Elections

The October 6 elections resulted in an unprecedented second majority win for the Social Democratic Party, giving rise to the fear that Portugal was becoming a one-party state. A democratically elected party had not won two consecutive absolute majorities since the founding of the republic eighty-one years earlier. To many, that kind of stability was reminiscent of the previous fascist dictatorship. Thus, the rival Socialists, despite holding the presidency, expressed concern that one-party rule by the Social Democrats was a danger to democracy. Voters obviously did not agree.

The Social Democrats received 50.4 percent of the vote, yielding 135 of the 230 seats in the assembly. (The number of seats in the Assembly of the Republic was reduced from 250 to 230 following the 1987 elections.) This resounding victory was attributed to the steadiness of Cavaco Silva's free market policies, economic privatization, and the encouragement of private initiative and foreign investment.

The Socialist Party made gains in 1991, garnering 29.3 percent of the vote and 72 seats compared with 22.2 percent and 60 seats 1987. One reason for the continued inability of the Socialists to overtake the Social Democrats was that both parties agreed on most key issues, such as the economy and the European Union. During this election, the Socialist Party tried to distinguish itself by emphasizing its concerns about social issues like health care, housing, education, and income inequalities.

1987 Parliamentary Elections

Prime Minister Anibal Cavaco Silva's Social Democrats captured an absolute majority of votes in the 1987 parliamentary elections, an astonishing feat given Portugal's history of democratic political instability.

Political Background. Portugal's first taste of democracy came in 1910 when the monarchy was overthrown following the 1908 assassination of King Carlos I and the crown prince. The ensuing Portuguese Republic had forty-five governments in fifteen years, finally giving way to an authoritarian "corporative" state led by economist António de Oliveira Salazar. The nearly bloodless coup of April 25, 1974, known as the Carnation Revolution, removed Salazar's successor, Marcello Caetano, from office. The provisional military government soon fell and was replaced by a parliamentary democracy, which although popular has not always been the picture of stability.

The 1987 elections were called two years early because former President Ramalho Eanes's small, left-of-center party, Democratic Renewal, sponsored a motion of censure that toppled Prime Minister Cavaco Silva's right-of-center minority government. Instead of asking the leftist majority in parliament to form a new government, Socialist president Mário Soares agreed with Cavaco Silva's call to dissolve parliament and hold early elections.

The timing of the 1987 elections certainly suited Cavaco Silva's purposes. With the economy in a strong growth cycle and the excitement surrounding Portugal's entry into the European Community, the prime minister was dealt an unbeatable hand to play. Throughout the campaign, there was never any doubt that the Social Democrats would remain the largest party. The only real question was whether they would win enough votes to form a majority government.

Past Parliamentary Election Results

Party	1987 % Votes	1987 Seats	1985 % Votes	1985 Seats	1983 % Votes	1983 Seats
PSD	50	148	30	88	28	75
PSP	22	60	21	57	37	101
CDU/APU [a]	12	31	16	38	19	40
CDS	4	4	10	22	13	30
PRD	5	7	18	45	—	—
Others	7	0	5	0	3	4
Total Seats		**250**		**250**		**250**

Note: Percentages may not add up to 100 due to rounding. PSD = Social Democratic Party, PSP = Socialist Party, CDU = Unified Democratic Coalition, APU = United People's Alliance, CDS = Social Democratic Center Party, PRD = Democratic Renewal Party.

[a] The CDU was part of the United People's Alliance until it dissolved in 1986; figures for 1987 are CDU only.

They did. The Social Democrats gained dramatically from 30 percent of the vote in 1985 to 50 percent in 1987. With 148 of its 250 seats in the hands of the Social Democrats, the parliament elected in 1987 was the first Portuguese parliament to complete a full four-year term.

The 1987 elections were considered crucial because, as a new member of the then European Community (EC), Portugal was going through a difficult period of social and economic adjustment. As the EC's least developed economy, Portugal desperately needed to catch up with the rest of Western Europe.

Leaders from across the political spectrum agreed that Portugal needed swift and sweeping political, economic, and social change to move ahead.

The Campaign. The 1987 parliamentary election was the seventh in Portugal since the fall of the fascist regime. While sharp ideological clashes marked the first years of democratic rule, the clear trend of political power seemed to be toward the center and away from the extremes.

During the campaign, Prime Minister Cavaco Silva freely criticized his opponents for their obstructionist tactics. He placed himself above the fray as the political leader who stood for the national interest. He skillfully positioned himself as the candidate who would be able to alleviate the national inferiority complex created by Portugal's ranking as the poorest country in Western Europe. The slogan "Portugal Cannot Stop" exploited the political capital built up during Cavaco Silva's eighteen months as prime minister.

An exceptionally favorable set of economic circumstances clearly swung votes in Cavaco Silva's direction. The U.S. dollar was weak, interest rates were low, and import costs—owing to the drop in oil prices—were falling. For an economy that imports 90 percent of its energy requirements, the drop in oil prices provided a major boost to the government's anti-inflation strategy. Cheaper imports helped keep price rises down to a little more than 10 percent in June. Cavaco Silva was able to paint a favorable picture of stabilizing prices, rising investment, growth in output, and job creation.

Cavaco Silva's "politics of success" had a positive influence on an important group of voters: the "floating voter." Close to 2 million individuals—25 percent of the electorate—switched their votes between 1985 and 1987. The expanding floating vote—identified as young, urban, and predominantly female—became a primary target for the parties during the campaign.

The second largest party, the Socialists had only recently emerged from an internal battle to succeed Mário Soares, their popular party leader who had been elected president of Portugal in 1986. The new secretary general, Vitor Constâncio, had not yet consolidated his authority as undisputed party leader.

The Socialists seemed to expect a victory by the Social Democrats, so they concentrated on fending off the challenge from the Democratic Renewal Party for the center-left vote and establishing their credentials as the main opposition party.

1994 European Parliament Elections

With the allocation of an additional seat, Portugal had 25 seats in the EP. The opposition Socialists won 10 of the seats and nearly 35

European Parliament Election Results

	1994		1989		1987	
Party	% Votes	Seats	% Votes	Seats	% Votes	Seats
PSP	35	10	29	8	23	6
PSD	34	9	33	9	37	10
CDS	12	3	14	3	15	4
Others	19	3	24	4	25	4
Total Seats		**25**		**24**		**24**

Note: Percentages may not add up to 100 due to rounding. PSP = Socialist Party, PSD = Social Democratic Party, CDS = Social Democratic Center Party.

percent of the vote to inch ahead of the ruling Social Democrats, who won 9 seats and 34.3 percent. This represented a substantial drop below the Social Democrats' 1991 general election showing when they won 50.4 percent of the vote.

The Social Democratic Center Party won 12.4 percent of the vote and 3 seats on an anti-EU platform. A new Communist-Green alliance secured the support of 11.2 percent of the vote, entitling it to 3 seats.

ELECTION LEXICON

Agrarian reform: After 1974, sweeping agrarian reform collectivized many private estates, but these collective farms proved inefficient. Throughout the 1980s and 1990s ongoing efforts have been made to decollectivize farming in favor of more private enterprise.

Carnation Revolution: Name given to the nearly bloodless coup in 1974 that overthrew the fascist dictatorship established in 1932 by António Salazar.

Classe politica: The political class, well-connected technocrats who get government jobs.

"Cunhal the Vampire": Unflattering reference to Communist Party leader Alvaro Cunhal's prominent eye teeth. Cartoonists often portrayed him as a vampire.

"Entra e sai": Literally, "entrance and exit." Portuguese expression referring to the "revolving door" between government and private sector jobs.

Estada novo: The "new state" established in 1932 by Salazar.

Estoril Accord: 1991 accord, with Portugal acting as mediator, that ended the sixteen-year civil war in Angola.

IMF: International Monetary Fund. To qualify for IMF economic assistance, Portugal has had to submit to austerity programs, including reducing government spending and raising taxes. IMF-imposed austerity measures are a frequent topic of political dialogue.

Junta of National Salvation: Formed in 1974 by members of the Carnation Revolution, this revolutionary group granted Portuguese colonies the right of self-determination, disbanded the secret police, and permitted political exiles to return to Portugal.

Lajes Accord: Agreement, first signed in 1951, that allows the United States to lease military bases in the Azores.

Movimento das forças armadas: Movement of the Armed Forces, an illegal group of lower-ranking military officers that opposed the fascist regime and instigated the 1974 coup.

"Poor man of Europe": Unflattering description of Portugal as the least economically advanced country in the European Union.

Portugal and the Future: Influential book by military hero General António de Spinola. It advocated a political solution to the colonial wars that played such a large part in the downfall of the dictatorship.

"Portugal cannot stop": Prime Minister Anibal Cavaco Silva's campaign slogan during the 1987 parliamentary election.

Retornados: The half million Portuguese living in the colonies who returned to live in Portugal after the colonies won self-determination in 1974.

Royal presidency: Term used to describe President Mário Soares's style in office. Observers liken it to that of a monarch.

"Second Salazar": Derogatory allusion to fascist dictator Salazar, referring to Prime Minister Cavaco Silva's seemingly unshakeable grip on political power.

"Small body with a big head": Popular expression referring to the power amassed by politicians in Lisbon, even though Portugal is such a small country.

Soares o sempre em pie: Literally, "Soares always lands on his feet." Familiar expression alluding to Mário Soares's uncanny ability to survive politically.

"Trial of the century": The term used by the press to describe the nineteen-month trial of General Otelo Saraiva de Carvalho for his continuing support of leftist revolution. De Carvalho and 47 codefendants were convicted in May 1987 of belonging to the terrorist organization Popular Forces of April 25, which was accused of assassinating at least fifteen businessmen and landowners and staging attacks on the U.S. embassy, NATO warships, and the residences of German airmen.

25th of April: Date of the 1974 Carnation Revolution.

Ultramar: Portugal's once-extensive overseas colonies. All but Maçao, a tiny island off the coast of China, have since been granted independence from Portuguese rule. Technically, Portugal still controls Portuguese Timor, but it was annexed by Indonesia in 1976.

"Uncle Mário": Nickname for President Mário Soares, who has cultivated a fatherly image as "president of all Portuguese," even renouncing his Socialist Party ties.

União National: The National Union, the only legal political party in Portugal during the Salazar years.

HISTORICAL SYNOPSIS

While the monarchy of Portugal (known in antiquity as Lusitania) existed more or less uninterrupted until the early part of the twentieth century, attempts toward representative government appeared as early as 1822 with the introduction of a liberal constitution with limited democracy.

1908	King Carlos I and crown prince are assassinated.
1910	King Carlos's eldest son is overthrown; the Portuguese Republic is established.
1926	After Portugal has forty-four civilian governments in fifteen years, army officers overthrow civilian government and establish a one-party dictatorship.
1932	António de Oliveira Salazar is named prime minister and establishes the *estado novo* ("new state").
1936	Salazar sends "Portuguese Legion" of 6,000 troops to fight on the side of General Francisco Franco's forces in the Spanish Civil War.
1949	Portugal becomes founding member of NATO.
1955	Portugal is admitted into the United Nations.
1960s	Portuguese colonies stage series of uprisings. Portugal becomes embroiled in various colonial wars.
1968	Marcello Caetano succeeds Salazar and retains single-party dictatorship.
1974	In Carnation Revolution, the Armed Forces Movement overthrows Caetano regime. The new government, with strong Marxist leanings, promises to decolonize.
1975	Most Portuguese colonies have won independence. Portugal holds its first free election in more than fifty years. Voters give overwhelming support to three moderate parties and reject the Marxist regime. Lt. Col. Ramalho Eanes puts down leftist coup attempt.
1976	Voters approve new constitution and Eanes is elected president.
1982	Portugal adopts new constitution, amending Constitution of 1976 by toning down Marxist rhetoric and abolishing the military Council of the Revolution.
1985	Social Democrat Anibal Cavaco Silva becomes prime minister and forms minority government.
1986	Socialist Mário Soares, a three-time prime minister, is elected as modern Portugal's first civilian president. Portugal is admitted into the European Community.

1987   No-confidence vote forces Cavaco Silva to hold elections. Cavaco Silva's Social Democrats win absolute majority in parliament and form Portugal's first majority government.

1991   Soares easily wins reelection as president. Cavaco Silva's Social Democrats again win absolute majority in parliamentary elections.

1994   With various minor governmental scandals and the prolonged recession sapping Prime Minister Silva's popularity, Silva announces that he will not seek reelection in 1995 and instead opt to run for president in 1996.

Spain

The Country in Brief

Official Name: Kingdom of Spain (*Reino de España*)
Capital: Madrid
Currency: Peseta
National Day: October 12 (Columbus Day)
Languages: Spanish, Basque, Catalan, Galician
Religion: Roman Catholic
Memberships: NATO and EU
Border Countries: Andorra, France, Morocco, Portugal
Embassy in Washington, D.C.: 2700 15th Street, N.W., 20009.
Telephone: (202) 452-0100.

Political Profile

Government Type: Constitutional monarchy/parliamentary
democracy
Head of State: King Juan Carlos I
Succeeded to Throne: 1975
Head of Government: Prime Minister Felipe González
Márquez
Political Party: Socialist
Assumed Office: 1982
Reelected: 1986, 1989, 1993
Legislature: Bicameral, Cortes (Courts)

Upper Chamber: Senate (*Senado*), 256 members, 208 directly elected and 48 designated by the seventeen autonomous regional legislatures.

Term of Office: Four years

Lower Chamber: Congress of Deputies (*Congreso de los Diputados*), 350 members, elected by proportional representation.

Term of Office: Four years

Last Election: 1993

Next Election: 1997

Comparative Data

Population: 39 million

GDP: $526 billion

GDP Per Capita: $12,600

Voting System: Party list proportional

Per Capita Representation Rate: 112,000

Big Government Index: 36%

Women in Parliament: 16%

Voter Turnout Rate: 70%

MAJOR POLITICAL PARTIES

Except for a smattering of regional and nationalist parties, Spain effectively has two main parties—the Spanish Socialist Workers' Party and the Popular Party.

Spanish Socialist Workers' Party (*Partido Socialista Obrero Español*, PSOE)

The Spanish Socialist Party, founded in 1879 and currently led by four-time prime minister Felipe González Márquez, has been a major force in Spanish politics since the 1930s. It has been Spain's largest party since 1977. The PSOE seeks a classless society based on democratic principles, liberalization of divorce and abortion laws, and continued Spanish integration into the European Union.

Popular Party (*Partido Popular*, PP)

The Popular Party was founded in 1976 as the Popular Alliance, which emerged as a right-wing challenger to the ruling Union of the Democratic Center (UDC). The party changed its name to the Popular Party in 1989 and moved slightly toward the center as a moderate alternative to the PSOE. The PP stands for traditional family values, public order, the middle classes, and free enterprise.

MINOR POLITICAL PARTIES

Basque Nationalist Party (*Partido Nacionalista Vasco*, PNV)
Basque Solidarity (*Eusko Alkartasuna*, EA)
Canarian Coalition (*Coalición Canaria*, CC)
Convergence and Union *(Convergència i Unió*, CiU)
Democratic and Social Center
   (*Centro Democrático y Social*, CDS)
Socialist Democracy *(Democracia Socialista*, DS)
Spanish Communist Party
   (*Partido Communista de España*, PCE)
United Left (*Izquierda Unida*, IU)
United Socialist Party of Catalonia
   (*Partit Socialista Unificat de Catalunya*, PSUC)

ELECTION REVIEW

1993 Parliamentary Elections:
How Low Can González Go?

The ten-year trend was not encouraging for the ruling Socialists (PSOE). Since 1982, when the party captured an astonishing 202 of the 350 seats in the Congress of Deputies, the PSOE had received a declining share of seats in each subsequent election: 184 in 1986 and 175 in 1989, when they just squeaked by with exactly half the seats. A further decline seemed inevitable in 1993.

1993 Parliamentary Election Results

Party	% Votes	Seats
Socialist Party (PSOE)	39	159
Popular Party (PP)	35	141
United Left (IU)	10	18
Convergence and Union (CiU)	5	17
Basque Nationalist Party (PNV)	1	5
Democratic and Social Center (CDS)	1	0
Others	9	10
Total Seats		350

Note: Percentages may not add up to 100 due to rounding.

The big surprise of the June 6, 1993, election was not the Socialists' continued slide, but that they managed—just barely—to retain power. Felipe González, the incumbent prime minister and PSOE leader, unexpectedly came out on top in the election with 38.7 percent of the vote and 159 seats. This margin was shy of an absolute majority but still made the PSOE the largest party in the Congress of Deputies. His fourth straight election victory allowed González to remain the EU's only Socialist prime minister (Andreas Papandreou of Greece joined González in this category following his election victory in September 1993).

To find a parallel to Spain's election result, one must look outside the EU to Norway. The outcome of the Norwegian elections of September 13, 1993, was strikingly similar: An incumbent Socialist regime winning just enough seats to continue in office as a minority government.

On the Spanish right, the Popular Party continued its upward climb, winning 34.8 percent of the vote and 141 seats in 1993 compared with 25.8 percent and 106 seats in 1989. Despite these gains, Popular Party supporters were disappointed. Pre-election polls had indicated that the party might emerge from the election as Spain's largest.

That was not to be, but the party's dramatic improvement was sure to make life more difficult for the ruling Socialists, who were forced to rely on the tacit support of other parties to remain in office. The possibility of an early election could not be ruled out, and the Popular Party certainly would benefit from such a development.

The other parties winning seats in 1993 included the United Left (IU) with 10 percent of the vote and 18 seats, the Catalan Convergence and Union (CiU) with 5 percent of the vote and 17 seats, two Basque nationalist parties together won 7 seats, and the Canarian Coalition secured 4 seats.

The Democratic and Social Center (CDS) lost all 14 of its 1989 seats, continuing its decline since former prime minister Adolfo Suarez resigned as CDS leader.

Background. The Spanish economy has grown impressively in the late 1980s, averaging more than 5 percent a year. However, unemployment still hovered close to 20 percent and inflation was above 7 percent. The real issue facing Spain in the coming election was how to maintain economic growth and distribute the wealth more equitably. The Popular Party suggested extensive privatization, tax cuts, and reducing social security contributions while raising pensions and benefits. The Socialists proposed moderate changes in welfare programs, continuing integration with Europe, and infrastructure projects. In the end, the Socialists attracted just enough votes to stay in power.

1989 Parliamentary Elections: González Hangs On

The European Community's youngest democracy held elections in 1989, eight months early, because the ruling Socialists, anticipating an economic downturn in the near future, opted to face the voters sooner rather than later. It is a testament to Spain's resilience as a still-new democracy that Spanish voters betrayed no sense of crisis. They calmly went to the polls to exercise their democratic privilege in what was only the fifth national election since the death of longtime dictator, General Francisco Franco Bahamonde.

Campaigning officially began on October 10, 1989, just nineteen days before the election. The only real question at the outset was whether the Socialists, led by popular incumbent prime minister Felipe González, would maintain their absolute majority in

Past Parliamentary Election Results

Party	1989 % Votes	1989 Seats	1986 % Votes	1986 Seats	1982 % Votes	1982 Seats	1978 % Votes	1978 Seats
PSOE	40	175	44	184	48	202	31	121
PP/AP	26	106	26	105	27	106	7	9
IU	9	17	4	7	4	4	11	23
CiU	5	18	5	18	4	12	3	8
CDS	8	14	9	19	3	2	—	—
PNV/EA	1	5	2	6	2	8	2	7
UCD	—	—	—	—	7	12	35	168
Others	11	15	10	11	5	4	11	14
Total Seats		**350**		**350**		**350**		**350**

Note: Seats may not add up to 100 due to rounding. PSOE = Socialist Party, PP = Popular Party, AP = Popular Alliance, IU = United Left, CiU = Convergence & Union, CDS = Democratic and Social Center, PNV = Basque Nationalist Party, EA = Basque Solidarity, UCD = Union of the Democratic Center.

Congress. In the end, the Spanish electorate returned González to office, but they denied him the outright majority in parliament that observers felt was of great psychological importance.

González was able to form a government, having captured 40 percent of the vote and 175 seats, but it was clear that his Socialist Workers' Party (PSOE) was losing ground, threatened from the right and the left. In this election the Communist alliance, known as the United Left (IU), gained 10 seats, bringing their total representation to 17. The conservative Popular Party (PP), which appeals to a middle class that feels overburdened by taxes, climbed slightly from 105 to 106 seats.

The PSOE in the early 1990s were not able to reverse the downward trend in their vote totals largely because the government was forced to follow an austere economic program during the critical period leading toward the European Single Market of 1992. This meant tightening credit to slow inflation and halt the growing trade deficit. These measures jeopardized the Socialist

European Parliament Election Results

Party	1994 % Votes	1994 Seats	1989 % Votes	1989 Seats	1987 % Votes	1987 Seats
PP	40	28	22	15	26	17
PSOE	31	22	40	27	42	28
IU	13	9	6	4	5	3
CDS	1	0	7	5	9	7
Others	15	5	25	9	18	5
Total Seats		**64**		**60**		**60**

Note: Percentages may not add up to 100 due to rounding. PP = Popular Party, PSOE = Socialist Party, IU = United Left, CDS = Democratic and Social Center.

Party's already tenuous hold on the rank-and-file workers who had always been its main supporters. To make matters worse, the popular González had hinted broadly that he might retire from elective politics.

1994 European Parliament Elections

Spain was alloted 4 additional seats in the new parliament, raising its total to 64.

When the balloting was completed, the opposition Popular Party had captured an impressive 40.2 percent of the vote and 28 seats—a gain of 13—in the June Euro-elections. In the process, the Popular Party dealt the ruling Socialist Party its first major defeat in many years. In winning only 30.6 percent of the vote (compared with 39 percent in the general election of 1993), the Socialists lost 5 of their previous 27 seats.

The Communists and allied left parties, known as the United Left (IU), increased their vote totals. The IU captured 13.4 percent of the vote and 9 seats—a 5-seat increase. Continuing to collapse as a political force, the Democratic and Social Center lost all 5 of its Euro-seats. The remaining 5 seats went to the Covergence and Union, Basque Nationalist, and Canarian Coalition parties.

ELECTION LEXICON

Blue-collar frustration: Term used to describe workers' frustration at not enjoying the fruits of the Spanish economic boom. This phenomenon is widespread and is credited for the Socialists' continuing loss of popularity.

"El Caudillo": Literally, "The Leader." A familiar term for former dictator General Francisco Franco.

Las Cortes: The bicameral parliament.

ETA: Euskadi tu Askatasnna (Basque Country and Freedom), a Basque Catholic nationalist terrorist group.

Falange Española: "Spanish Phalanx," the fascist political party governing Spain during the Franco era. It was the only legal political organization at that time.

Fontaneros: Literally, "hydraulic engineers." Reference to the behind-the-scenes players who actually do all the work and make the government function.

Fraga "Ceiling": The upper level of support it was assumed that the Popular Party (PP) could never exceed because its former president, Manuel Fraga, was best known for being a minister under Franco. Fraga had been regarded as the PP's biggest handicap in attracting greater support at the polls. In 1993, the Popular Party made dramatic gains under the leadership of José María Aznar.

El Golpe: Name for the attempted coup in 1981.

Herri Batasuna: The political wing of the Basque nationalist movement.

Izquierda Unida: Literally, "united left." An electoral coalition involving the Communists and various small left-leaning parties.

Kuwait Investment Office: After the abrupt withdrawal of extensive Kuwaiti holdings in Spain in 1992, the Popular Party demanded that a complete parliamentary inquiry be conducted. The Popular Party suspected that the ruling Socialist Party had allowed Kuwaitis to evade Spain's foreign investment laws.

Law of Fundamental Reform: The 1976 government proposal that changed Spain from the corporatist arrangement based on functional representation under Franco to a parliamentary democracy. The referendum held on December 15, 1976, was a precursor to the 1978 constitution.

Moncloa Palace: The prime minister's residence outside Madrid.

Socialist Democracy: A faction within the Socialist Workers' Party that emerged just before the 1989 election campaign and became a separate party in 1990. The group accused González of being too stubborn and conservative.

Tener Enchufas: "To have connections," a reference to having the right "connections" to find gainful employment.

23F: Reference to the large national strike held February 23, 1982 (thus, 23F). Following this, when there is a strike, it is referred to by the date, followed by the letter of the month. For example, the strike of December 14, 1988, is referred to as 14D.

HISTORICAL SYNOPSIS

The Spanish Empire reached its height during the latter half of the sixteeth century, began to decline, and lost its throne to the Bonapartes in 1808. The country regained its sovereignty in the Peninsular War five years later but lost its major colonies at the end of the century.

1914–1918	Spain remains neutral during World War I.
1931	King Alfonso XIII flees the country, and Spain becomes a democratic republic.
1936	The elections of 1936 produce a strong majority for the Popular Front. General Francisco Franco leads a rebellion against the republican government. The Spanish Civil War begins.
1939	Franco wins the civil war and becomes dictator of Spain.

1947	In a referendum, Spanish voters approve Franco's proposed succession law and reestablish Spain as a monarchy.
1955	Spain is admitted to the United Nations.
1969	Franco and the Cortes designate Prince Juan Carlos Alfonso Victor María de Borbón to become king at the end of Franco's rule.
1975	Franco dies on November 20. Seven days later, Juan Carlos is proclaimed king of Spain. Spain begins setting up a new democratic government to replace Franco's dictatorship.
1978	Spanish voters approve a new democratic constitution.
1982	Spain joins NATO. Socialist Felipe González wins the parliamentary election and forms a government.
1986	Spain, along with Portugal, joins the European Community. In June, voters approve a referendum to remain in NATO but, like France, outside its military command. González is returned to power in the parliamentary elections, although his majority in parliament is reduced.
1989	González wins again, but with exactly half of the seats in parliament, just enough to form a government.
1992	Spain ratifies the Maastricht Treaty on European Union.
1993	On September 6, the Socialists, led by González, secure 159 seats in the Congress of Deputies and form a minority government based on support from smaller parties.
1994	Ongoing political scandals continue to rock and weaken, but fail to unseat, the Socialist government.

Sweden

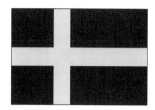

The Country in Brief

Official Name: Kingdom of Sweden (*Konungariket Sverige*)
Capital: Stockholm
Currency: Krona
National Day: June 6 (National Day)
Language: Swedish
Religion: Swedish Lutheran
Memberships: Non-NATO
Border Countries: Denmark, Finland, Norway
Embassy in Washington, D.C.: 600 New Hampshire Avenue, N.W., 20037. Telephone: (202) 467-2600.

Political Profile

Government Type: Constitutional monarchy/parliamentary democracy
Head of State: King Carl XVI Gustaf
Succeeded to the Throne: September 19, 1973
Head of Government: Prime Minister Ingvar Carlsson
Political Party: Social Democratic Party
Assumed Office: 1994 (also prime minister from 1986 to 1991)
Legislature: Unicameral. Riksdag, 349 members, elected by proportional representation; 310 members are elected from twenty-eight constituencies and 39 seats come from national pool to

provide greater proportionality to all parties reaching the 4 percent threshold.
Term of Office: Three years
Last Election: 1994
Next Election: 1997

Comparative Data

Population: 8.6 million
GDP: $235 billion
GDP Per Capita: $26,700
Voting System: Party list proportional (4% threshold)
Per Capita Representation Rate: 25,000
Big Government Index: 64% (1989)
Women in Parliament: 41%
Voter Turnout Rate: 86%

MAJOR POLITICAL PARTIES

Social Democratic Party
(*Socialdemokratiska Arbetareparti*, SD)

Founded in 1889, the Social Democratic Party has been the dominant party in Swedish politics for many decades. It has been in government, often as the leading or only ruling party, every year except nine since 1932. The party advocates a fully developed welfare state and an equal distribution of wealth and power. It seeks to achieve these ends through a mixed economy guided by central planning and government regulations. The party supports a nuclear-free zone in Scandinavia, nuclear arms reduction, and peaceful settlement of disputes.

Moderate Coalition Party (*Moderata Samlingspartiet*, M)

The Moderate Coalition Party was founded in 1904 and has become the largest nonsocialist party in recent years. Its voter support has fluctuated between around 12 percent to just above 20 percent. The Moderates advocate a free market economy and individual freedom, but allow a role for limited government regulation to safeguard the public welfare.

Center Party (*Centerpartiet*, C)

Formed as a rural-based party in 1910, the Center Party advocates an economy based on free enterprise and competition. It opposes cartels and monopolies and promotes diversity in industry and decentralization of power. Personal initiative, entrepreneurship, and small business ventures are encouraged. It strongly opposes nuclear power.

Liberal People's Party (*Folkpartiet Liberalerna*, FP)

Founded in 1934, the Liberal People's Party advocates a socially oriented market economy. It supports a free market economy but believes the state should act as a check on the undesirable tendencies of unbridled capitalism to protect the society as a whole.

Left Party (*Vänsterpartiet*, VP)

This party was formed in 1917 as the Left Social Democratic Party, but changed its name to the Communist Party in 1921, the Left Party-Communists in 1967, and to just Left Party in 1990. It is one of the oldest Communist parties in the world and has been represented in the Riksdag throughout its history. Moderate in ideology, the Left Party has been a passive partner to many Social Democratic governments—never holding ministerial power but voting with (or at least not against) the Social Democrats in government.

MINOR POLITICAL PARTIES

Christian Democratic Community Party
  (*Kristdemokratiska Samhällspartiet*, KDS)
Green Ecology Party (*Miljöpartiet de Gröna*, Greens)
New Democracy (*Ny Demokrati*, NYD)
Communist Workers' Party
  (*Arbetarepartiet Kommunisterna*, APK)

ELECTION REVIEW

1994 Parliamentary Elections: A Move to the Center-Left

In September 1994, Swedish voters did just as all the pre-election opinion polls predicted: They returned former Social Democratic prime minister Ingvar Carlsson to power, ending the three-year conservative coalition government of Prime Minister Carl Bildt. The Social Democrats (SD) won 45 percent of the vote, more than 7 points better than their dismal 1991 showing of 37.6 percent. This gave them 161 seats, just 14 short of the 175 seats they needed for an absolute majority in parliament. The Left Party (VP) secured 22 seats, while the environmentalist Greens won 18 seats. Altogether, these three parties of the center-left won a total of 201 seats—a whopping 47-seat gain from 1991.

This shift was at the expense of the center-right parties, which suffered a stunning setback. Prime Minister Carl Bildt, the chairman of the Moderate Coalition Party, was forced to relinquish the reins of government. He had headed the government since 1991, when a four-party coalition government was formed by the Moderates, the Liberal People's Party, the Center Party, and the Christian Democratic Community Party. The Moderates held their own in the election, retaining the 80 seats they had won in 1991, but the Liberal, Center, and Christian Democratic parties lost 7, 4, and 11 seats, respectively. The right-leaning New Democracy Party failed to clear the 4 percent threshold, thus losing all 25 seats it had captured in the previous election. Altogether, the center-right parties lost 47 seats, from 195 in 1991 to 148 in 1994.

The percentage of women elected to the Swedish parliament rose dramatically in 1994, increasing from 34 percent to 41 percent. This was spurred largely by the policy of the Social Democrats requiring a fifty-fifty balance between men and women among its office holders.

1991 Parliamentary Elections: Carl Bildt's Conservative Coalition

Except for a six-year hiatus beginning in 1976, the Social Democratic (SD) juggernaut had controlled the government for more

1994 Parliamentary Election Results		
Party	% Votes	Seats
Social Democratic Party (SD)	45	161
Moderate Party (M)	22	80
Center Party (C)	8	27
Liberal Party (FP)	7	26
Left Party-Communist (VP)	6	22
Greens	5	18
Christian Democratic Party (KDS)	4	15
New Democracy (NYD)	1	0
Others	2	0
Total Seats		349

Note: Percentages may not add up to 100 due to rounding.

than half a century. But in 1991, led by Prime Minister Ingvar Carlsson, the Social Democrats went down to defeat.

In fact, the popularity of the SD had been declining steadily leading up to the September 15, 1991, elections. In 1989, favorable ratings for the SD were at 40 percent—not very good and declining fast.

Two reasons for the slide stand out. First, a new centrist party had emerged. New Democracy became a convenient populist protest party, draining away disgruntled SD supporters. Second, Prime Minister Carlsson was not highly popular. He was viewed as a rather colorless and uncharismatic figure.

In order to counter the rise of the New Democracy movement in the center, the ruling SD tried to co-opt some traditionally nonsocialist issues, like supporting cuts in marginal income tax rates and postponing the planned phaseout of nuclear energy, reversing a longstanding policy that would have shut down two reactors in 1995-1996 and the remaining ten by 2010.

The Social Democrats also announced support for Sweden's entry into the EU, a commitment to fighting inflation, and the intention to cut back and restructure some elements of Sweden's vaunted welfare state. Despite these efforts, the SD had a hard time convincing voters that the party truly had changed its ways.

Voters blamed the SD's policies throughout the 1980s for causing many of the economic problems that Sweden had faced in the 1990s.

The SD was not the only party to seek out middle-of-the-road positions. In fact, since most of the parties seemed to agree on most issues, one political commentator called the election a "campaign in felt slippers."

While moving to the center on many issues, the SD oddly refused to drop a high-profile, Socialist-sounding scheme that engendered a good deal of controversy. They proposed allowing five government-owned National Pension Insurance Funds to buy shares in publicly traded Swedish companies. These merged funds would be allowed to invest up to 60 percent of the assets in company stock, raising the specter of publicly owned private companies. The idea was seen by many as a kind of backdoor nationalization program. It was great campaign fodder for the various nonsocialist parties, who were quick to label it "a relapse into socialism."

Another factor in the Social Democrats' defeat was the apparent willingness of the largest nonsocialist parties to form a coalition. For decades, the inability of the opposition to unite gave the SD an open playing field for governing. Carl Bildt, the Moderate Party leader, and Bengt Westerberg, leader of the Liberal People's Party, announced in October 1990 that they agreed on many major issues such as EU membership, tax cuts, public-sector savings, deregulation, privatization, and the continued operation of nuclear power plants. In April 1991, they announced an economic plan called "A New Start for Sweden."

Results. In the end, the Social Democratic Party suffered its worst defeat since 1928, winning just 37.6 percent of the vote and 138 seats, down from 43.2 percent of the vote and 156 seats in 1988.

Carl Bildt's Moderate Party gained ground, collecting 21.9 percent of the vote and 80 seats in 1991 compared with 18.3 percent and 66 seats in 1988. The Center, Liberal, and Left (former Communists) parties all declined in both percentage of votes and seats won. The Green Party, which had shocked the political establishment in 1988 by winning 5.5 percent of the vote and 20 seats, failed to clear the 4 percent threshold in 1991.

Past Parliamentary Election Results

Party	1991 % Votes	1991 Seats	1988 % Votes	1988 Seats	1985 % Votes	1985 Seats	1982 % Votes	1982 Seats
SD	38	138	43	156	45	159	46	166
M	22	80	18	66	21	76	24	86
C	9	31	11	42	12	44	16	56
FP	9	33	12	44	14	51	6	21
VP	5	16	6	21	5	19	6	20
KDS	7	26	3	0	2	0	1	0
NYD	7	25	—	—	—	—	—	—
Greens	3	0	6	20	2	0	—	—
Total Seats		349		349		349		349

Note: Percentages may not add up to 100 due to rounding. SD = Social Democratic Party, M = Moderate Party, C = Center Party, FP = Liberal Party, VP = Left Party, KDS = Christian Democratic Party, NYD = New Democracy.

Two upstart parties scored major gains. The New Democracy Party, with 6.7 percent of the vote, won 25 seats. The Christian Democratic Party, which had been trying for thirty years to clear the threshold for entering parliament, garnered 7.1 percent of the vote and 26 seats.

When all the votes were tallied, the three center-left parties (Social Democratic, Left, Green) won 45.6 percent of the 1991 vote and 154 seats. This compares unfavorably with their showing in 1988, when these three parties collected 54.6 percent of the vote and 197 seats.

The 1991 vote totals pointed to a rightward shift in Swedish politics. The five nonsocialist parties that won seats in parliament in 1991 (Moderates, Liberals, Center, Christian Democrats, and New Democracy) secured 53.3 percent of the vote and 195 seats, compared with 44.7 percent of the vote and 152 seats in 1988 (New Democracy had not been formed in 1988).

After the 1991 elections, King Gustaf asked Moderate leader Carl Bildt to form the new government. The new ruling coalition included the Moderates, Liberals, Center Party, and Christian Democrats, but it was also forced to rely on New Democracy to either vote for government proposals or abstain.

The Bildt government's priorities included joining the EU and revitalizing the economy through deregulation, tax cuts, and by introducing the idea of choice into the state welfare system.

SWEDEN JOINS THE EUROPEAN UNION

On November 13, 1994, 52.2 percent of Swedish voters cast ballots in support of Sweden's entry into the European Union. The historic referendum, in which 82 percent of eligible voters participated, meant that Sweden joined Finland and Austria as the three newest EU members, effective January 1, 1995.

The urbanized southern half of the country, geographically and economically more closely bound to Europe, out-voted the rural, pro-neutralist north.

The pro-EU vote was a victory for Social Democratic prime minister Ingvar Carlsson, who urged reluctant Social Democrats to vote "yes." The party had been split on the issue for years.

Oddly, Sweden now becomes a member of EU but not of NATO, while its Nordic neighbor Norway remains a NATO member but voted on November 28, 1994, against joining the EU. Hence, Sweden retains a measure of military neutrality, and Norway clings to a degree of economic independence.

ELECTION LEXICON

All These Days: Title of former finance minister Kjell-Olof Feldt's book, which features the memoirs of his government years from 1982 to 1990. Published just prior to the 1991 election, the book accuses the ruling Social Democrats of not taking advantage of the devaluation of the Krona policy, which he created. He said the government waited too long to cut back the public sector and shift national resources to industry.

AMS: *Arbetsmarknadsverket,* the Labor Market Board, composed of employers and trade union representatives. AMS is a key element of the "Swedish Model" (*see below*). It is the agency that carries out Sweden's system of centralized collective bargaining and administers the entire labor market, including retraining programs and active recruitment for vacancies nationwide.

"A new start for Sweden": The economic program unveiled by the alliance of the Moderate and Liberal parties in April 1991.

Bert & Ian: Reference to Bert Karlsson and Ian Wachtmeister, leaders of the New Democracy Party. They are sometimes referred to as "the odd couple."

Bofors: A major scandal involving this weapons-producing company and a questionable 1985 arms transfer to India. The scandal caused considerable embarrassment to the government, especially in view of Sweden's international posture and reputation of supporting arms reduction and the peaceful settlement of disputes.

"Campaign in felt slippers": Phrase used to describe the rather sedate election campaign of 1991.

Chernobyl: Site of the Soviet nuclear power plant accident, which caused enormous anxiety about contamination in Sweden. This incident dramatized the environmental issue and helped the Greens enter parliament in 1988.

"Comrade 4 Percent": Nickname for the Social Democrats who traditionally vote for the Left Party (formerly the Communist Party) in order to help the party make it over the 4 percent threshold, thus giving the SD enough support in parliament to form a government.

"Concrete Party": A Green-inspired derogatory term for the Social Democrats, referring to the party's alleged past neglect of the environment.

Consensus: Swedish-style politics relies upon a degree of conciliation and consensus that exists in few other countries.

Dead seals: The mysterious epidemic that struck Sweden's seal population along the western coast also had a profound political effect. Leading up the 1988 election, news programs routinely showed footage of dead seals on the shoreline, heightening environmental concerns that were already elevated due to the Chernobyl accident.

Ebbe Carlsson Affair: The bizarre, private investigation conducted by Ebbe Carlsson, apparently with the knowledge and support of the Swedish justice minister, into the assassination of Prime Minister Olof Palme.

"Evergreen issues": The perennial social and economic issues in Swedish politics, such as taxes, unemployment insurance, and health care.

Freedom: As a backlash against big government, there is an increasing demand in Swedish society that individuals be given greater freedom of choice in many areas of daily life. For instance, Swedes are demanding a greater range of options in choosing doctors, schools, and child care providers.

Lagom: "Just so," a Swedish expression that has political implications, suggesting moderation, balance, and a shunning of extremes.

LO: Landsorganisationen, the powerful Swedish Trade Union Confederation. It consists of twenty-four nationwide unions representing approximately 90 percent of all blue-collar workers.

Lost innocence: Reference to the traumatic murder on February 28, 1986, of Prime Minister Olof Palme, the first Swedish leader assassinated since King Gustaf III was shot in 1792 and the first European head of state to be killed in office in forty-seven years. Until the assassination, Swedes had considered their country somehow immune from the plague of violence in other parts of the world. The botched investigation into the murder did little to restore the country's self-confidence.

"Middle way": Reference to Sweden's unique approach to socialism, a kind of "market socialism."

Mistrust of politicians: Because the investigation into the assassination of Prime Minister Olof Palme was handled so poorly, many Swedes came away with a very cynical and distrustful attitude toward politicians.

National Pension Insurance Funds: Social Democrats proposed using these funds to buy stock in publicly traded companies. The nonsocialist parties accused the SD of using these funds as a back-door approach to nationalization.

New Democracy: A new populist political party formed in 1991 as a type of centrist protest party. It received enough votes in the 1991 election to enter parliament.

Neutrality: A fundamental principle of Sweden's foreign policy. Following this policy, Sweden has been at peace since 1814. The decision to join the EU cast some doubt about the future of strict Swedish neutrality.

Nordic Council: An organization created in 1952, made up of the parliaments and cabinets of Denmark, Finland, Iceland, Norway, and Sweden. Its goal is to coordinate policy on economics, foreign affairs, social welfare, and cultural affairs. It has helped establish substantial uniformity in the legislation of these countries.

Nuclear-free zone: A proposal, supported largely by the parties on the left, that Sweden should join with the other Scandinavian countries to establish a zone that would be devoid of nuclear weapons.

Ombudsman: A uniquely Swedish invention, which has been copied elsewhere, where the Riksdag appoints independent officers to respond to citizen concerns and complaints and launch investigations into official actions. Ombudsmen are elected by the parliament for four-year terms.

Pettersson, Christer: Man convicted of assassinating Prime Minister Olof Palme in 1986. He claimed he was innocent. A judicial tribunal later overturned his conviction because of lack of evidence.

Regering: Swedish for "government." The Swedish government consists principally of the prime minister and his or her cabinet. Most power rests in this body.

"Relapse into socialism": Slogan used by nonsocialist leaders to describe the proposal by the Social Democrats to use National Pension Insurance Funds to buy stock in publicly traded companies.

Riksdag: The 349-member, unicameral Swedish parliament.

SAF: *Svenska Arbetsgivareföreningen*, the Swedish Employers' Confederation, to which most private-sector employers belong.

Statsminister: The prime minister.

Sveavägen: Name of the street where Prime Minister Olof Palme was assassinated.

Swedish Model: Sweden's famed welfare state coexists with—and is supported by—a market-oriented economy. Key elements of the model include a goal of full employment, elimination of wage differentials, and a redistribution of the wealth through taxes and benefit transfers. At the same time, market forces are allowed to determine which companies fail or thrive, and generous unemployment benefits are matched with equally generous job training and labor marketing assistance.

HISTORICAL SYNOPSIS

Sweden was established as a national state in 1523, following a rebellion against Denmark. In 1809, it adopted a new Instrument of Government, based on a balance of power between the king and parliament. It is the second oldest constitution after that of the United States.

1920	Universal suffrage is adopted.
1939	Sweden declares policy of neutrality during World War II.
1949	Efforts to create a Nordic Defense Community fail as Norway, Denmark, and Iceland join NATO. Sweden continues policy of neutrality.
1960	Stockholm Convention establishes European Free Trade Association.
1969	Olof Palme succeeds Tage Erlander as prime minister.
1971	One-chamber Riksdag is created, replacing the previous two-chamber parliament.
1976	Olof Palme leads Social Democrats to their first loss of power since 1932. Nonsocialist Center Party leader

Thorbjörn Fälldin becomes prime minister, leading a three-party nonsocialist coalition. Four different nonsocialist cabinets rule during the next six years.

1982　The Social Democrats regain power under the leadership of Olof Palme.

1986　Olof Palme is assassinated. Social Democrat Ingvar Carlsson becomes prime minister.

1988　Social Democrats retain power in Sepember elections.

1991　Carl Bildt, leader of the Moderate Coalition Party, leads nonsocialist coalition to victory in parliamentary elections. Bildt becomes first conservative prime minister in sixty-six years. Social Democrats suffer worst electoral defeat in more than a half century.

1994　The parliamentary elections in September result in the return to power of Social Democrat Ingvar Carlsson. On November 13, 52.2 percent of Swedes support the referendum to join the European Union.

1995　On January 1, Sweden (along with Austria and Finland) officially joins the EU.

Switzerland

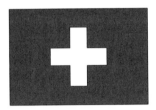

The Country in Brief

Official Name: Swiss Confederation (*Schweizerische Eidgenossenschaft* [German], *Confédération Suisse* [French], *Confederazione Svizzera* [Italian])
Capital: Bern
Currency: Swiss franc
National Day: August 1 (anniversary of the founding of the Swiss Confederation)
Languages: German, French, Italian, Romansch
Religions: Roman Catholic, Protestant
Memberships: Non-NATO (formally applied to join EU, on hold)
Border Countries: Austria, France, Germany, Italy, Liechtenstein
Embassy in Washington, D.C.: 2900 Cathedral Avenue, N.W., 20008. Telephone: (202) 745-7900.

Political Profile

Government Type: Federal republic/parliamentary democracy
Head of State: President Otto Stich
Political Party: Social Democratic Party
Assumed Office: January 1, 1994
Election Method: Presidency rotates yearly among the seven members of the Federal Council (*Bundesrat*).

Term of Office: Four years
Last Election: 1991
Next Election: 1995
Legislature: Bicameral, Federal Assembly
(*Bundesversammlung/Assemblée Fédérale*)
Upper Chamber: Council of States (*Ständerat/Conseil des Etats*), 46 members (two from each of the twenty territorial divisions [cantons] and one each from the six half-cantons), the majority directly elected, but procedures vary in the cantons.
Lower Chamber: National Council (*Nationalrat/Conseil National*), 200 members, directly elected within each canton by proportional representation.
Last Election: 1991
Next Election: 1995

Comparative Data

Population: 6.8 million
GDP: $230 billion
GDP Per Capita: $33,100
Voting System (Lower House): Modified party list proportional/preference voting for individual candidates
Per Capita Representation Rate: 34,000
Big Government Index: 34.2%
Women in Parliament: 18%
Voter Turnout Rate: 47%

MAJOR POLITICAL PARTIES

Switzerland basically has four governing parties: Radical Democrats, Social Democrats, Christian Democrats, and the Swiss People's Party.

Radical Democratic Party (*Freisinnig-Demokratische Partei*, FDP; *Parti Radical-Démocratique*, PRD)

The FDP dates to 1894. In recent years, the FDP has emerged as Switzerland's strongest party. The party believes in individual rights, a free economy, Switzerland's armed neutrality, autonomy for the cantons, and social security.

Social Democratic Party (*Sozialdemokratische Partei*, SPS; *Parti Socialiste/Partito Socialista*, PSS)

The SPS was founded in 1870. After 1991, the SPS emerged as Switzerland's second largest party. Since its party congress in Lugano in 1982, the SPS has been more reformist minded and adopted a less radical Socialist ideology. The party advocates an end to discrimination between the sexes, social justice, world peace, and environmental protection.

Christian Democratic People's Party (*Parti Populaire Democrate-Chretien*, PDC; *Christlichdemokratische Volkspartei*, CVP)

The PDC was formerly known as the Conservative Christian-Social Party, founded in 1912. It is currently Switzerland's third largest party. The PDC advocates strong family life, protection of the individual, a healthy environment, increased aid for the Third World, entry into the United Nations, and disarmament.

Swiss People's Party (*Schweizerische Volkspartei*, SVP; *Parti Suisse de l'Union Démocratique du Centre*, UDC)

Founded in 1971 and formerly known as the Agrarian (or Peasant) Party, the SVP maintains a "liberal" (i.e., conservative) democratic philosophy. The SVP advocates Swiss neutrality, a strong family, and environmental protection.

MINOR POLITICAL PARTIES

Green Party (*Grüne Partei*, GPS; *Parti Ecologiste*, PES)
Independents' Alliance (*Landesring der Unabhängigen*, LdU; *Alliance des Indépendants*, AdI)
Liberal Party (*Liberale Partei*, LPS; *Parti Libéral*, PLS)
Swiss Car Party (*Schweizerische Partei der Autofahreren*, SPA; *Parti Suisse des Automobilistes*, PSA)

Swiss Democrats (*Schweizer Demokraten*, SD;
  Democrates Suisses, DS)
Swiss Party of Labor (*Partei der Arbeit der Schweiz*, PdAS;
  Parti Suisse du Travail, PST)
Ticino League (*Lega dei Ticinesi*, TL)
Vigilance Party (*Parti Vigilance*, PV)

ELECTION REVIEW

1991 Parliamentary Elections: Not Much New, As Usual

In a country ruled by consensus, in a country in which the voter appeal of at least eight parties has not changed more than a few percentage points in forty years, in a country with a semipermanent ruling coalition composed of four parties from both the right and left, little new seems to happen each election. That was true for the most part for the October 20, 1991, elections.

There was a perceptible shift from the center to the right and left in the elections. The ruling four-party coalition was shaken slightly by the loss of 10 seats in 1991 compared with its 1987 showing. But with 149 seats in the 200-seat National Council, the ruling coalition was not threatened with defeat.

The relative support for the parties within the ruling coalition shifted only marginally. Totals for the two largest coalition parties—the Radical Democrats (FDP) and the Christian Democrats (PDC)—declined since the last election. Specifically, the FDP won 21 percent of the vote and 44 seats in 1991 compared with 23 percent and 51 seats in 1987. The PDC garnered 18 percent of the vote and 37 seats in 1991 compared with 20 percent and 42 seats in 1987.

Meanwhile, the other two coalition partners recorded slightly more votes in 1991. The Social Democrats (SPS) won 19 percent of the vote and 43 seats in 1991 compared with 18 percent and 41 seats in 1987. The Swiss People's Party (SVP) held steady, securing 12 percent of the vote and 25 seats, as it had done in 1987.

1991 Parliamentary Election Results

Party	% Votes	Seats
Radical Democratic Party (FDP)	21	44
Social Democratic Party (SPS)	19	43
Christian Democratic People's Party (PDC)	18	37
Swiss People's Party (SVP)	12	25
Greens	7	14
Liberal Party (LPS)	3	10
Independents' Alliance (LdU)	3	6
Others	17	21
Total Seats		**200**

Note: Percentages may not add up to 100 due to rounding.

Thus, the FDP remained the largest party in the National Council with 44 seats, followed by the SPS with 43 seats, the PDC with 37, and the SVP with 25.

No other party in the National Council won more than 10 percent of the vote. The Green Party became the biggest party outside the coalition, picking up 14 seats, a 5-seat increase. The Liberals (10 seats), the Swiss Car Party (8 seats), and the Swiss Democrats (5 seats) all increased their share of representation in the National Council.

The Ticino League, a new nationalist group from the largely Italian-speaking Canton of Ticino, entered parliament for the first time by capturing 2 seats.

Controversy at the Federal Council. While the parliamentary election of 1991 was relatively uneventful, a stir was caused in 1992 when a French-speaking Social Democrat resigned from the Federal Council. The Federal Council functions as Switzerland's executive. It consists of seven members who are elected by and from the Federal Assembly in a joint session of the two chambers.

The same four-party coalition—Radical Democrats (FDP), Christian Democrats (PDC), Social Democratic Party (SPS), and Swiss People's Party (SVP)—has been in power on the federal level since 1959. The FDP, the PDC, and the SPS each have two members on the Federal Council; the SVP supplies the remaining member.

The SPS nonimated French-speaking Christiane Brunner as a replacement for René Felber. She proved to be a very controversial nominee. For starters, she was a woman, and would have been only the second woman ever to serve on the Federal Council. In addition, her lifestyle and manner of dress were a bit too free-wheeling for the political establishment. An outspoken feminist, she had been married three times and an anonymous source claimed to have nude photographs of her. She was also attacked for voting in favor of a 1989 referendum to disband the Swiss Army.

On March 3, 1992, the Federal Assembly voted against Brunner's nomination to join the Federal Council. After the vote, Brunner said, "I am disappointed not for myself, but for all women in Switzerland." Women's groups protested the vote and vowed to continue the battle for equality.

Ruth Dreifuss, another Social Democrat, eventually filled the vacancy, becoming only the second woman on the Federal Council.

1987 Parliamentary Elections:
Greens Gain, Social Democrats Decline

The big story of 1987 was the nearly two-thirds jump in support for the environmentalist Green Party, which increased its share of the vote from less than 3 percent in 1983 to nearly 5 percent in 1987. Its seat count went from 3 to 9 in the 200-seat National Council.

Meanwhile, the Social Democratic Party—one of the "big four" ruling parties—suffered its biggest loss since the proportional representation system began in 1919. The loss continued a downward trend that began in 1975. That year, the party polled just over 25 percent of the vote; in 1979 this slipped to just under 25 percent. In 1983, it fell to below 23 percent. In 1987, the Social Democratic vote plummeted to just over 18 percent, representing a decline of 7 percent in twelve years—a loss of support that by Swiss standards can only be called precipitous.

Past Parliamentary Election Results

Party	1987 % Votes	1987 Seats	1983 % Votes	1983 Seats	1979 % Votes	1979 Seats	1975 % Votes	1975 Seats
FDP	23	51	23	54	24	51	22	47
SPS	18	41	23	47	24	51	25	55
PDC	20	42	20	42	22	44	21	46
SVP	12	25	11	23	12	23	10	21
Greens	5	9	2	3	1	0	—	—
LPS	3	9	3	8	3	8	2	6
LdU	4	8	4	8	4	8	6	11
Others	16	15	14	15	11	15	14	14
Total Seats		200		200		200		200

Note: Percentages may not add up to 100 due to rounding. FDP = Radical Democratic Party, SPS = Social Democratic Party, PDC = Christian Democratic People's Party, SVP = Swiss People's Party, LPS = Liberal Party, LdU = Independents' Alliance.

The four-party coalition suffered a slight loss in the 1987 elections, but they continued to dominate Swiss politics and were able to again elect the ruling Federal Council.

The Kopp Affair. In 1989, the coalition suffered serious embarrassment with the resignation of one of its members, Radical Democrat Elisabeth Kopp, who gained renown in 1984 by being the first female member of the Federal Council. Kopp resigned amidst a drug trafficking/money laundering scandal involving some $1 billion. It was alleged that Kopp, as the head of the Justice and Police Department, breached secrecy rules by warning her husband, Hans, that a company of which he was a board member, Shakarchi Trading, was being investigated. Hans Kopp resigned from the firm two days before the investigation was made public.

Elisabeth Kopp was later acquitted on a technicality. She was replaced on the Federal Council by Radical Democrat Kaspar Villiger. The case caused a good deal of controversy in a country not accustomed to it.

ELECTION LEXICON

Amicable agreement: The principle inherent in Swiss politics of reaching decisions through consensus and decentralization.

"Asylum seekers": Those people seeking refuge in Switzerland. They are often economic and not political refugees.

Availability: This principle of Swiss foreign policy suggests that Switzerland makes herself available to mediate disputes between other countries or parties.

Bundesrat: A seven-member Federal Council exercising executive (presidential) authority on a rotating, one-year basis. The members are elected by the entire Federal Assembly.

Cantonal sovereignty: Each canton enjoys a high degree of independence and self-determination, sharply limiting the role and powers of the central government. The official title of Geneva, for instance, is the Republic and Canton of Geneva.

Fifth Switzerland: Reference to the large population (estimated at almost 400,000) of expatriate Swiss citizens who prefer to live abroad. The other "four" Switzerlands are the major language groups: German, French, Italian, and Romansch speakers.

"First among equals": Reference to the presidency, a one-year assignment that rotates among the seven members of the Federal Council.

Foreign workers: Nearly one-third of the Swiss workforce is comprised of foreign workers, mainly Italians. This has become a major political issue. Two right-wing political parties—the Swiss Republican Movement and the National Action for People and Homeland—have stridently opposed this influx. A 1987 referendum tightened the rules governing both workers and asylum seekers.

International Red Cross: Headquartered in Geneva, this humanitarian organization was founded in 1864 by Swiss philanthropist Henri Dunant. The Red Cross symbol itself was taken directly from the Swiss flag, except the colors are reversed.

"Magic formula": Reference to the method established in 1959 for selecting the seven members (councilors) of the Federal Council. Each of the three largest parties in the National Council gets two members and the fourth largest party gets one. In addition, a canton may not have more than one councilor and at least two councilors must come from the French- or Italian-speaking areas. One councilor usually comes from each of the largest cantons: Zurich, Bern, and Vaud.

Permanent neutrality: A fundamental principle governing Swiss foreign policy. Switzerland declared its neutrality in 1815. This policy has kept Switzerland out of war, including World Wars I and II, for nearly two centuries. It also complicates any effort to establish a closer relationship with the European Union.

Romansch: Switzerland's fourth, and smallest, language minority. Spoken by roughly 50,000 citizens in isolated valleys in the canton of Grisons, Romansch is a Latin-based language that some experts believe is a living linguistic vestige from the late Roman Empire.

Solidarity: Swiss belief that the country has a moral obligation to provide humanitarian assistance to developing nations.

"Switzerland has no army": A group of Young Socialists wanted to have this phrase inserted into the federal constitution. A referendum on November 26, 1989, defeated the proposal, but 35 percent of the voters supported complete abolition of the army.

"Togetherness" Proposition: Referendum defeated in 1981 that would have recognized foreign residents as having rights completely equal to those of Swiss citizens.

Universality: Swiss policy of maintaining diplomatic relations with many nations, regardless of ideology.

HISTORICAL SYNOPSIS

The Swiss Confederation dates back to 1291, when three cantons united to form an "eternal alliance" against the Hapsburgs. The league became formally independent of the Holy Roman Empire at the 1648 Peace of Westphalia, only to be occupied by Napoleon the following century. In 1815, the Congress of Vienna recognized Switzerland's independence and guaranteed its neutrality. A new constitution, modeled after that of the United States, soon followed.

1914–1918	Determined to preserve its neutrality, Switzerland stays out of World War I.
1940–1945	Switzerland remains neutral during World War II.
1959	Four-party ruling coalition government is established and continues to rule without interruption into the 1990s.
1971	Women's suffrage is approved on the national level.
1986	March referendum rejects Swiss membership in the United Nations by three-to-one margin.
1987	By a two-to-one margin, voters approve a referendum that tightens the rules on immigration and political asylum.
1988	Elisabeth Kopp resigns from the Federal Council, the result of scandal.
1989	Voters reject referendum to abolish the Swiss Army.
1991	March referendum lowers the voting age in federal elections from twenty to eighteen.
1992	In May, government applies for membership in the European Union, and voters, in a referendum, approve Swiss membership in the International Monetary Fund and the World Bank. In a setback for the government, voters in a December referendum narrowly reject (50.3 percent to 49.7 percent) Swiss participation in the proposed European Economic Area, linking the European Free Trade Association countries with the European Union. This vote against economic integration with the EU certainly delays and probably derails the idea of Swiss membership in the EU.

Turkey

The Country in Brief

Official Name: Republic of Turkey (*Türkiye Cumhuriyeti*)
Capital: Ankara
Currency: Turkish Lira
National Day: October 29 (proclamation of Republic)
Language: Turkish
Religion: Islam (Sunni)
Memberships: NATO (formally applied to join EU)
Border Countries: Armenia, Bulgaria, Georgia, Greece, Iran, Iraq, Syria
Embassy in Washington, D.C.: 1714 Massachusetts Avenue, N.W., 20036. Telephone: (202) 223-2343.

Political Profile

Government Type: Presidential/parliamentary democracy
Head of State: President Süleyman Demirel
Political Party: True Path (Conservative)
Assumed Office: 1993
Election Method: Elected by Grand National Assembly
Term of Office: Seven years (nonrenewable)
Next Election: 2000
Head of Government: Prime Minister Tansu Ciller
Political Party: True Path (Conservative)
Assumed Office: June 1993

Legislature: Unicameral, Turkish Grand National Assembly (*Türkiye Büyük Millet Meclisi*), 450 members, elected by party list proportional representation.
Term of Office: Five years
Last Election: 1991
Next Election: 1996

Comparative Data

Population: 56.5 million
GDP: $112 billion
GDP Per Capita: $1,900
Voting System: Party list proportional (10% threshold)
Per Capita Representation Rate: 125,000
Big Government Index: 24.1%
Women in Parliament: 2%
Voter Turnout Rate: 92%

MAJOR POLITICAL PARTIES

Turkey's present multiparty system has greatly expanded over the last forty years. Until the 1950s, the Republican People's Party had monopolized political power. The 1982 constitution subsequently widened the political landscape.

True Path Party (*Dogru Yol Partisi*, DYP)

The True Path Party (also known as the Right Path Party) was founded in 1986 from the remnants of the right-of-center Justice Party, founded in 1961. The DYP advocates a program similar to that of the Motherland Party and is viewed as that party's major competitor for right-of-center votes. Unlike the Motherland Party, however, True Path followers prefer a radical free market approach. They have been dubbed "Turkey's new Jacksonians."

Motherland Party (*Anavatan Partisi*, ANAP)

The right-of-center Motherland Party was established May 20, 1983. Its main goal has been establishing an economic program that strikes a balance between the private and public sectors. The party seeks economic growth through targeted investments, encouraging competition, and increasing the role of the private sector. The Motherland Party has initiated sweeping privatization proposals, with the goal of transforming Turkey into a major industrial power.

Social Democratic Populist Party (*Sosyal Demokrat Halkçi Parti*, SHP)

The left-of-center Social Democratic Populist Party emerged in 1985, when it combined forces with several center-left parties, including the Populist Party and the Social Democratic Party. The SHP also attacted a number of former members of Turkey's oldest established political party, the Republican People's Party (which had dissolved in 1981). Like its sister Democratic Left Party, the SHP advocates land reform and a strong central government.

Welfare Party (*Refah Partisi*, RP)

Created by former members of the Islamic National Salvation Party, the Welfare Party is an Islamic fundamentalist party. The RP entered parliament in 1991 with 17 percent of the vote and 62 seats.

Democratic Left Party (*Demokratik Sol Parti*, DSP)

The DSP is another spinoff from the Republican People's Party. Its appeal is mainly among intellectuals, public employees, and trade union members. It advocates a centralized economy and loosening ties with NATO.

MINOR POLITICAL PARTIES

Democracy Party (*Demokrasi Partisi*, DeP)
Great Unity Party (*Büyük Birlik Partisi*, BBP)
Nationalist Action Party (*Milliyetçi Haret Partisi*, MHP)
Nation Party (*Millet Partisi*, MP)

ELECTION REVIEW

1991 Parliamentary Elections: Starting Down the "True Path"

The center-right Motherland Party had reason to be smug about its prospects in the 1991 parliamentary elections. The party held a commanding majority in the Grand National Assembly, and Turgut Ozal, the party's founder, was serving as president of Turkey.

Once the votes were counted in the October 20 election, however, the Motherland Party had not done well. It dropped from 37 percent of the vote and 292 seats in 1987 to a disappointing 24 percent and 115 seats in 1991. That poor showing meant the Motherland Party would not be able to retain its hold on governmental power.

The reigns of power would now be held by the center-right True Path Party, headed by Turkey's legendary political survivor and six-time prime minister, Süleyman Demirel. The True Path Party emerged as Turkey's largest, rising from 19 percent of the vote and 59 seats in 1987 to 27 percent and 178 seats in 1991. Because he lacked a majority in the 450-seat parliament, Demirel had to go shopping for a coalition partner.

Despite ideological similarities, and despite the fact that the Motherland Party's 115 seats would give a Demirel-led government an overwhelming 293-seat majority, joining forces with the Motherland Party was out of the question for the True Path Party. The personal rivalry between Demirel and Ozal was simply too intense for the two leaders to form a coalition government. As it was, Ozal and Demirel would be forced to "cohabit" with each other—Ozal in the presidency and Demirel as prime minister.

Demirel's True Path Party was forced to turn to the Social Democratic Populist Party, which had won 21 percent of the vote and 88 seats. Together, the two parties commanded a solid 266 seats in the 450-member assembly.

Aside from Demirel, the biggest winners in the 1991 elections turned out to be the Welfare Party, led by Islamic conservative Mecmettin Erbakan, and the Democratic Left Party. These two parties managed to clear the 10 percent threshold for entering

1991 Parliamentary Election Results

Party	% Votes	Seats
True Path Party (DYP)	27	178
Motherland Party (ANAP)	24	115
Social Democrat Populist Party (SHP)	21	88
Welfare Party (RP)	17	62
Democratic Left Party (DSP)	11	7
Total Seats		**450**

Note: Percentages may not add up to 100 due to rounding.

parliament. The Welfare Party captured 17 percent of the vote and 62 seats; the Democratic Left Party won 11 percent of the vote and 7 seats. Only three parties received the requisite 10 percent of the vote in 1987. In 1991, five parties conquered the threshold, suggesting a growing volatility in Turkish politics and a dissatisfaction with the status quo.

Aftermath. The new government had plenty of work to do. The coalition's top priorities included attacking the 70 percent inflation rate, cutting the huge budget deficit, and privatizing more state-owned enterprises. Outside the economic arena, the Kurdish insurrection in the southeast grew worse by the day. Turkey was widely criticized for numerous human rights violations.

After the 1991 election, Ozal said he no longer wanted to preside over a government that was not controlled by the Motherland Party. "The Ozal era is finished," he said at one point. "I don't want any role from now on."

But he refused to resign. In 1992, he stated publicly that Motherland Party's leader, Mesut Yilmaz, had been an incompetent foreign minister and that he was an even worse prime minister. Ozal challenged the Motherland Party to dismiss Yilmaz. If they refused, Ozal said he would resign from the presidency to form a rival party composed of Motherland deserters.

End of the Ozal Era. In the meantime, one of Prime Minister Demirel's goals in office was to force Ozal from the presidency.

Demirel stated frequently that the president had usurped too much authority. Demirel wanted to strip the presidency of what he regarded as unconstitutional powers, but taking those actions would have required a constitutional amendment supported by two-thirds of parliament. The Motherland Party had just enough support in parliament to prevent a constitutional change of that type.

What Demirel could not achieve politically was handed to him by fate. Ozal's unexpected death from massive heart failure on April 17, 1993, cleared the way for Demirel's elevation to the presidency. Demirel was elected by the Grand National Assembly and assumed the presidency on May 16, 1993.

Demirel's move to the presidency left the office of the prime minister vacant. This triggered a leadership fight within the True Path Party. On the second ballot, the True Path Party elected Economics Minister Tansu Ciller as its party leader. This, in turn, made Ciller Turkey's first female prime minister.

Ciller vowed to continue the ruling coalition with the Social Democrats, but that task was made much more difficult with the defection of two groups of Social Democratic dissenters. The first of the dissenters was a group of Kurdish Nationalist deputies. The second group left the party to restart one of the parties that had been disbanded by the army in 1980.

As a result of these defections, the True Path Party's majority, which started out at more than 40 seats, was reduced to just 5. The next parliamentary election is not due until 1996.

1987 Parliamentary Elections:
Ozal Wins Two Offices at Once

In the 1987 parliamentary election, Turkey's incumbent prime minister, Turgut Ozal, got a two-for-one deal he could not refuse. He led his Motherland Party to a strengthened majority in the Turkish Grand National Assembly (TGNA). Because the TGNA elects the country's president, Ozal was able to use his party's unassailable majority as a springboard to the presidency in 1989. He was elected president on October 31, 1989, garnering 263 votes on the third ballot. He took office with thoughts of calling the shots from that high office for a secure seven years.

Under the 1982 Constitution, a Turkish president is limited to a single term.

Political Background. The fact that parliamentary elections were even held in 1987 deserves explanation, and so does the fact that political leaders and parties that had been banned in the early 1980s were allowed to compete in the election—Ozal's strenuous objections notwithstanding.

In the late 1970s, Turkey's economy and political apparatus were in serious danger of going into a tailspin of total chaos. Terrorism was rampant. Twenty terrorist killings a day were not uncommon. Inflation was running at 130 percent—and rising. Civilian authorities showed every sign of not being able to cope.

Finally, on September 12, 1980, under the leadership of General Kenan Evren, the military intervened. All administrative power was placed in the hands of the military National Security Council until the political situation could be stabilized. Political parties were dissolved and major party leaders arrested. A ten-year ban on these "pre-1980" party leaders was imposed.

This ban forced a wholesale reshuffling of Turkey's major political parties, as well as the creation of a few new parties. In 1982, a new constitution was approved by referendum and General Evren was simultaneously elected to a single seven-year term as president.

By 1983, the chaos had subsided sufficiently to allow a partial return to civilian rule. In the parliamentary election of that year, Turgut Ozal—who as deputy prime minister had spearheaded Turkey's economic austerity program under General Evren's military government—led his recently established Motherland Party to 46 percent of the vote and a 211-seat majority in the Turkish Grand National Assembly, which contained 400 seats at that time. Although General Evren retained his position as president, Ozal established the first civilian government in years that enjoyed a majority in the TGNA.

A referendum passed narrowly in 1987 lifting the ban on pre-1980 political leaders and parties. Ozal opposed lifting the ban, arguing that a "yes" vote was a vote for a return to the anarchic and violent years of the late 1970s. On the eve of the referendum,

Past Parliamentary Election Results

| | 1987 | | 1983 | |
Party	% Votes	Seats	% Votes	Seats
ANAP	37	292	46	212[a]
SHP	25	99	—	—
DYP	19	59	—	—
RP	—	—	—	—
DSP	—	—	—	—
HP	—	—	29	117
MDP	—	—	22	71
Total Seats		**450**		**400**

Note: Percentages do not add up to 100 because totals are not available for parties not surpassing the 10 percent threshold. ANAP = Motherland Party, SHP = Social Democrat Populist Party, DYP = True Path Party, RP = Welfare Party, DSP = Democratic Left Party, HP = Populist Party, MDP = Nationalist Democracy Party.

[a] Seat total was later reduced from 212 to 211 by the Turkish National Security Council.

Ozal announced that he would schedule new elections in November rather than wait until the end of his term.

Key issues during the campaign included terrorism, Turkey's effort to join the European Community, rising inflation, the privatization plan initiated by the Motherland Party, the dismantling of state industries and the role of Islam—the so-called prayer-rug vote—in the secular state.

Results. Fulfilling expectations, Prime Minister Ozal's Motherland Party won a sizable majority in the newly expanded Turkish Grand National Assembly, garnering 292 of the 450 seats. That impressive result would be considered a landslide were it not for the fact that the Motherland Party's share of the vote actually declined from 46 percent in 1983 to 37 percent in 1987.

Erdal Inönü's Social Democratic Populist Party received 25 percent of the vote and 99 seats, while former prime minister

Süleyman Demirel's True Path Party captured 19 percent of the vote and 59 seats.

The remaining 20 percent of the vote was scattered among the additional four parties on the ballot, none of which attained the 10 percent vote threshold needed to enter the Turkish Grand National Assembly.

President Evren's tenure as president was unaffected by the vote. Yildirim Akbulut, whom Ozal would later tap to become prime minister, was elected speaker of the TGNA.

ELECTION LEXICON

Atatürkism: A unique mixture of secularism, nationalism, and Western orientation that has been the guiding ideology of the Turkish Republic since its founding. This political orientation is named after Kemal Atatürk, founder of the Turkish Republic.

Baba: "Father," what President Süleyman Demirel's followers call him.

Bee: Ari in Turkish, the industrious, productive bee is a symbol of the Motherland Party.

Bridge between East and West: With its Eastern heritage but having opted for Western ideals and values, Turkey regards itself as a unique and valuable geopolitical bridge to further peace and understanding.

Bulgarization: Reference to Bulgaria's suppression in the late 1980s of its Turkish minority by forbidding the use of the Turkish language and hindering the pratice of Islam. Bulgaria began expelling its Turkish minority, while Turkey, economically unable to meet the needs of these refugees, petitioned for UN assistance.

Coffee house: Kahvehane, the culturally and politically important gathering area present in every village. The coffee house is the place where men gather to discuss current topics and where politicians come to make campaign speeches.

"A Greek lake": Reference to the Aegean Sea and the ongoing dispute between Greece and Turkey regarding fishing and mining rights in the Aegean.

"Holy Alliance": Electoral alliance among the right-wing nationalists, the Islamic fundamentalists, and the Motherland Party.

Language Society: Functioning within the framework of the Atatürk High Institution of Culture, Language, and History, this organization has worked since 1932 to reform and purify the Turkish language.

Lemon: Campaign symbol used by Turgut Ozal's opposition, the suggestion being that "Ozal will squeeze you like a lemon"—an allusion to Ozal's economic austerity program.

Meclis: Turkish word for the Turkish Grand National Assembly (TGNA), the country's 450-member unicameral legislature.

Party centers: Each party maintains a party headquarters in every city of any size in the country. Citizens come to the party centers seeking help and favors in return for political support. The party centers symbolize the system of political patronage that is endemic—although hardly unique—to the Turkish political culture.

"Peace at home; peace in the world": Motto of Kemal Atatürk and the ongoing official policy of Turkey.

"Prayer-rug vote": Reference to the fundamentalist Islamic voting bloc.

Secularism: Although the population is 99 percent Muslim, Turkey maintains strict secularism as a fundamental principal of government.

"Still a lot of work left to do": Campaign slogan of the Motherland Party during the 1991 elections.

TRT: Turkish Radio and Television. All political groups with at least ten members have access to free time on the state-run television to criticize or discuss government policies. Televised debates are central to Turkish political campaigns and are of an intensity and vigor that is not seen in the European or American media.

"Trust in Ozal": Campaign slogan of the Motherland Party.

Turban and fez: This traditional headwear, symbols of the old order, have been forbidden since 1925, suggesting the end of class, rank, and religious discrimination.

"Young Turks": Term for the group of liberal reformists who revolted in 1909 and forced Sultan Abdul Hamid to institute constitutional government.

HISTORICAL SYNOPSIS

The present day Turkey is the remaining center of the Ottoman Empire, which was established in 1300 and greatly expanded from 1520 to 1566 by Süleyman the Magnificent to include much of central Europe, North Africa, and the Middle East. Over the years the empire was reduced and it was ultimately dissolved in the aftermath of World War I, following its disastrous alliance with Germany.

1909   Revolt of the liberal "Young Turks." They force Sultan Abdul Hamid to institute constitutional government.

1914–1918   Turkey signs secret pact with Germany, and Allies declare war against Turkey. Ottoman Empire is defeated, dismembered, and Turkey is occupied by Greek and other Allied forces.

1920   National Assembly elects Mustafa Kemal (who later adopts the name Kemal Atatürk) president. Under his leadership, foreign forces are driven from Turkey.

1922   The sultanate, the temporal ruling institution of the defunct empire, is abolished.

1923   Atatürk proclaims the Turkish Republic.

1924   Caliphate, the religious ruling institution associated with the former empire, is abolished. Atatürk launches ambitious reform effort to modernize and industrialize Turkey.

1938   General Ismet Inönü succeeds Atatürk and is reelected three times until his defeat in 1950, when the one-party

	rule of Atatürk's Republican People's Party comes to an end.
1945	Turkey enters World War II, declaring war against Germany and Japan just before the end of the war.
1947	Truman Doctrine is proclaimed, and Turkey, along with Greece, begins to receive large amounts of U.S. military and economic assistance.
1952	Turkey joins NATO.
1960	Military coup overthrows ten-year rule of the Democratic Party.
1961	New constitution establishes Turkish Grand National Assembly (TGNA) and a National Security Council, which gives Turkish military great sway in government.
1965-1971	The Justice Party of Süleyman Demirel holds majority of seats in the TGNA.
1973	Atatürk's Republican People's Party emerges as largest party and Bülent Ecevit becomes prime minister.
1975-1980	Anarchy and terrorist violence spread throughout Turkey. A series of unstable governments, headed alternately by Ecevit and Demirel, are replaced in 1980 by a military government led by General Kenan Evren.
1982	In a nationwide referendum, 91 percent of the electorate approves the new constitution and, simultaneously, elects General Evren president for a single seven-year term and imposes a ten-year ban on "pre-1980" political party leaders from politics.
1983	Formation of new political parties is permitted so long as the founding members were not party leaders or members of parliament before 1980. Turgut Ozal's Motherland Party is formed and wins 211 seats of the 400-member TGNA. Ozal becomes prime minister.
1987	In April, Turkey formally applies to join the European Community, but prospects for acceptance appear dim. In September, a referendum narrowly passes lifting the ban on pre-1980 political leaders. Ozal calls for new national elections, held November 29. Ozal is reelected prime minister.
1989	TGNA elects Ozal president on third ballot.

1991   Elections held on October 20 result in the True Path
Party replacing the Motherland Party as Turkey's
largest party. Six-time prime minister Süleyman
Demirel becomes prime minister again by forming a
coalition with the Social Democrats. Demirel vows to
force President Ozal from office.

1993   President Ozal dies on April 17 and is succeeded on
May 16 by Prime Minister Süleyman Demirel. On July
5, Tansu Ciller is elected Turkey's first female prime
minister.

1994   Turkey's economic crisis intensifies, as inflation
reaches triple digits, threatening to undermine the
Ciller government and force new elections. The prime
minister manages to survive politically and enters 1995
looking as if her government might last until new elections in 1996.

United Kingdom

The Country in Brief

Official Name: United Kingdom of Great Britain and Northern Ireland
Capital: London
Currency: Pound Sterling
National Day: Ruling monarch's birthday
Languages: English, Welsh, Gaelic
Religions: Church of England, Presbyterian, Roman Catholic
Memberships: NATO and EU
Border Countries: Ireland; France lies south across the English Channel and Strait of Dover
Embassy in Washington, D.C.: 3100 Massachusetts Avenue, N.W., 20008. Telephone: (202) 462-1340.

Political Profile

Government Type: Constitutional monarchy/parliamentary democracy
Head of State: Queen Elizabeth II
Succeeded to Throne: 1952
Head of Government: Prime Minister John Major

Political Party: Conservative
Assumed Office: 1990
Term of Office: Five years
Last Election: 1992
Next Election: 1997
Legislature: Bicameral, Parliament
Upper Chamber: House of Lords, 1,194 peers, approximately two-thirds are hereditary while one-third are created appointments.
Lower Chamber: House of Commons, 651 members, directly elected using the winner-take-all voting system.
Term of Office: Five years
Last Election: 1992
Next Election: 1997

Comparative Data

Population: 57.4 million
GDP: $1 trillion
GDP Per Capita: $17,000
Voting System: Winner-take-all plurality/single-member districts
Per Capita Representation Rate: 90,000
Big Government Index: 39.8%
Women in Parliament: 9%
Voter Turnout Rate: 76%

MAJOR POLITICAL PARTIES

National party organizations influence the selection of candidates and the governing of the country far more in the United Kingdom than in the United States. Once these national organizations have approved the candidates selected by the local affiliates, the candidates are expected to adhere strictly to national party manifestoes in their campaigns. Similarly, after being elected, British members of parliament almost invariably vote as instructed by party leaders.

Conservative Party (CP)

Since 1979, the United Kingdom has been governed by the Conservative Party (formally known as the Conservative and Unionist Party), first under the leadership of Prime Minister Margaret Thatcher and now under John Major. Often obscured by the many twists and turns of its long history (going back to the seventeenth-century Tories), the Conservative Party's philosophy has been the defense of tradition and the unity of society against utopian social engineering and divisive class conflict. Such a vague ideology allows for a variety of permutations. Under Thatcher and Major, the party has stood for vigorous competition in the economy, including free trade with other countries, the curtailment of trade union power, and a rather stern attitude toward those on welfare (referred to as "the dole"), all positions that would have horrified Tories at various times in the past—not to mention so-called Wet Tories of the present.

Labour Party (LP)

The Labour Party has been the United Kingdom's second largest party since the 1920s. It was formed in the early 1900s by a fusion of Socialist intellectuals and the trade union movement, with the former providing an ideology that promised to advance the interests of the latter. This ideology has provided a fairly cohesive program for the party but can also paralyze it when that program collides with political or economic reality. Although the party's recent leaders have been comparatively moderate, the party and its sometimes strident Socialist ideology have inspired more suspicion than confidence in the electorate.

Liberal Democratic Party (LDP)

In early 1981, tensions between "fundamentalist" Socialists and moderates within the Labour Party led four prominent Labour leaders to form the Social Democratic Party (SDP), which called for more decentralization and more attention to creating growth in the economy and a proportional voting system. Shortly thereafter, the Social Democrats worked out an agreement with the Liberal Party to campaign together in general elections.

The Liberal Party, with roots in nineteenth-century laissez-faire capitalism, had evolved to the point that it agreed with the SDP on a number of issues: support for state intervention to achieve worthy social goals, but with an emphasis on individuals, rather than their "guardians" in government and the trade unions. Together, these two parties formed the Alliance, which contested the 1983 and 1987 elections and later collapsed. The Alliance evolved into the current Liberal Democratic Party, which has emerged as a strong third party in British politics.

Any third party in Britain faces an uphill struggle to gain not just power but credibility. The first-past-the-post electoral system is a virtually insurmountable obstacle for any third party, even a proven vote-getter like the Liberal Democrats, to overcome. The results of the 1983 elections dramatize the difficulty. That year the Liberal-SDP Alliance polled an astounding 25.4 percent of the total vote, compared with 27.6 percent for Labour. However, the Alliance only won 23 seats in parliament, whereas Labour captured 209 seats.

MINOR POLITICAL PARTIES

Green Party (GP)
Scottish National Party (SNP)
UK Independence Party (UKIP)
Ulster Unionist and Loyalist (UUL)
Welsh Nationalist Party (*Plaid Cymru*, WNP)

ELECTION REVIEW

1992 Parliamentary Elections:
Major Wins a Narrow Victory

According to all the opinion polls, John Major and his Conservative (Tory) Party were destined to lose the parliamentary election on April 9, 1992. After all, the Tories had been in power for

1992 Parliamentary Election Results		
Party	% Votes	Seats
Conservatives	42	336
Labour	34	271
Liberal Democrats	18	20
Others	6	24
Total Seats		651

Note: Percentages may not add up to 100 due to rounding.

thirteen years. The country was going through a bad recession. Unemployment had reached 10 percent. All signs pointed to a Labour victory. At the very least, Labour could expect to join with the Liberal Democrats to form a coalition government.

But it was not to be. A higher than expected turnout—combined with last-minute fears about Labour's possible high-taxing, Socialist intentions—tipped the scale in favor of the Conservatives.

Both Labour and the Tories waged campaigns that raised fears among the voters. The Tories claimed that the economy, already plagued by the longest recession since the 1930s, would get even worse under a Labour government. Labour countered that the Tories were planning to dismantle the National Health Service.

The third party in the race, the Liberal Democrats, campaigned almost exclusively on the issue of changing the electoral system to proportional representation. Paddy Ashdown, the Liberal Democratic Party leader, said that in the event of a hung parliament, the Liberal Democrats would insist on voting system reform as its price for joining a government coalition.

With polls showing that the Liberal Democrats were pulling support away from the Tories, Chris Patten, chairman of the Conservative Party, told millions of television viewers that a vote for the Liberal Democrats was tantamount to a vote for Labour and could lead to a Labour government. That line of attack against the Liberal Democrats, raising the specter of a Labour government, seemed to have the desired effect.

Defying the odds, the Conservatives escaped with a narrow victory. It was their fourth consecutive "minority" government and the longest winning streak in British politics since the 1820s. It was also the closest general election in a generation.

When the dust settled, the Conservatives had won 336 seats in the House of Commons on the strength of 42 percent of the vote. In 1987, the Conservatives won a similar percentage of the vote but 40 more seats than they did in 1992. The Labour Party, although denied victory, improved on its dismal 1987 results, winning 34 percent of the vote and 271 seats. In 1987, Labour collected only 31 percent of the vote and 229 seats.

Meanwhile, the Liberal Democrats earned 20 seats with 18 percent of the 1992 vote. This showing compares with the similar performance of the Liberal Democratic precursor, the Alliance, which garnered 22 seats and 22.5 percent of the vote in 1987. All told, the Tory majority had declined to a mere 21 seats in 1992.

The outcome left all sides scratching their heads and wondering how the opinion polls could have been so wrong. A number of explanations have been advanced for the embarrassing failure of the poll-takers. The unexpectedly high turnout probably had an effect. These late-to-decide voters, by and large, supported the Conservatives due to fear about the Labour Party's proposed tax plan. In addition, some voters may have decided to punish Labour because the party appeared to predict a Labour victory before the voters had a chance to vote.

Background: Thatcher Dispatched. The second half of 1989 and the first half of 1990 had not been an easy time for Margaret Thatcher. The Conservatives took a drubbing in the June elections to the European Parliament. Following that debacle, Thatcher decided to do some house cleaning. No one was prepared for the complete renovation of July 1989, when thirteen of twenty-two Cabinet posts were refilled. Perhaps the most startling step was the removal of the widely respected Geoffrey Howe from the post of foreign secretary.

Howe was regarded by many as too supportive of further economic integration with Europe. This was followed by Nigel Lawson's resignation as chancellor of the Exchequer, comparable to a combination of the U.S. Treasury secretary and director of the Office of Management and Budget. John Major replaced him, and a few other posts had to be refilled to round out the cabinet. Thatcher may have had succession on her mind when she elevated the relatively youthful Major to the Exchequer post.

Lawson's surprise resignation on October 26, 1989, caused a major uproar. He had raised nettlesome issues involving Britain's role in the European Community. Lawson had long been lobbying Thatcher on the benefits of a pro-European policy, but Thatcher would not budge. She remained steadfastly suspect of the exchange rate mechanism of the European Monetary System (EMS). Thatcher's view of the entire EC-'92 program, which was put forth as a program for economic integration, differed sharply from other European leaders and many leading political figures in Britain. She saw the 1992 plan as an opportunity for completely open markets with little or no government regulation; others saw it as opportunity for cooperation with coordinated regulation. Thatcher remained adamantly opposed to the idea of supranationalism.

All this disruption in the Thatcher government gave rise to the obvious question: "Is this the beginning of the end for Thatcher?"

The municipal elections held on May 3, 1990, resulted in widespread losses for Thatcher's Conservatives, but analysts regarded it as less of a drubbing than had been expected. The Labour Party won 42 percent of the vote compared with 31 percent for the Conservatives. Riots in the streets over the unpopular "poll tax" and abysmal approval ratings in the opinion surveys, however, seemed to be loosening Margaret Thatcher's grip on the Conservative Party leadership.

All this disruption led up to Margaret Thatcher's unceremonious demise in November 1990. The proximate cause of Thatcher's defeat was her policy toward Europe. The fatal blow came when Sir Geoffrey Howe delivered a devastating speech in parliament, saying Thatcher's obstructionist policies vis-à-vis Europe carried "serious risks for our nation."

Many Conservatives were itching for new leadership because they believed Thatcher was leading them toward defeat in the next election. The party had been trailing Labour in opinion polls for the last eighteen months. Contributing to the concerns of Conser-

Past Parliamentary Election Results

Party	1987 % Votes	1987 Seats	1983 % Votes	1983 Seats	1979 % Votes	1979 Seats	1974 % Votes	1974 Seats
CP	42	376	42	397	44	339	36	277
LP	31	229	28	209	37	269	39	319
Lib/SDP[a]	23	22	25	23	14	11	18	13
UUL	1	13	1	15	1	10	2	10
Others	3	10	3	6	4	6	5	16
Total Seats		650		650		635		635

Note: Percentages may not add up to 100 due to rounding. CP = Conservative Party, LP = Labour Party, Lib = Liberal Party, SDP = Social Democratic Party, UUL = Ulster Unionist and Loyalist.

[a] There was no SDP prior to 1983; figures for 1979 and 1974 refer only to the Liberal Party.

vatives was the fact that Labour itself had begun to moderate its tone and ideology.

After losing the first round of a party leadership vote among Conservative members of parliament, Margaret Thatcher resigned. On November 27, 1990, the Conservative Party elected Thatcher's protégé and designated successor to lead their party. John Major, at age forty-seven, became prime minister on November 28, 1990.

1987 Parliamentary Election: Thatcher Thrice

After eight years in power, Conservative Prime Minister Margaret Thatcher's unique anti-government, free-market philosophy had produced some amazing results. Under her leadership, the British economy had recovered substantially from the malaise of the 1970s. Going into the 1987 election, Margaret Thatcher was such a dominant force in British politics that her third election as prime minister surprised no one.

On reflection, however, her longevity in office was remarkable. After all, no previous British prime minister had won a third consecutive term in office. In the past, longstanding British governments had frequently fallen victim to the public's desire for change. Even the legendary Winston Churchill was unceremoniously voted out of office just months after V-E Day in 1945.

Not so with Margaret Thatcher. In May 1987, the Tory Party was riding high in the polls and had just done rather well in local elections. Thatcher was eager, as she told her Conservative colleagues, "to get the election behind us." On May 11, she asked Queen Elizabeth II to dissolve parliament and announced that a general election would be held on June 11.

Her confidence was well placed. The Conservatives won the election decisively against a divided opposition.

Results. Thatcher's Conservative Party came out of the election with 376 seats to Labour's 229 and the Alliance's 22, with 23 scattered among other small parties. This was a very comfortable majority, but the Conservatives had declined somewhat from their 1983 totals of 397 seats.

Under the leadership of Neil Kinnock, Labour picked up 20 seats and firmly reestablished itself as the chief opposition party. Within the party, he could claim that the perception of leftist control and especially the suicidal policy of unilateral nuclear disarmament had hurt the party and would continue to do so if he was not permitted to reform matters.

The Alliance's leaders had less reason to celebrate. Labour's success came at the expense of the Alliance. Its strategy had been confused, first attacking the Tories and then switching against Labour without doing either much damage. All the founders of the Social Democratic Party except David Owen had lost their seats in parliament. Within the Alliance, the hand of those who were calling for a formal merger of the SDP and Liberal Party was strengthened, and in fact the merger took place in March 1988, although David Owen and a rump SDP declined to join the new Liberal Democrat Party, led by Paddy Ashdown.

1994 European Parliament Elections

In the June Euro-elections, Prime Minister John Major's Conservative Party suffered a stunning defeat, winning just under 28

European Parliament Election Results

Party	1994 % Votes	1994 Seats	1989 % Votes	1989 Seats	1984 % Votes	1984 Seats	1979 % Votes	1979 Seats
LP	44	62	39	45	35	32	32	17
CP	28	18	33	32	39	45	48	60
LDP[a]	17	2	6	0	19	0	—	—
Others	11	5	22	4	7	4	20	4
Total Seats		87		81		81		81

Note: Percentages may not add up to 100 due to rounding. LP = Labour Party, CP = Conservative Party, LDP = Liberal Democratic Party.

[a] Tallies for the LDP include votes cast for the Social Democratic and Liberal Party Alliance in 1989 and 1984.

percent of the vote and a mere 18 seats—a 14-seat loss. This result was a precipitous drop from the 42 percent of the vote the Conservatives had won in the 1992 general election.

The main beneficiary of the Conservative decline was the Labour Party, which collected 44 percent of the vote—nearly 10 percent above its 1992 general election results—and 62 seats. The Liberal Democratic Party, with 17 percent of the vote and 2 seats, also greatly increased its totals and finally managed to win representation in the EP.

ELECTION LEXICON

Backbenchers: The rank-and-file members of parliament. The leading members and spokespersons sit on the front benches.

"The Dole": Term to describe the welfare system.

Downing Street Declaration: The joint peace initiative on Northern Ireland issued on December 15, 1993, by John Major and Albert Reynolds, the British and Irish prime ministers.

Dry Tory: A hard-line member of the Conservative Party in the "Thatcherite" mold.

"The English disease": Phrase referring to the decline of Britain's economy and the end of British influence in world affairs.

"Europe, open for business": The Conservative view of Europe in 1992. Thatcher had hoped to keep European unity strictly business-oriented.

First past the post: British electoral system that awards victory to the candidate winning the most votes cast in single-member districts. This system contrasts with majoritarian systems that require a runoff election and proportional representation, which is the most commonly used system in Europe.

Her Majesty's Opposition (or the Loyal Opposition): The party having the second-largest share of seats in the House of Commons.

Iceberg manifesto: Conservative term for the 1987 Labour manifesto, suggesting Labour had a hidden agenda it was afraid to reveal.

"Iron Lady": One of many terms referring to Thatcher's toughness as a leader; another is "Attila the Hen."

"It's time for a change": Labour Party campaign slogan in the 1992 election. The party hoped to make the election a referendum on Tory rule.

"The longest suicide note in history": Reference to the Labour Party's 1983 manifesto, which was so dubbed because of its length and radical Socialist content.

Loony Left: Conservatives' derisive term for left-wing members of the Labour Party.

Man from Mars: Reference to Nigel Lawson, former chancellor of the Exchequer, who reportedly once sold Mars chocolate bars.

1922 Committee: Committee composed of most backbench members of the Conservative Party in the House of Commons. The name refers to the 1922 revolt of the backbenchers that deposed the Conservative Party leader at the time.

"Nightmare on Downing Street": Slogan of the Conservative

Party predicting what would happen if Labour won the 1992 election. They claimed Labour's policies would lead to higher taxes and a return to socialism.

Number 10 Downing Street: The prime minister's address.

Oxbridge: Reference to the dominance of Oxford and Cambridge as the source of Britain's top government administrators.

Party Manifesto: Term used for any political party's platform or plan of action issued during an election campaign.

Poll tax: Controversial "community" or local tax plan passed into law by Thatcher's government. It replaced taxes based on property assessments with a direct levy on all adults—"per head" tax. Its critics argue it places an unfair burden on the poorer members of society. Street riots and widespread opposition led John Major to abolish the poll tax in 1991.

Proportional Representation (PR): A major topic of debate leading up to the 1992 elections. The Liberal Democrats asserted that if there was a hung parliament, they would insist on adoption of PR as their price for joining a coalition government. In general, PR voting systems allocate legislative seats in "proportion" to the percentages of votes received by political parties or candidates.

Queen's speech: The monarch opens parliament each year with a speech, prepared by the government, laying out the government's programs and priorities.

"Safe Seats": About half of the members of parliament do not reside in their "constituencies" (districts) prior to the election. National party leaders search for districts in which their party has historically dominated and offer candidates for these races; local leaders accommodate the national leadership by helping party leaders get elected in these safe seats.

Shadow cabinet: In the House of Commons, the opposition party sets up a "government-in-waiting" with party members assigned to be future ministers, should their party come into power. These members act as the party's chief spokespersons on issues under the jurisdiction of their respective "ministries."

Supply-side socialism: Neil Kinnock's term for his Labour

Party's doctrine that called for a mixed economic system instead of Labour's traditional reliance on nationalization and other "big government" solutions.

"The Two Davids": Reference to David Owen, the SDP leader, and David Steel, the Liberal Party leader. These two parties merged to contest the 1983 and 1987 elections.

Unwritten constitution: Britain has no written constitution.

Wet Tory: A moderate member of the Conservative Party who takes more socially concerned positions than the hard-line "Dry" Tories.

Westminster: The parliament building.

Whitehall: London street where key government ministries, including the ministries of defense, foreign affairs, and agriculture, are located.

HISTORICAL SYNOPSIS

The signing of the Magna Carta in 1215 established the United Kingdom as the birthplace of parliamentary democracy. The Magna Carta introduced the principle that the monarch's power is limited—an idea enforced with the temporary abolishment of the monarchy in 1649 and the confirmation of the power of parliament in 1688.

1707	Act of Union joins England and Scotland.
1775	Thirteen American colonies begin War of Independence.
1783	In Peace of Paris, England recognizes American independence.
1812	War of 1812 against the United States. England sacks and burns Washington.
1815	Wellington defeats Napoleon at Waterloo. Congress of Vienna redraws map of Europe.
1874-1880	Under Disraeli, Tories develop ideas of "social harmony," including beginnings of the welfare state, and establish broad base of support among working class.

1924	First Labour government. Labour supplants Liberals as second largest party.
1928	Women granted franchise on equal terms with men.
1940	Prime Minister Neville Chamberlain resigns and is replaced by Winston Churchill.
1945	May 7, V-E Day. July parliamentary elections give Labour Party an overwhelming victory. Churchill steps down. Labour government under Clement Attlee begins to lay foundations of modern British welfare state.
1949	United Kingdom becomes a founding member of NATO.
1951	Churchill returns to Number 10 Downing Street as head of Conservative government.
1952	King George VI dies on February 6. Elizabeth II becomes queen.
1955	Churchill is replaced as prime minister by Anthony Eden.
1960	United Kingdom joins European Free Trade Association (EFTA) as founding member.
1972	United Kingdom, along with Denmark, leaves EFTA to join the European Community.
1979	Margaret Thatcher becomes United Kingdom's first woman prime minister.
1982	On April 2, Argentina invades the Falkland Islands (Malvinas in Spanish). Thatcher sends a forty-ship task force. On June 14, Argentine troops surrender.
1983	Thatcher is reelected, handing the Labour Party its worst defeat since 1922.
1987	Thatcher wins another term. Labour Party under Neil Kinnock bounces back slightly from 1983 showing.
1990	Margaret Thatcher is challenged for Conservative Party leadership and resigns from office. John Major becomes prime minister on November 28.
1992	On April 9, John Major's Conservatives win an unexpected victory in parliamentary elections, gaining a slender majority of seats with only 42 percent of the vote.
1993	The British parliament ratifies the Maastricht Treaty on European Unity but at considerable political cost to

Prime Minister John Major. Following months of secret negotiations, on December 15 Major and Irish prime minister Albert Reynolds issue the so-called Downing Street Declaration, their landmark joint initiative on peace in Northern Ireland.

1994 On August 31, the Irish Republican Army (IRA) announces a surprise "complete cessation of military operations," thereby halting its twenty-five-year campaign of terrorist violence against the British in Ireland. Youthful, moderate Tony Blair becomes Labour Party leader after the unexpected death of John Smith. Labour's popularity ratings soar in opinion polls.

INDEX

Bildt, Carl (Sweden), 240, 242, 243, 249

Bjornsson, Sveinn (Iceland), 148

Blair, Tony (United Kingdom), 287

BLEU. *See* Belgium-Luxembourg Economic Union

Boeynants, Paul Vanden (Belgium), 67

Bofors (Sweden), 245

Borgariflokkurinn (CP). *See* Citizen's Party

Bossi, Umberto (Italy), 167

Brandt, Willy (Germany), 123, 125-126

Brinkman, Elco (Netherlands), 195, 196, 202

Britain. *See* United Kingdom

Brundtland, Gro Harlem (Norway), 206, 207-208, 211, 213

Brunner, Christine (Switzerland), 255

Brussels Treaty (1948), 67

Bruton, John (Ireland), 154, 161, 164

Bulgaria, 6, 268

Bundesrepublik Deutschland. *See* Germany

Buske, Erhard (Austria), 51

Caetano, Marcello (Portugal), 219, 225

Candidates, 4-5

CAP. *See* Common Agricultural Policy

"Capital of Europe," 65, 189

Caretaker government, 178

Cariglia, Antonio (Italy), 176

Carlos I (king of Portugal), 219, 225

Carlsson, Ebbe (Sweden), 246

Carlsson, Ingvar (Sweden), 240, 241, 244, 249

Carnation Revolution. *See* Portugal

Carvalhos, Carlos Gomes (Portugal), 217

CDA (*Christen Democratisch Appel*). *See* Christian Democratic Appeal

CDU (*Christlich-Demokratische Union*). *See* Christian Democratic Union

Centerpartiet (C). *See* Center Party (Sweden)

Center Party. *See also* Political parties
  Finland (*Keskustapuolue*, KP), 81, 87, 92, 93
  Ireland, 151
  Norway (*Senterpartiet*, SP), 205, 206, 207, 208, 210, 213
  Sweden (*Centerpartiet*, C), 239, 240, 242, 243-244, 248-240

Chamberlain, Neville (United Kingdom), 286

Charlotte (grand duchess of Luxembourg), 191

Chernobyl nuclear accident, 88-89, 245, 246

Chirac, Jacques (France)
  campaign slogan, 108
  "cohabitation," 22, 85, 111
  decade of renewal, 107
  economic factors, 101
  as prime minister and president, 98, 100, 105, 111
  Rally for the Republic, 96

Christelijke Vokspartij (CVP). *See* Christian Democratic Party, Belgium

Folkpartiet Liberalerna (FP). *See*
  Liberal People's Party
Forlani, Amintore (Italy), 181
Former Yugoslav Republic of
  Macedonia (FYROM), 131, 136
Fortress Europe, 43
Forza Italia (Go, Italy, FI), 38,
  167, 170, 175. *See also* Political
  parties
FP (*Folkpartiet Liberalerna*). *See*
  Liberal People's Party
FP (*Fremskrittspartiet*). *See* Prog-
  ress Party
FPO (*Freiheitliche Partei
  Osterreichs*). *See* Austrian
  Freedom Party
Fraga, Manuel (Spain), 234
Framsóknarflokkurinn (PP). *See*
  Progressive Party
France (Republic of; *République
  Française*). *See also* Europe
  "battle of the seat," 41
  cohabitation, 21-22, 23, 84-85,
    101-105, 107, 108
  country summary, 95-96, 110
  economic factors, 96, 100, 101,
    102, 103, 105
  election lexicon, 107-109
  election review, 98-106
  emergency blood supply, 103
  Euro-elections, 36-37, 40, 106
  European Union, 30, 31, 33,
    111
  foreign policies, 110
  head of government/state, 8, 95,
    96, 101
  historical synopsis, 110-111
  Maastricht Treaty, 27
  political issues, 23, 96, 99-101,
    110
  political parties, 10, 36, 96-100,
    102-103, 104-106, 111
  prime minister of, 8
  rapid action force, 109
  Republics, 101, 107, 110
  treaties, 67
  voter turnout, 18, 96
  voting system, 6, 10, 23, 33, 96,
    98-99, 101-102
  women in parliament, 16,
  World War II, 110
Franco Bahamonde, Francisco,
  231, 234, 235
Free Democratic Party (*Freie
  Demokratische Partei*, FDP;
  Germany), 37, 114-115, 117, 120,
  122, 125, 126. *See also* Political
  parties
Freedom Alliance (*Pollo delle
  Liberta*, PL; Italy), 167, 170,
  182. *See also* Coalition politics
Freedom and Progress Party
  (*Partij voor Vrijheid en
  Vooruitgang*, PVV; Belgium), 59.
  See also Liberal Party
Freie Demokratische Partei
  (FDP). *See* Free Democratic
  Party
Freiheitliche Partei Osterreichs
  (FPO). *See* Austrian Freedom
  Party
Freisinnig-Demokratische Partie
  (FDP). *See* Radical Democratic
  Party
Fremskrittspartiet (FP). *See*
  Progress Party
FRG (Federal Republic of
  Germany). *See* Germany
Front National (FN). *See* National
  Front
FYROM. *See* Former Yugoslav
  Republic of Macedonia

Mussolini, Alessandra, 174
Mussolini, Benito, 168, 178, 181

NA (*Alleanza Nazionale*). *See*
National Alliance
Napoleon, 259, 285
National Alliance (*Alleanza
Nazionale*, NA; Italy), 38, 168,
176. *See also* Italian Social
Movement; Political parties
National Coalition Party
(*Kansallinen Kokoomus*, KoK;
Finland), 82, 83, 84, 86, 87, 88-
89, 91-92, 93. *See also* Coalition
politics; Political parties
National Front (France), 37,
97-98, 100-101. *See also* Political
parties
NATO. *See* North Atlantic Treaty
Organization
Nazi Germany, 113, 114, 124, 125,
126, 135, 212. *See also* Germany;
Hitler, Adolph; World War II
Nea Democratia (ND). *See* New
Democracy Party, Greece
Netherlands (Kingdom of;
Koninkrijk der Nederlanden).
See also Belgium, Netherlands,
and Luxembourg Economic
Union; Europe
country summary, 192-193, 202
economic factors, 193, 197, 198,
200
election lexicon, 200-201
election review, 195-199
environmental issues, 197-198,
200, 201
Euro-elections, 36, 38, 199
European Union, 30-31, 33, 202
head of government/state, 192
historical synopsis, 202
legislature/parliament, 201

Maastricht Treaty, 27
monarchy, 192, 200-201, 202
neutrality, 202
North Atlantic Treaty Orga-
nization, 193, 194, 202
political issues, 193, 194,
196-197, 200
political parties, 193-199
treaties, 65, 67
voting system, 193
World War II, 202
Neutrality
Austria, 53, 55
Denmark, 212
Finland, 89, 90, 93
Iceland, 146, 148
Ireland, 151, 152, 163
Luxembourg, 190
Netherlands, 202
Norway, 212
Spain, 235
Sweden, 212, 244, 247, 248
Switzerland, 252, 258, 259
New Democracy Party. *See also*
Political parties
Greece (*Nea Democratia*, ND),
37, 128-130, 131, 132, 133,
135, 136, 138
Sweden (*Ny Demokrati*, NYD),
240, 241, 243, 244, 245, 247
New Ireland Forum, 161
New Zealand, 1, 6
NL (*La Lega Nord*). *See* Northern
League
Nordic Council, 78, 92, 93, 147,
211, 247
Nordic Defense Community, 248
North Atlantic Treaty
Organization (NATO)
Denmark, 77, 79, 248
France, 108
founding of, 67